No Method to the Madness

No Method to the Madness

Making Sense of the Psychiatric Treatment of Our Youth

Robert Foltz

BLOOMSBURY ACADEMIC
NEW YORK • LONDON • OXFORD • NEW DELHI • SYDNEY

BLOOMSBURY ACADEMIC
Bloomsbury Publishing Inc, 1359 Broadway, New York, NY 10018, USA
Bloomsbury Publishing Plc, 50 Bedford Square, London, WC1B 3DP, UK
Bloomsbury Publishing Ireland, 29 Earlsfort Terrace, Dublin 2, D02 AY28, Ireland

BLOOMSBURY, BLOOMSBURY ACADEMIC and the Diana logo are trademarks
of Bloomsbury Publishing Plc

First published in the United States of America 2025

Copyright © Bloomsbury Publishing Inc 2025

Cover design by Dustin Watson
Cover image © istock/RichVintage

All rights reserved. No part of this publication may be: i) reproduced or transmitted in any form, electronic or mechanical, including photocopying, recording or by means of any information storage or retrieval system without prior permission in writing from the publishers; or ii) used or reproduced in any way for the training, development or operation of artificial intelligence (AI) technologies, including generative AI technologies. The rights holders expressly reserve this publication from the text and data mining exception as per Article 4(3) of the Digital Single Market Directive (EU) 2019/790.

Bloomsbury Publishing Inc does not have any control over, or responsibility for, any third-party websites referred to or in this book. All internet addresses given in this book were correct at the time of going to press. The author and publisher regret any inconvenience caused if addresses have changed or sites have ceased to exist, but can accept no responsibility for any such changes.

A catalog record for this book is available from the Library of Congress.

ISBN: HB: 979-8-8818-0602-6
       PB: 979-8-8818-0603-3
     ePDF: 979-8-7651-5537-0
    eBook: 979-8-8818-0604-0

Typeset by Integra Software Services Pvt. Ltd.
Printed and bound in the United States of America

For product safety related questions contact productsafety@bloomsbury.com.

To find out more about our authors and books visit www.bloomsbury.com
and sign up for our newsletters.

I want to thank my wife Lynn, and the girls, Kelly, Christin, and Kathleen. This project could not have been completed without their ongoing support and encouragement. Not only in the many years of working in the field, but tackling the long, challenging task of research, practice, and writing this book could not have happened without them. My brother, Mark, has also been a source of support and encouragement for this project, as well as many other events throughout my life.

I also want to thank my lifelong friends, Jason, Jon, Scott, and our memories of Jim. Over the decades of knowing them, we've always enjoyed relationships that supported debate and challenged our assumptions. I believe these many years of "critical thinking" began in these friendships—wanting to recognize others' opinions, examine those positions, and determine what works and what doesn't, and all that stuff in between.

Contents

List of Figures and Tables   viii
Note on Author   ix

1   **Introduction**   1
2   **Arriving at a Diagnosis**   15
3   **The Role of Trauma**   35
4   **Medicating Attention Deficit Hyperactivity
    Disorder (ADHD)**   49
5   **Rethinking the Treatment of Adolescent Depression**   83
6   **Containment vs Treatment: The Use of Antipsychotic
    Medications**   121
7   **Child Welfare and Intensive Services**   151
8   **Deprescribing: Is It an Option?**   169

Index   179

Figures and Tables

Figures

2.1	From *Anatomy of an Epidemic*, Whitaker, 2011	30
6.1	From: Leucht, S., Kane, J., Kissling, W., Hamann, J, Etschel, E. and Engel, R. (2005). What does the PANSS mean? *Schizophrenia Research*, 79(2–3), 231–238	135
7.1	An Example of Episodes of Crisis Behavior	161

Tables

2.1	DSM-5 Inter-Rater Reliability Scores	22
4.1	Trials Used to Establish Efficacy in the Management of ADHD Symptoms	62
4.2	A Sample of Items from the SKAMP Scale Used to Evaluate Symptom Presentations in ADHD	63
4.3	Intervention Recommendations from the American Academy of Pediatrics in the Treatment of ADHD	64
4.4	A Summary of Outcome Domains and Evaluators in the MTA Study	72
5.1	Placebo-Controlled Fluoxetine (Prozac) Studies in the Treatment of Major Depression in Youth	93
5.2	Antidepressant vs. Fluoxetine vs. Placebo Studies in the Treatment of Major Depression in Youth	95
5.3	CDRS-R Scores for TADS Treatment Groups at Baseline, 6 Weeks, 12 Weeks, and Study Endpoint	98
5.4	FDA-Approved Indications for Antidepressant Medications in Youth	108
5.5	Receptor Affinity for Popular Antidepressant Medications	109
6.1	Popular Antipsychotic Medications	123
6.2	Antipsychotic Receptor Site Affinity	133
6.3	PANSS Scores at Baseline, Study Endpoint, and Average Improvement	137

Note on Author

Robert Foltz, PsyD, is a clinical psychologist and associate professor of Clinical Psychology with over thirty-five years of experience in the field, including inpatient, residential, and outpatient services. Throughout his career, he has focused on more severe conditions in young people, working for over fifteen years as a clinician and administrator in residential treatment centers, and maintaining a private practice for over twenty years. He has been teaching graduate students in psychology since 2009. Courses he teaches include Psychopathology (understanding the disorders), Pediatric Psychopharmacology (the use of psychiatric medications in youth), Foundations in Research and Practice, Trauma-Informed Care, Psychotherapy strategies, and Ethics in Psychology. Across these decades, it became clear that medications were assumed to be quite effective in the management of severe conditions, but after many years of meeting with these youth and families, critically examining the literature, and searching for more effective interventions, Dr. Foltz raises serious questions about our current assumptions in both diagnosing and treating troubled youth. These decades of experience have established the foundation for *No Method to the Madness*.

1
Introduction

The Problem in Perspective: The 10,000-Foot View

The goal of *No Method to the Madness* is to critically review the mental health services being provided to children and adolescents in the United States. *Critical* doesn't have to mean negative, however. *Critical*, in this sense, means to dig into the current strategies of our system, closely examine the results, and challenge many of the assumptions that come with the current climate of care for our troubled youth. Through a more transparent and accurate understanding of the situation, clinicians, parents, and policymakers will be in a better position to make informed, data-driven decisions.

My Background

I am a clinical psychologist. I completed a doctoral degree in clinical psychology called the PsyD (similar to a PhD). I cannot prescribe psychiatric medications. But, with more than thirty-five years of work in the field, I have encountered countless people—young and old—who had been prescribed psychiatric medications to "treat" their symptoms. Early in my career, it made sense to me. I have spent virtually all my clinical work in settings working with individuals struggling with the severe conditions, such as schizophrenia, bipolar disorder, major depression, etcetera. Doctors, nurses, counselors, and my teachers all explained that these conditions were "chemical imbalances," or brain problems, and the most effective treatments were medications. A mountain of articles continued to support these claims.

In my undergraduate abnormal psychology courses, the theories of psychological causes for severe disorders were waning. While the ideas of "nature versus nurture" were being tossed about, it was more often purported that our experiences didn't matter as much as the chemicals flowing through our brain, or those powerful genetic predispositions that leave many of our outcomes predetermined. It was many years before I realized that these "conclusions," put forth by my professors and other professionals I was working with, were incomplete, if not false. More specifically, our science—even today—does not offer the sophistication required to answer these complex questions. Yet I wonder why very smart people chose to promote these "conclusions" as fact.

One day, many years ago, while working on an inpatient psychiatric unit, I was speaking with a middle-aged man diagnosed with paranoid schizophrenia. He had dark hair, was of a slight build, wore a worried look on his face, and smoked throughout the day. He walked the halls, gently patting his chest. At times he would stop, his eyes wide with fear, and then resume his slow walk up and down the halls. Eventually, he shared that the gentle patting of his chest was his effort to ensure that his heart kept beating. He was suspicious of most people, but as I was on the unit regularly throughout the week for eight hours at a time, he became quite comfortable sharing his thoughts and feelings with me. But early on, one day when we were chatting in the smoke room, I leaned on the door frame and crossed my arms to relax. He froze. Eyes wide, he said, "I can tell you hate me." Surprised, I asked, "What would make you think that? We're having a good conversation." He said he could tell by the way I crossed my arms. Over time, we looked forward to our conversations. On a day nearing his discharge, he was recounting his many hospitalizations and his perceptions of what he found helpful. To my stunned surprise, he said he couldn't wait to get out of the hospital so he could stop taking his medications. I asked, "But don't your medications help you?" His response, "No, they don't. I think they make me worse."

This statement made me pause. It planted a seed of skepticism that didn't begin to grow until I was well into my graduate studies. As I continued to work with adults struggling with severe conditions throughout my educational process, I started to more regularly ask about their experiences. More and more frequently, I would hear about the lack of effectiveness of medications in managing or resolving their symptoms. Equally puzzling was that other treatment providers were either not being told those same patient experiences or were not incorporating them into the treatment planning.

After almost ten years of working primarily with adults in hospitals, I began working in residential treatment settings for troubled children and adolescents. Most of these young people had endured horrible, traumatic childhoods. The pain of their lives evolved into anger, aggression, depression, fear, and psychosis, among many other reactions. In this setting, they received multidisciplinary care, meaning many providers offered services to help them. Indeed, one of the most common interventions is medication. And in these settings, many youth are on multiple medications. However, residential treatment—and the severely troubled youth within them—are some of the least researched topics within the mental health field.

Critically reviewing the research for troubled youth is a daunting task. Having been immersed in it for years, I often talk to parents who are confused, overwhelmed, not sure who to trust, and frustrated in their efforts to help their children. The internet is filled with information—some accurate, some not. Much of it is designed to sell products. Research articles may be difficult to obtain or are filled with complicated statistics or jargon that makes them appear to be written in a different language. But these dilemmas are not unique to parents. Even well-trained clinicians struggle to understand this information and how to integrate the conflicting results into their actual treatment efforts.

For therapists working with adolescents, a solid foundation of training is essential, and continued education on the evolutions in the field must be obtained. But in recent research related to topics in *No Method to the Madness*, many doctoral level psychologists may not have foundational training in key topics. For example, a survey of doctoral programs was conducted in 2022 to determine how many programs, accredited by the American Psychological Association, required a course on psychopharmacology. Remarkably, only 31 percent of programs required a course (Foltz et al., 2023b) Even more stunning, only 5 percent of these programs required a course on the impact and treatment of trauma (Foltz et al., 2023a).

Goal of This Book

The goal of this book is to provide a thorough examination of the practice of diagnosing and medicating youth in distress. Empowered by catchy marketing terms like "chemical imbalance," we have, as a society, come to accept the perfunctory use of medications. Based on their pervasive use, we assume they must be safe, effective, and well established in science. The goal of this book is not to uncover a conspiracy, demonize prescribing physicians, or recommend that people not use medications.

- You should *always* discuss any concerns you may have with your prescriber.
- You should *never* abruptly stop or change your medications without the supervision of your prescriber.

These medications are developed to change the way we think, feel, and behave. That goal does not come easily. Nor does it come with clear, or reliable, scientific outcomes. The use of medications is complicated and motivated by far more than politics, research, and profits. People use psychotropic medications because they are in distress and are looking for relief. The challenge, therefore, is to examine the evidence of how these medications can enhance or impair someone's functioning. In that endeavor, we will take a critical look at the science that creates the foundation for medication use in children and adolescents.

The medications used to control the symptoms of common diagnoses will be closely examined to illuminate the benefits and drawbacks of typical psychotropic strategies. To provide an exhaustive review of medication research is not the goal, nor is it practical. Hundreds of studies emerge every year. The research within this work will be focused on those studies offering the best methodology and the largest sample of participants. Major organizations, such as the American Academy of Child and Adolescent Psychiatry also create "Practice Parameters" or "Practice Guidelines." These thorough reviews of the research will also be incorporated, as they represent many studies reviewed and synthesized by experts in the field. As a result, it is hoped that the studies examined will provide the best estimates of how medication research can be applied to the overall population of youth.

A Statement on Ethics

Ethical standards for a clinical psychologist are established by the American Psychological Association (APA, 2017) and the state in which they are licensed. Because I cannot prescribe medications, I am not permitted to make specific recommendations for or against prescribing. Surprisingly, it is quite common that psychologists will refer to a psychiatrist (based on an assumption that medications may be beneficial) when completing an evaluation. For example, a psychologist may complete psychological testing and conclude that a child meets the diagnostic criteria for major depressive disorder. As a result, they may include a statement like, "Recommend a psychiatric referral to consider antidepressant treatment." While this is a recommendation to a trained professional that is licensed to prescribe, it is also close to a recommendation *for* medication. I do not believe this is appropriate unless it includes a review of the research to support or challenge those recommendations, which would serve to educate on the topic. I believe that the recommendations should include a review of treatment options, and the evidence that supports (or does not support) those treatments. The same could be said in relation to other treatments being suggested, such as occupational therapy, educational supports, and so on. This is, in part, based on the power that a professional has in the relationship with clients. When a recommendation comes from "a doctor," there is often recognition that it's coming from "an expert." But doctors are not experts in everything, and providers are not free from bias in their beliefs of human behavior, treatments, and expected outcomes. All these factors should be openly discussed with clients in the collaborative process.

Psychologists are permitted to provide education to those receiving care for mental health conditions. The goal is to support and advocate for the client with a focus on optimizing outcomes in the process of treatment. As a result, if evidence does not support a particular treatment, and the psychologist has that knowledge, it is ethically supported to convey that knowledge to their client. Of course, this information needs to be provided in a way that is understandable and applicable to the client's situation. Finally, the clinician should be mindful of their limitations in knowledge. For example, in my career, I have not focused my study or clinical practice on eating disorders. As a result, this limitation in my own education and experience should contextualize any information I would share with a client or caregiver.

In reading this book, you may have questions. It is essential that you speak to your treatment provider before making any specific changes to your treatment based on the information here. One aim of this book is to empower more critical thinking around diagnoses and treatments. If the information here raises questions for you, take this to your provider and discuss it. No one has a monopoly on truth in the field of mental health. They may disagree with the material here. In that case, I always recommend creating clear, measurable outcomes for your care. If, with a particular treatment, a specific goal is not achieved in the set amount of time, it should be reviewed and reconsidered.

For students and clinicians: It's OK to admit, "I don't know." But as a provider, you should establish strategies to research symptom presentations, intervention strategies, and ways to measure outcomes. Your honesty and humility will further support developing a genuine rapport with your client. It also helps establish the reality that the treatment process is a journey to be taken together. Even if you have certainty about a diagnosis, for example, the client in front of you is different from every other one you have worked with. Appreciate the uniqueness of the relationship. Appreciate the power of your role. Recognize the limitations of your knowledge and expertise. If you are working with multiple providers, encourage them to communicate, have collaborative meetings, and create a shared vision of what successful treatment looks like.

For parents: Providers are licensed to provide a specific range of services. They are expected to adhere to the rights and privileges of their discipline but not step beyond those abilities. However, knowledge across disciplines may overlap. You will likely have discussions with a psychiatrist about therapy techniques, discussions about medications with your therapist, or raise concerns about educational interventions with an occupational therapist. It is not that these discussions should not occur or won't be helpful but communicating openly and honestly with each provider will offer the greatest advantage. If you are working with multiple providers, encourage them to communicate, have collaborative meetings, and create a shared vision of what successful treatment looks like.

Foundations of Critically Examining the Science

Whether you are a parent, clinician in training, clinician in practice, or policymaker, you may often hear phrases that describe psychiatric disorders in children and teens as neurobiological, neurodevelopmental, or neurological. It implicates the brain being involved in the disorder; specifically, something abnormal is happening in the brain and a treatment that addresses this abnormality would seem to be the most appropriate strategy. Early in my training, I jumped onto these beliefs. It sounds sophisticated, and with the complexity of these disorders, the brain must be the cause! In my years of study, I've come to realize that this formulation equates to explaining a mystery with a mystery.

The brain is involved in everything we do. In that way, abnormal thoughts and behaviors are indeed based in brain function. But as science tries to understand this, some that describe disorders as neurological assume that we have identified areas or systems in the brain that are malfunctioning, resulting in abnormal thoughts and behaviors. This is not the case. If it were true, we could use more precise neuroimaging technologies to confirm psychiatric diagnoses. The *Diagnostic and Statistical Manual of Mental Disorders* (DSM) highlights throughout the idea that neurological imaging, laboratory tests, or other measures of biological functioning cannot be used to determine the existence of a psychiatric disorder. We'll discuss this further below.

In examining research, one concept you should understand is "internal validity." From the American Psychological Association, "internal validity is the degree to which a study or experiment is free from flaws in its internal structure and its results can therefore be taken to represent the true nature of the phenomenon. . . . Internal validity pertains to the soundness of results obtained within the controlled conditions of a particular study, specifically with respect to whether one can draw reasonable conclusions about the cause-and-effect relationships among variables" (APA, 2018).

As an example of internal validity, consider a study testing the effectiveness of psychotherapy in the treatment of depression. One group of participants receives a therapy session once a week for two months, the other group is on a wait list for that time. At the end of the study, the results show that while most people receiving therapy improved, over half of those on the wait list also showed improvement. Is it safe to conclude that a wait list can be effective treatment? Obviously, there are many problems with this simple example. No information is known about what happened in the lives of those on the wait list. Having made the effort to seek treatment (and were now on a wait list), had they become more optimistic about their futures? Had they started becoming more active, exercising, engaging more with friends? All these factors could reduce depression but are unknown in the results. Therefore, interpreting any results from this study must be done cautiously, meaning that this is an example of weak internal validity.

External validity is another important concept to understand when you're evaluating research. External validity is "the extent to which the results of research or testing can be generalized beyond the sample that generated them" (APA, 2018). Unfortunately, research outcomes are commonly generalized to groups that may have little relationship to the study population. Consider a study investigating the effectiveness of Risperdal (an atypical antipsychotic medication) to control aggressive behavior in youth diagnosed with autism. In this study, researchers may give Risperdal to half of the group and a placebo to the other half. They will then examine the occurrences of aggressive behaviors during the study. If Risperdal is shown to reduce depression in this study, can you confidently conclude that Risperdal is an effective treatment to reduce aggressive behaviors across other disorders? No. Generalizing this finding to other groups has weak external validity. It is not safe to assume that aggressive behaviors presented in autistic youth are the same as aggressive behaviors shown in, say, conduct disordered youth. As a result, the effectiveness of Risperdal may not be consistent across different diagnostic groups.

Failure to Replicate Successful Studies

Throughout our era of evidence-based treatment, clinicians are expected to utilize intervention strategies that have demonstrated effectiveness in rigorously controlled studies. Repeating the study and achieving comparable results can give practitioners confidence that the techniques and strategies they are using are more likely to succeed. Unfortunately, replicating successful research is easier said than done.

In 2018, researchers sought to replicate twenty-one social science studies (Camerer et al., 2018). They were able to replicate just thirteen of them. However, even in those replicated studies, they also found that the estimated effect sizes were notably smaller than in the original published studies. In other words, the effectiveness of the intervention was less potent than originally determined. These researchers also found that, among those studies that were not successfully replicated, "there was essentially no evidence for the original finding" (Camerer et al., 2018, p. 640).

The "failure to replicate" dilemma has plagued the field of mental health for many years. There is no simple solution to the problem, but the walkaway message is this: Be critical consumers of information. It is easy to find a variety of studies or headlines that make claims of effective and safe treatments. Yet be aware that one enthusiastic headline or new article, even in top tier journals, may be overestimating their results and we need to be cautious until the study is replicated with a comparable group of participants.

Universal and Exclusive

In my decades of evaluating research, a theme has emerged that informs my threshold to arrive at conclusions. Every year, thousands of articles are published in the fields of psychology, psychiatry, counseling, social work, and so on. Many of them have dazzling titles and their abstracts summarize impressive research, making conclusions that a particular diagnostic strategy has identified the abnormality of a condition, substantiated a treatment that achieved amazing results, or created a test to finally clarify a diagnosis. With time, unfortunately, these exceptional claims dissolve.

When I review research, I look to align the findings on two fronts: *universal* and *exclusive*. With the concept of universal, to be truly unique to the condition, the finding should apply across every participant in the study. It should be universal. Take the idea of "frontal lobe dysfunction." People will often make claims of frontal lobe problems for a psychiatric disorder. But in this research, to be definitive, their findings should be found across every participant in the study. If one hundred children with ADHD receive functional magnetic resonance imaging (fMRI) and only seventy-eight are found to have frontal lobe deficiencies, it is interesting, but not universal to ADHD.

With the concept of exclusivity, to be a signature characteristic for the disorder, it should only occur in that particular disorder. Again, with frontal lobe deficiencies, these "abnormalities" can be found in ADHD, depression, OCD, among many other conditions. Because the problems within the frontal lobe can be found across many diagnoses, they are indeed interesting but are not unique to the specific diagnosis. Refined research methodologies could ameliorate both issues, but we are not at a point in our science to establish neurological "signatures," or pathognomonic features, for any psychiatric condition.

Scientific Research Papers

In 2023, the prestigious journal *Science* published a paper entitled, "Fake Scientific Papers are Alarmingly Common" (Brainard, 2023). Remarkably, the author highlights that a recent review of nearly five thousand papers in 2020 estimated that a third were plagiarized or faked. The dilemma of "paper mills" was identified; covert businesses that generate papers to multiply the publications of authors—giving them greater exposure, with little to no real authorship in the work. This creates a staggering challenge for clinicians trying to utilize evidence-based strategies. As a clinician, when I go to the literature looking for explanations, formulations, or treatment recommendations for a particular issue, I read those articles with the assumption that the work has been vetted, critiqued, and peer reviewed. These mechanisms provide a reassurance that the work has withstood scrutiny.

Within academia, many institutions create the "publish or perish" culture. For prestigious institutions, if their faculty members are not publishing—that is, actively contributing to professional literature—they run the risk of losing their position at the university. As a result, this culture could create an environment of falsifying data, exaggerating research findings, or financial corruption, among other factors. Let's be clear: Most researchers are doing their best to maintain integrity in their work and create projects that will enhance our understanding of disorders and treatment. However, without transparency in the "real" research versus that which is faked, the masses of clinicians looking to use published literature to guide their interventions could fall victim to faulty data.

All of this speaks to the "business" of academia, research, and evidence-based treatments. Universities are tuition driven. That is, their business model is driven by students enrolling and attending. Students choose their colleges based on reputation and opportunity. If a student can be accepted into a prestigious university, they assume they'll have a more successful future. If universities generate noteworthy research, not only does it attract students but it also increases their chances of securing additional funding from grants, donations, collaboration, etcetera. Moreover, powerful corporations may also leverage the influence of these researchers to expand their reach into different "markets." Basically, they target children and adults with any sort of disorder or disease to highlight the products that have been developed to treat these conditions.

In recent years, academia has come under particular scrutiny. Claiming that researchers, professors, their conclusions, and recommendations are corrupt, inaccurate, or driven by an alternative agenda to work against the betterment of the public. I'm sure this has happened, but it is the rare exception to the rule. As a society, being able to Google a topic, read a few websites and blogs, does not make you an expert. Those that have arrived in academic positions, or administrative roles in large public health institutions are not there by accident. In most cases, they have achieved the highest degrees in their field, have demonstrated their ability to think critically through research and publication, have shown the cognitive sophistication to adapt their formulations with emerging science, have devoted thousands of hours to their work, and have created a tangible benefit in their field. They are experts.

As noted in the important book, *The Death of Expertise* (Nichols, 2024), there is a growing, casual dismissal—even angry rejection—of expertise driven by the above assumptions of corruption or inaccuracy. Simply finding a conflicting view does not mean the "expert" should be dismissed. Experts are wrong less often. Experts have a foundation of knowledge that the novice does not have. Experts have thought far longer about their area of specialty than the novice and have a better understanding of other factors that may impact conclusions. Assuming that someone without qualifications has the same level of intellectual rigor on a topic comes with clear risks. When these topics are related to health, policies, and systemic processes, the risks are amplified.

Popular Beliefs in Academia

During my years as a graduate student, financial demands required that I also work part-time. I was fortunate to work in psychiatric hospitals, most often with adults diagnosed with schizophrenia. These experiences were, in many ways, just as valuable as the education I was receiving. While the academic foundation is essential, real-world experiences with those struggling with psychological challenges proved to be invaluable.

Working with adults diagnosed with schizophrenia provided keen insights into those experiences of psychosis, but more importantly, revealed the humanness of the condition. Seeing the distress, the fear, the frustration, and the resiliency, courage, and determination in these individuals highlighted to me that our current treatments were insufficient. In fact, these early experiences were my first realizations that our medication strategies were not what these patients wanted most. Beyond symptom control through medications, they wanted to be safe, feel productive, and be understood.

I took these experiences into my classrooms as a graduate student. My earliest interests were in severe conditions, such as schizophrenia and other psychotic experiences. I thought, "if we can figure *this* out, everything else is easy." But patients telling me that they didn't want to keep taking their medications made me curious to find other treatments that were available. As a psychologist in training, our emphasis was on providing psychotherapy, so I started examining the literature, which was encouraging. But what I was hearing from professors was something quite different.

Decades ago, the research on schizophrenia was quite different. Today, most research generated on schizophrenia is focused on neurochemistry, neuroanatomy, and genetics. In contrast, required readings for graduate school included theoretical formulations to consider how childhood experiences, parenting, and life events may contribute to the emergence of psychotic symptoms. However, rather than embracing these to guide treatment, I was repeatedly told by professors that "insight-oriented psychotherapy for schizophrenia is contraindicated. You can't do therapy with them until they are effectively medicated." In other words, therapy strategies to explore and expand one's understanding of their childhood, early attachment relationships, foundations of coping strategies, and so on., should *not* be utilized as a treatment strategy. Rather, "supportive therapy" should be offered to ensure their compliance with medication. Only then could you use psychotherapy. I came to realize that neither of these "conclusions" were supported by research.

As a graduate student, I had an inherent respect for my professors. Their years of experience, knowledge, and range of skills were attributes I still hoped to achieve. Yet I was curious, and quite honestly, skeptical about what I was hearing. So, I went to the research. In fact, my doctoral dissertation was focused on the experience of being medicated in schizophrenia, and I included questions about psychotherapy, so examining the literature became part of the task of my completing my degree.

While not mainstream, I delved into a legacy of literature supporting the use of insight-oriented treatments for schizophrenia. I began to contact, attend conferences with, and be mentored by experts providing psychotherapy strategies to those diagnosed with schizophrenia. These experiences upended my academic training. I also realized that many clinicians in the field have not received training specific to the psychotherapy of psychotic conditions. It is a unique skillset not sought out or provided in the typical training of a therapist or psychologist. It made me acutely aware of how information can be used in political and powerful ways. For example, in today's training environment, only a small fraction of psychology graduate students has any access to learning about therapy for schizophrenia. Fewer clinicians are in the field doing that work, fewer people are being trained, and the skillset of providing insight-oriented therapy to those with schizophrenia is disappearing. Being able to influence the curriculum of mental health training can have profound downstream effects. It's not surprising, then, to realize that the pharmaceutical industry's influence in medical school training could be a powerful force in our society's embrace of a medication response to any particular disorder we may identify (Kluger, 2009).

This book represents the culmination of my decades of study and clinical practice. It is intended to provide a critical analysis of our current diagnostic and treatment strategies for young people. I decided to write this book after many years of conference presentations, publications, and teaching. Encouraged by my colleagues for years, my perspective on our treatment processes may not be mainstream, but I believe it offers a valuable addition to the decision-making of clinicians, students, and parents.

References

American Psychological Association. (2017). Ethical principles of psychologists and code of conduct. https://www.apa.org/ethics/code

American Psychological Association. (2018). Internal validity. *APA Dictionary of Psychology*. https://dictionary.apa.org/internal-validity

Brainard, J. (2023). Fake scientific papers are alarmingly common: But new tools show promise in tackling academia's growing symptom of "publish or perish" culture. *Science*, May 9.

Camerer, C., Dreber, A., Holzmeister, F., Ho, T., Huber, J., Johannesson, M., . . . Wu, H. (2018). Evaluating the replicability of social science experiments in *Nature* and *Science* between 2010 and 2015. *Nature: Human Behavior*, (2): 637–644.

Foltz, R., Fogel, K., Kaeley, A., Kupchan, J., Mills, A., Murray, K., . . . Rubright, C. (2023). The psychopharmacology training gap in accredited clinical psychology programs. *Training and Education in Professional Psychology*. https://doi.org/10.1037/tep0000442

Foltz, R., Kaeley, A., Kupchan, J., Mills, A., Murray, K., Pope, A., . . . Rubright, C. (2023). Trauma-informed care? Identifying training deficits in accredited doctoral programs. *Psychological Trauma: Theory, Research, Practice, and Policy*, *15*(7): 1188–1193. https://doi.org/10.1037/tra0001461

Kluger, J. (2009). Is drug-company money tainting medical education? *Time Magazine*, March 6. https://time.com/archive/6933271/is-drug-company-money-tainting-medical-education/

Nichols, T. (2024). *The death of expertise: The campaign against established knowledge and why it matters* (2nd ed.) Oxford University Press.

2
Arriving at a Diagnosis

The Diagnostic Process

An important step in critically examining the "science" is understanding the assumptions and framework of our diagnoses and disorders. When I entered the field, the *Diagnostic and Statistical Manual, Third Edition, Revised* (DSM-III-R) was the current catalog of diagnostic options. With my inexperience, I believed that this book was grounded in rigorous scientific study. I have since learned that there are many influences that create, maintain, and perpetuate psychiatric diagnoses. I've come to learn that many diagnoses are eliminated from versions of the DSM while others are created to address the failings of previous editions. Moreover, issues of reliability and validity remain problematic for the DSM. In other words, there continues to be considerable disagreement about what characterizes a particular "disorder" and even when a diagnosis is chosen, it is not safe to assume that a valid condition has been identified. If you are a parent or clinician, you should know that the diagnoses are "best guesses." In fact, the DSM-5 (APA, 2013) concedes this in a densely worded passage,

> Indeed, the once plausible goal of identifying homogeneous populations for treatment and research resulted in narrow diagnostic categories that did not capture clinical reality, symptom heterogeneity within disorders, and significant sharing of symptoms across multiple disorders. The historical aspiration of achieving diagnostic homogeneity by progressive sub-typing within disorder categories no longer is sensible; like most common human ills, mental disorders are heterogeneous at many levels, ranging from genetic risk factors to symptoms.
> (American Psychiatric Association, 2013, p. 12)

To decipher that psychobabble, it could more simply be stated as "the effort to establish diagnostic groups, characterized by similar characteristics (homogeneity), is no longer sensible because disorders are too heterogeneous (made up of characteristics that are not similar)." The lack of similar characteristics includes everything from genetic and neurological findings to behaviors and emotions. So, even though a diagnosis may be determined (and treatments are initiated based on that diagnosis), it is openly acknowledged that the symptoms for that diagnosis may be inconsistent, reflect another diagnosis, or overlap with another disorder. Keep in mind, this includes things like feelings of depression, irritability, anxiety, impulsivity, distorted thoughts, impaired relationships, and so on. The DSM authors also try to minimize the magnitude of this confession. Equating the heterogeneity of psychiatric disorders to "most common human ills" is quite an oversimplification. For example, having the sniffles, sneezing, and a sore throat may be a "common cold" or seasonal allergy (e.g., heterogeneity of symptoms across different diagnoses). Having a battery of tests to determine the "accurate" diagnosis for these symptoms is unnecessary. While inconvenient, the impact on your functioning is likely minimal and temporary. However, cancer is unfortunately a common human illness that may present symptoms that could initially be confused with other conditions. Accurate diagnostic testing, including blood tests, MRIs, and a variety of other tools, is essential to determine the presence of cancer and administer the appropriate treatment. Unfortunately, the precision available in diagnosing cancer and other physical ailments is not available in psychiatric diagnoses.

Diagnostic Ambiguity

The DSM-5-TR notes that the goal of a diagnosis is to create a "clear and concise description" of a condition (APA, 2022, p. 5). This suggests that the latest edition has refined diagnostic descriptions to the extent that clinicians, researchers, and others can arrive at a clear, concise view of what they are dealing with. It would make sense that a new edition should offer an even greater advantage.

Later in the Introduction of the DSM-5, the American Psychiatric Association also concedes that they've come to realize that "the boundaries between disorders are more porous than originally perceived" (APA, 2013, p. 6). Most recently, in the DSM-5-TR, "the boundaries between many disorder 'categories' are more fluid over the life course than has been recognized" (APA, 2022, p. 14). But wait, how do you make sense of that? The DSM purports to provide clear and concise definitions of mental disorders, yet they acknowledge disorders actually blur together. I've often talked with parents who expressed a "sigh of relief" after they received a diagnosis for their child. However, it is common—if not expected—that these symptoms and conditions will change over time.

The problem is worse than you can imagine. Recent research highlights the "heterogeneity" of diagnoses, meaning the diversity or varying presentations of the disorders. In fact, when you consider how many different symptom combinations can meet the requirements for certain diagnoses, one begins to question how all of those could represent the same condition.

- There are 270,000,000 symptom combinations that meet the criteria for comorbid PTSD and Major Depressive Disorder (Allsopp et al., 2019).
- There are over 630,000 symptom combinations that meet the criteria for PTSD (Cloitre, 2020).
- There are over 18,000 combinations that can be diagnosed as ADHD, Combined Type, the most common form.

Function of a Diagnosis

In what may be one of the least-read portions of the DSM-5-TR, the Introduction, it says that a diagnosis should have clinical utility. That is, it should help a "clinician determine prognosis, treatment plans, and potential treatment outcomes . . . and support clinical, public health, and research purposes" (APA, 2022, p. 14). There is a pragmatic value in this. For example, if a colleague calls me to refer an adolescent for psychotherapy and the teen is described as having oppositional defiant disorder, I have a general sense of some of the challenges facing the youth and family. Or, when designing a study, researchers may want to include individuals currently meeting the criteria for major depressive disorder. However, embedded in any of these diagnoses is that they reflect the current life experience of the person, their relationships, and the world around them. There is nothing within a diagnosis that establishes a cause for those symptoms (except within posttraumatic stress disorder). Thus, our treatment recommendations based on a diagnosis are driven to reduce or eliminate symptoms. But simply reducing symptoms may be insufficient. This is an important difference to be discussed later (cure versus containment).

Arriving at a diagnosis does not identify any "source" or cause of the symptoms (except for trauma-related diagnoses that stem directly from the experience of trauma exposure). The American Psychiatric Association acknowledges that "a diagnosis does not carry any necessary implications regarding etiology or causes of the individual's mental disorder or the individual's degree of control over behaviors that may be associated with the disorder" (APA, 2022, p. 29). This important concept has direct implications in the popular beliefs around these conditions. For example, if major depressive disorders were proven to be the result of a "chemical imbalance," a diagnosis would establish the need for medications to correct that imbalance. But the cause (or etiology) of these disorders has not been established. Thus, our perfunctory use of medications needs to be considered carefully.

The American Psychiatric Association (2022) extends this further as it considers the role of a psychiatric diagnosis in forensic settings (situations related to court or legal proceedings).

> In most situations, the clinical diagnosis of a DSM-5 mental disorder such as intellectual developmental disorder (intellectual disability), schizophrenia, major neurocognitive disorder, gambling disorder, or pedophilic disorder *does not imply that an individual with such a condition meets legal criteria for the presence of a mental disorder or 'mental illness' as defined in law*, or a specified legal standard (e.g., for competence, criminal responsibility, or disability) . . . additional information is usually required beyond that contained in the DSM-5 diagnosis.
>
> (APA, 2022, p. 29, italics added)

While the standards of evidence, parameters of a legal argument, or defining culpability of specific behaviors can become a complicated legal process, it remains a bit confusing why the criteria that have been established to create "clear and concise" definitions of a disorder are not sufficient to identify the presence of the disorder in most legal circumstances. The DSM is what actually defines those specific disorders. However, it has been argued that neither the reliability nor the validity of diagnoses used to categorize millions of youth and adults across the country every day, are sufficient to withstand rigorous challenges in court proceedings (Faust, 2011).

Rule Out Trauma First. Then Do Your Diagnosing

With decades of experience in the field, I have come to feel confident in one conclusion: A reaction to traumatic experiences can mimic many different psychiatric disorders. Trauma exposure will be explored in greater depth in the next chapter, but this relates directly to understanding the diagnostic process. It is well understood that traumatic events are not limited to a life-threatening event (such as a car accident or war exposure). Moreover, those experiences referenced in the diagnostic criteria for posttraumatic stress disorder (PTSD) are only a short list of what people may experience as trauma.

The reason I recommend ruling out trauma before considering other diagnoses is because many symptoms that emerge from trauma exposure can look like a range of common psychiatric disorders. Failing to recognize this results in diagnostic confusion, leading to ineffective treatments, poor outcomes, and frustrated youth and parents. As we'll see, a diagnostic impression drives decision-making around treatment. If the dysregulated emotions in a teen are diagnosed as bipolar disorder, specific treatment recommendations will be made. But if those emotions are caused by a traumatic experience, the treatment would be very different. Moreover, the recommended treatment for bipolar disorder would do little to alleviate the trauma-exposed teen's distress in the long run.

Diagnosis Leading to Treatment

Arriving at a diagnosis is the first step in determining the scope of symptoms and level of impairment that a person is struggling with. Aside from the complications noted above, every day, clinicians meet with people to assist them in identifying "what's wrong." Once a diagnosis is established, the clinician is expected to examine the available evidence-based treatments to determine how they can most effectively assist their client in reducing their distress and improve their functioning.

The American Psychiatric Association concedes that "the diagnosis of a mental disorder is not equivalent to a need for treatment" (APA, 2022, p. 14), recognizing that while people may not meet the full array of symptoms required for a diagnosis, they may present with a clear need and/or benefit from treatment. In this way, a diagnosis should not be considered determinative in whether one needs treatment (although for insurance to pay for your treatment, a diagnosis is required).

As you will realize in reading *No Method to the Madness*, selecting an intervention strategy is a complicated endeavor. There are countless psychotherapy strategies, wide-ranging medications, self-help recommendations, psychoeducational approaches, as well as many other possibilities within other disciplines (e.g., occupational therapy, nutritional, etc.), depending on the condition. With all these options, it is difficult to have a comprehensive, balanced understanding of what may be best for your specific situation. As a result, you may receive a variety of recommendations depending on the service provider. Their suggestions may also be rooted in what they're most comfortable with, or most familiar with in the literature they review, or from their training.

Generally, every disorder is a combination of symptoms that must occur together for a specified amount of time, and create distress or impairment in the person's functioning. This impairment must occur across different settings (such as at home, with friends, and at school). Disorders within the DSM-5-TR have many different symptom options, and the person must have a specified number to reach the diagnostic threshold. If the person meets more than the required number of symptoms, they may have a "severe" qualifier for the diagnosis. Amazingly, for some categories, someone may *not* meet the minimum threshold of symptoms required for the disorder but may still receive the diagnosis under the creative label, "Other Specified, *disorder*" (e.g., Other Specified ADHD). That's right. A clinician can give you a diagnosis even if you have not met the minimum threshold of symptoms that defines the disorder.

While the DSM is the most prevalent model for diagnosing psychiatric conditions in the United States, the International Classification of Diseases (ICD) published by the World Health Organization (WHO) is also a significant model. Moreover, with ongoing criticism and recognition of the weaknesses of the DSM model, emerging strategies, to be explored below, are offering compelling modifications to how we conceptualize psychiatric disturbance.

Identifying a disorder is done in a "diagnostic interview." The time to complete the diagnostic process should take hours. Understanding the development, maintenance, and contextual factors that have created symptoms is critical to an accurate picture of the problem. However, a diagnosis is often recklessly determined in a matter of moments. This compressed procedure may also be influenced by the restrictions of insurance companies to reimburse the clinician for the diagnostic process. Giving a diagnosis requires that some level of impairment occurs across different settings. If it's just in one setting, it likely says more about that setting than a disordered child. This diagnostic process should include the parent/caregiver, youth, and any other collateral information that could be integrated (e.g., feedback from a teacher). But the interview should also try to understand the child's interpersonal world. Like a tree falling in the woods, symptoms are "heard" in relationships. Therefore, when and how relationships are disrupted can be very revealing as to the factors leading to "symptoms."

A diagnosis also requires that the symptoms are creating distress within the individual. For children, this distress is often described by the adults in their lives. "Billy can't go to sleep without someone in his bedroom with him . . . " or "can't stay in his seat at school" . . . or "is disrespectful and doesn't follow directions" . . . or "can't finish his homework" . . . or "seems to worry a lot." You get the idea. As a psychologist, I've never had a child come into therapy distressed about how often he gets out of his seat. But when they *do* express distress, it's critical to pay close attention to their concerns. Too often, adults dismiss complaints/concerns expressed by children because "adults know better." My view, however, is that it is essential to respond to what the youth can share with you about their experience. A child saying, "I can't slow my thoughts down . . . " "My parents don't understand me . . . " "I'm sad all the time . . . " "the rules aren't fair . . . " is clearly sharing a level of distress that needs attention.

Medical causes for the symptoms must also be ruled out. The clinician should make sure that the child has had a physical or recent evaluation by a physician. If this hasn't occurred by the time you have a therapy appointment, it may provide an opportunity to then set up an appointment with the physician, letting them know that you have concerns about your child's behavior/emotions and want to make sure that it does not have a medical basis. There are a range of medical conditions that can create behavioral or emotional symptoms and if those are present, psychotherapy may do little to alleviate the distress.

Clinicians are also afforded the ability to make "Provisional" diagnoses. A provisional diagnosis is a tentative determination of the disorder but recognizes that more information is required (and will be gathered in the future) to confirm the diagnosis. As mentioned, it is imperative that clinicians always consider exposure to trauma as a factor in a clinical presentation.

Many of life's common challenges may result in a psychiatric diagnosis if you enter treatment. For example, there are conditions called "adjustment disorders" which reflect one's struggle to manage the stress of life events. There is no doubt that life can throw many difficult experiences at us and indeed may result in the need to get help. An adjustment disorder requires a stressful event (e.g., divorce, going off to college) that creates distress and/or impairment in a person's life. It may disrupt relationships, job performance, and so on. It can include anxiety, depression, behavioral symptoms, or other disruptions in a person's life. People handle stress differently, some better than others. And while the availability of this diagnostic label can support the payment of insurance companies for services, we need to be careful about the assumptions we make about the word *disorder*.

The Accuracy of Diagnosing

When the criteria for a diagnosis are being developed, researchers and clinicians meet to generate a list to capture the experience of the condition. Once the list is created, it is often sent out for field trials. These trials allow clinicians to use the diagnostic criteria to determine its utility and accurate applicability to clients they may be working with in different clinical settings.

Within these field trials, different clinicians will use the diagnostic criteria. Through this work, a measure of "inter-rater reliability" is created. Measuring inter-rater reliability allows researchers to understand the extent to which people agree on the diagnosis when presented with the symptom presentation. When there is agreement across the symptom presentation and clinicians arrive at the same diagnosis, there is perfect inter-rater reliability. In statistical terms, this measurement is represented as a kappa score. While the level of 0.60 is considered moderate agreement, it is the level pursued to be "acceptable" for DSM diagnostic purposes. You will see in Table 2.1, though, that 0.60 is the exception rather than the rule in common child/adolescent disorders.

Table 2.1 DSM-5 Inter-Rater Reliability Scores

	DSM-5	DSM-IV	ICD-10	DSM-III
Generalized Anxiety Disorder	0.20	0.65	0.30	0.72
Posttraumatic Stress Disorder	0.67	0.59	0.76	0.55
Schizophrenia	0.46	0.76	0.79	0.81
Bipolar Disorder Type I	0.32	0.59	0.53	0.80
Bipolar Disorder Type II	0.40			
Major Neurocognitive Disorder	0.78		0.60	0.91
Antisocial Personality Disorder	0.22			
Autism Spectrum Disorder	0.69	0.85	0.77	0.01
Attention-Deficit Hyperactivity Disorder	0.61	0.85	0.85	0.50
Disruptive Mood Dysregulation Disorder	0.25*			
Oppositional Defiant Disorder	0.41	0.55		0.66
Conduct Disorder	0.48	0.57	0.78	0.61

Adapted from Frances, A. (2012, May 8). Newsflash from APA meeting: DSM-5 has flunked its reliability tests. *Huff-Post*. https://www.huffpost.com/entry/dsm-5-reliability-tests_b_1490857. Scores represent the kappa score. A threshold of 0.60 is considered acceptable agreement.
* DMDD kappa score was retrieved from Freedman et al., 2013.

The Evolution of Diagnosing

As discussed, the dominant model of diagnosing psychiatric conditions is the *Diagnostic and Statistical Manual of Mental Disorders, Fifth Edition, Text Revision*. But the evolution of our diagnostic models, championed by the American Psychiatric Association, began in 1952 with the DSM-I. Prior to that, there was a very concise *Statistical Manual for Institutions for the Insane* published in 1918, by the National Committee for Mental Hygiene, Bureau of Statistics. So, diagnosing as we know it only began about seventy years ago. There have long been efforts to categorize and describe behavioral and emotional abnormalities, but the editions of the DSM have attempted to do so in a more organized, purportedly "scientific" way.

Centuries before the DSM, the efforts to identify and explain "insanity" were guided by spiritual beliefs. For example, in the 1400s, bizarre behaviors were considered to be caused by evil spirits or witches (Whitaker, 2019). Even today, you will occasionally see stories about exorcisms being performed, but as a foundation for mental illness, these ideas have changed. As our thinking and beliefs about health evolved, so did our ways of explaining behavioral and emotional oddities. For example, imbalances in the body's "humors" (yellow bile, blood, phlegm, and black bile) were thought to be connected to the behaviors of the insane. This framework to conceptualize pathology established the foundation for our current beliefs about chemical imbalances (Whitaker, 2019) and reliance on medications. That is, something was out of balance and if restored, the individual would recover.

Through the history of efforts to improve symptoms of the mentally ill, many strategies were attempted, from abusive to compassionate. As Whitaker (2019) details, the "treatment" of mentally ill has included bloodletting, ice baths, spinning chairs, lobotomies, induced seizures, shock therapies, removing potential sites of infection, among many others. At one time, more compassionate efforts, such as Moral Therapy, found success with impressive outcomes. But pressure again grew to integrate physically based treatments, resulting in an elevation of physicians into a decision-making role in most models of mental health care (e.g., in "asylums" and mental health institutions).

It should also be noted that the thought-leaders many years ago were simply well-educated individuals that may have had the opportunity to publish a paper, a book, present at a conference, or hold an academic position at an influential institution. Times were very different even just several decades ago in terms of distributing scientific information. Before the internet, opportunities to distribute information (such as a research project) were much more limited, so if a paper or book was published, it could have tremendous influence over practices in the field, even if the research methodology was flawed. At the other extreme, we are now inundated with countless journals, online resources, books and e-books, and Google to guide our decision-making. In the past, treatment strategies could have been developed despite a paucity of scientific study. Now, deciphering the science to make treatment decisions is like wading through a morass of good and bad science, hoping to discover a strategy that will benefit the person in distress. This may sound a bit pessimistic, but we'll explore the strengths and weaknesses of our science throughout the book.

In a remarkable example of how time can influence our conceptualization of "disorders," in 1851 Dr. Samuel Cartwright, a physician appointed to be chairman of the state medical convention in Louisiana, published a paper on what he believed to be a disorder, one he identified as drapetomania. This condition was exclusive to all Africans and characterized by the uncontrollable urge to run away from their owners (Myers, 2014). Dr. Cartwright had considerable status and authority in the field giving him influence on how others perceived and conceptualized enslaved Africans. While this diagnosis by today's standards is absurd, it is important to appreciate how a socially constructed idea became the foundation for a mental illness. Moreover, assumptions embedded in drapetomania are not completely absent from racist beliefs about African Americans today. Though thoroughly debunked as a mental illness, we need to take that lens to other labels and disorders we use today. We do not have a monopoly on truth and wisdom in the field of mental health. Indeed, things we believe today will be debunked and discarded in the future.

Also reflective of the influence of these "thought leaders," a conference in 1921 convened experts from the elite academic institutions such as Johns Hopkins, Princeton, Harvard, Columbia, and others. Remarkably, this conference focused on the "defectives" in society, examining "the Jewish Problem" and "Negro-White Intermixture" among others. Guided by the status of these presenters, it quickly provided an intellectual foundation for eugenics (Whitaker, 2019). Yet just one hundred years later, our understanding of genetics has expanded exponentially, frankly leading to more questions than answers. So again, the scientific foundation of these genetically attributed causes remains uncertain, but unfortunately continues to influence our policies, public perceptions, etc. Let's be clear: our genes influence our behavior, but we cannot use this understanding to explain psychiatric disorders to date.

People will subscribe to ideas like this when they are delivered with certainty, are provided by a person in authority, explain a narrative or bias (confirmation bias), or enhance a person's sense of predictability. Not too dissimilar from some of our diagnostic labels today, when a parent is told by an "expert" that their child has ABC diagnosis, they may feel a sense of relief thinking, "Finally, we know what is going on with Billy and we can seek the best care." When in fact, the diagnosis only provides an umbrella term for a collection of observed symptoms, offering no real understanding of *why* the problems are occurring, or *how* to correct the situation.

These questions, of course, are valid. When we are faced with challenges, we want to make sense of it. If our child is in distress, not doing well in school, or losing friends, we naturally want to know what is happening. It is also a good decision to seek help when we need it. When parents go to an expert for help, this expert completes a diagnostic evaluation and arrives at identifying a disorder. Now knowing that an expert has determined that ABC disorder is impacting their child, the next obvious question is, "what could be causing this?" An honest answer to that question is "we really don't know." Some clinicians will engage in some psychobabble gymnastics, such as "Billy has anger problems because he has Disruptive Mood Dysregulation Disorder, but he has DMDD because he has anger problems." I have had discussions with countless parents, students, and even colleagues about the causes of these disorders but no one can answer that question with certainty.

Trauma adds dimension to that discussion, to be explored later. Traumatic or adverse events are highly correlated to having difficulties later in behavior, emotion, interpersonal relationships, physical health, and so on. However, not all victims of trauma experience those difficulties. We must consider other factors in the life of the person to understand the impact of events and the protective factors that may have shielded them from problems afterward.

One final thought before we explore the evolution of the Diagnostic Manuals. If you are seeking assistance from a mental health professional, have an open discussion about their diagnostic impressions. I would often bring out the DSM and go over the diagnostic criteria of the disorder that I'm considering to see if it makes sense to the person I'm working with. There should be no secrets about this, as it will drive the treatment strategy. This transparency often strengthens the relationship, as well as clarifying goals for our work together.

The Diagnostic and Statistical Manuals of Mental Disorders

This brief review of the Diagnostic Manuals will be through the lens of understanding their impact on child and adolescent disorders and our beliefs about these conditions. As you will see, the way we describe, classify, and understand these conditions has changed significantly over time. So, it is worth asking, did those who authored the earlier versions of the DSMs know that they were incorrect by today's standards? I suspect not. And if that's the case, should we also be concerned about the disorders we've identified today?

The number of diagnoses has also changed considerably over time. Believe it or not, there are inconsistencies related to how many diagnoses are included in each manual. As we'll discuss, there are general categories (e.g., Mood Disorder) and specific disorders (e.g., Major Depression) within those categories, but there are many other details or "specifiers" that are added then to the diagnostic code (e.g., chronic or in remission). As a result, the exact count of diagnoses in each manual varies in the available literature.

In 2024, Judy Kupchan, MA (a doctoral student in clinical psychology) completed a sophisticated analysis of the DSM-5-TR. In addition to detailing the overarching categories of diagnoses, her analysis included a methodology to account for all the specifiers within those categories (that is, variations of the disorders). This additional layer of analysis has revealed thousands upon thousands of unique diagnoses within the DSM diagnostic system. These findings are critically important. Take a common example of major depressive disorder. This condition can be diagnosed as a single episode or recurrent, with or without psychotic features, and so on. These forms of major depression represent important, complex differences in the presentation, cause, and potential treatments of the condition. In total, there are over 37,000 different diagnostic formulations that can be established within the DSM-5-TR. The majority of these are bipolar disorders (representing 26,545 or 71.68 percent of diagnoses) (Foltz & Kupchan, 2025).

DSM-I (1952)

The DSM-I included just over one hundred diagnoses (Kawa & Giordano, 2012). Of these, few focused specifically on young people. It is not, of course, because children and teens did not have behavioral and/or emotional challenges in the mid-1950s, but they were apparently not of sufficient concern to be considered psychiatric disorders.

DSM-II (1968)

The DSM-II included approximately 180 diagnoses (Kawa & Giordano, 2012). As noted above, the exact count of diagnoses is debated. The DSM-II did include a range of disorders related to infancy and childhood, including conditions such as encopresis, enuresis, and disturbances in feeding. However, the DSM-II did include disorders specifically assigned to Behavior Disorders of Childhood and Adolescence. These included:

- Hyperkinetic reaction of childhood (or adolescence)—This diagnosis was seemingly the first iteration of what is known today as attention deficit hyperactivity disorder. It was characterized by restlessness, overactivity, and short attention span.

- Withdrawing reaction of childhood (or adolescence)—This diagnosis was characterized by a general inability to form close relationships, shyness, detachment, and timidity.
- Overanxious reaction of childhood (or adolescence)—This condition was diagnosed when the child was overly anxious, had unrealistic fears, lacked self-confidence, and was overly approval-seeking.
- Runaway reaction of childhood (or adolescence)—This disorder is worth quoting directly. "Individuals with this disorder characteristically escape from threatening situations by running away from home for a day or more without permission. Typically, they are immature and timid, and feel rejected at home, inadequate, and friendless. They often steal furtively" (p. 50). Quite simply, if one feels rejected and inadequate at home, and finds it threatening, running away—while risking a worse outcome—is not irrational thinking. To label this as a disorder of the child seems odd.
- Unsocialized aggressive reaction of childhood (or adolescence)—This disorder includes a resistance to authority, as well as verbal and/or behavioral aggression. In today's paradigm, these behaviors would likely be diagnosed as Oppositional Defiant Disorder or Conduct Disorder.
- Group delinquent reaction of childhood (or adolescence)—This disorder included breaking rules, stealing, skipping school, and staying out late at night. They note that in girls, this disorder may also include sexual delinquency and shoplifting.
- Other reaction of childhood (or adolescence)—This diagnosis was reserved for other behavioral problems that were not included in other categories.

Criticism of psychiatry grew in the years of the DSM-II era. Challenging the legitimacy of psychiatry, one of the most pointed critiques was "the lack of clear demarcations between mental health and illness, and the relatively low reliability of psychiatric diagnoses" (APA, 1968, p. 4). It is worth restating here that our *current* diagnostic manual highlights the lack of clear boundaries between disorders as well as ambiguous thresholds for what qualifies as a "disorder." While the American Psychiatric Association attempted to deal with these criticisms decades ago, one must wonder why these same vulnerabilities remain to this day.

DSM-III (1980)

Adding over 80 diagnoses to the DSM-II, there are approximately 265 diagnoses in the DSM-III (Kawa & Giordano, 2012). Related to our discussion here, the following disorders were some of those included in the "Disorders Usually First Evident in Infancy, Childhood, or Adolescence":

- Attention Deficit Disorder—This category included specifiers of "with Hyperactivity," "without Hyperactivity," and "Residual forms." This was the first iteration of what is known today as ADHD.
- Conduct Disorder—This category included four subtypes of Undersocialized, Socialized, Aggressive, and Nonaggressive. Overall, this disorder is characterized by repetitive patterns of behavior that violate social norms, the rights of others, and noncompliance with rules.
- Anxiety Disorders of Childhood or Adolescence—This category comprised several anxiety-based disorders including separation anxiety disorder, avoidant disorder, and overanxious disorder.
- Other Disorders of Infancy, Childhood, or Adolescence included reactive attachment disorder, schizoid disorder, selective mutism, oppositional disorder, and identity disorder. While these other diagnoses have persisted over time, identity disorder no longer exists in this form. In this DSM-III era, identity disorder was characterized by severe distress related to uncertainty around long-term goals, career choice, friendship patterns, sexual orientation and behavior, religious identification, moral value systems, and/or group loyalties.
- Pervasive Developmental Disorders—Included infantile autism, childhood onset pervasive developmental disorder, and atypical pervasive developmental disorder.

The DSM-III provided inter-rater reliability details. For the child and adolescent diagnostic categories, authors note that reliability was only "fair." Indeed, reliability scores were just .50, .61, and .44 for attention deficit disorder, conduct disorder, and anxiety disorders, respectively (p. 471).

DSM-III-R (1987)

The DSM-III-R included 292 diagnoses (Kawa & Giordano, 2012). Regarding the "Disorders Usually First Evident in Infancy, Childhood, or Adolescence," there were some modifications. Updated information was also provided in this revised edition.

- Pervasive Developmental Disorders did include modifications. This category was reduced to just two diagnoses. "Autistic disorder" was identified as a severe form of pervasive developmental disorder. The diagnosis of "pervasive developmental disorder, not otherwise specified" was now in place to capture developmental impairments that did not qualify for autistic disorder.

- The Category of "Disruptive Behavior Disorders" was created and included "attention-deficit hyperactivity disorder," which required eight of fourteen symptoms. This edition also notes that the symptoms in the list of diagnostic criteria for ADHD "are in descending order of discriminating power based on data from a national field trial." (p. 53). This category also included conduct disorder (with subtypes of Group Type, Solitary Aggressive Type, and Undifferentiated Type), and oppositional defiant disorder.
- The Anxiety Disorders remained unchanged with separation anxiety disorder, avoidant disorder, and overanxious disorder.

The DSM-III-R noted that field trials were conducted to examine the reliability of the Disruptive Behavior Disorders category. However, reliability (kappa) scores were not provided. Interestingly, authors indicate "the clinicians assessed 550 children in four diagnostic groups (many with multiple diagnoses)" (p. 493), raising questions about the diagnostic specificity of these conditions. Of these 550 children, there were 311 diagnosed with ADHD, 140 with oppositional defiant disorder, 130 with conduct disorder, and 134 with Other and No Mental Disorder.

DSM-IV (1994)

The DSM-IV included 297 diagnoses (Kawa & Giordano, 2012). There were some noteworthy modifications to diagnostic categories, to be described below. In the years soon following the release of the DSM-IV, a major trend emerged in the diagnosing of bipolar disorder in young people. In the earlier, DSM-III-R, the average age of onset of a manic episode was the early 20s. Indeed, as of the release of the DSM-IV, people younger than 20 years old were rarely diagnosed with the condition. But as depicted in Figure 2.1, things quickly changed.

The rate of diagnosing bipolar disorder in youth skyrocketed from 25 per 100,000 (in 1994–1995) to 1,003 per 100,000 (in 2002–2003) (Moreno, 2007). But given what we assume about the causes of bipolar disorder, how could this be true? Does this 4,000 percent increase reflect improved identification? Could it indicate a proliferation of the biological foundations of this disorder? Or could it reflect an aggressive pattern of overdiagnosis?

Figure 2.1 From *Anatomy of an Epidemic*, Whitaker, 2011.

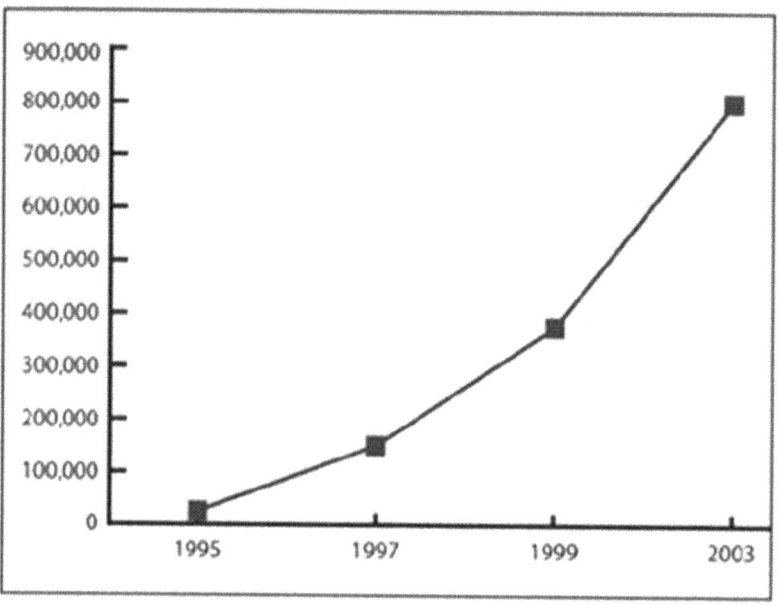

This movement proved to be horribly flawed. After a generation of identifying and medicating young people as bipolar, the field realized that these young people did not become adults with bipolar disorder. But the remedy for this mistake emerged in the DSM-5, to be discussed below.

The DSM-IV included changes to major categories, compared to the DSM-III-R.

- Pervasive Developmental Disorders now included autistic disorder, Rett's disorder, childhood disintegrative disorder, Asperger's disorder, and pervasive developmental disorder, not otherwise specified.

- Attention-Deficit and Disruptive Behavior Disorders—This category combines the disorders of ADHD, oppositional defiant disorder, and conduct disorder (now only identifying childhood onset or adolescent onset). It also includes disruptive behavior disorders, not otherwise specified. In the DSM-IV, the ADHD criteria (now only requiring six of eighteen symptoms) were used to identify three subtypes of the condition, Predominantly Inattentive, Predominantly Hyperactive, and Combined Type. Further, it maintained that "there are no laboratory tests that have been established as diagnostic in the clinical assessment of Attention-Deficit Hyperactivity Disorder. . . . There are no specific physical features associated with" ADHD (p. 81). It is worth noting that as of 2013, the American Psychiatric Association decided that ADHD is a neurodevelopmental disorder, categorized with autism, rather than keeping it associated with Disruptive Disorders, to be discussed below.

DSM-IV-TR (2000)

As its title indicates, the DSM-IV-TR provided text revisions to the DSM-IV version but did not substantially alter any of the diagnostic conditions or criteria for those described above in the DSM-IV. For conditions most relevant for *No Method to the Madness*, it is noteworthy that for ADHD, the DSM-IV-TR notes "there are no laboratory tests, neurological assessments, or attentional assessments that have been established as diagnostic in the clinical assessment of Attention-Deficit / Hyperactivity Disorder" (p. 89). Moreover, for ADHD, the DSM-IV-TR states that "there must be clear evidence of clinically significant impairment in social, academic, or occupational functioning" (p. 93).

DSM-5 (2013)

The DSM-5 emerged with significant changes from the DSM-IV-TR. It presented nearly three hundred diagnoses across twenty categories. The overarching category of "Disorders Usually First Evident in Infancy, Childhood, or Adolescence" was eliminated. Some of those disorders were now subsumed under a category of Neurodevelopmental Disorders. In this category, Autism Spectrum Disorders was created but it was with the elimination of Asperger's disorder, Rett's disorder, childhood disintegrative disorder, and pervasive developmental disorder.

The Neurodevelopmental Disorders also include ADHD in the DSM-5. Remarkably, the diagnostic requirement of clinically significant impairment resulting from ADHD symptoms was noticeably softened. In the DSM-5, ADHD symptoms must only "interfere with or reduce the quality of social, academic, or occupational functioning" (p. 60).

One of the most noteworthy additions to the DSM-5 is the introduction of the diagnosis of disruptive mood dysregulation disorder (DMDD). This disorder was created to address the diagnostic confusion related to pediatric bipolar disorder. Irritable children with outbursts were a group commonly diagnosed with bipolar disorder and DMDD was purported to be a more accurate conceptualization. This new diagnosis was placed in the category of depressive disorders. The invention of this condition, though, was not without controversy.

Respected experts in the field of child/adolescent psychiatry raised concerns about the new DMDD diagnosis (originally called temper dysregulation disorder, TDD). These authors concluded there was "insufficient scientific support to include TDD as a unique diagnostic entity" (Axelson et al., 2011, p. 1257). They highlight that the symptoms of this disorder commonly exist across other disorders which will lead to comorbidity and diagnostic confusion. Finally, they accurately predicted that this disorder would be an easy target for pharmaceutical intervention—likely the antipsychotic class of medications—to control the irritability and outbursts.

The DSM-5 also eliminated the subtypes of schizophrenia and the Multiaxial Assessment system of diagnostic summary to name two additional, significant changes from the DSM-IV-TR.

DSM-5-TR (2022)

The DSM-5-TR did not offer any changes to specific diagnostic criteria, though the supporting text was revised. Importantly, the American Psychiatric Association added valuable content related to the association of trauma and adverse experiences to the emergence and exacerbation of psychiatric symptoms. While this has been known for decades, discussion of the influence of trauma was minimally offered in earlier editions of the DSM.

After more than a decade of using the DMDD diagnosis, discussed above, the DSM-5-TR acknowledged the large role that trauma may play in that disorder. Like so many other conditions, "factors associated with disrupted family life, such as psychological abuse or neglect, parental psychiatric disorder, limited parental education, sing-parent household, early trauma, death of a parent, parental grief, divorce, and malnutrition, are associated with the core behaviors of disruptive mood dysregulation disorder" (p. 181).

While the DSM-5-TR represents the latest framework for identifying psychiatric disorders, it is anticipated that changes will continue, new disorders will be created, and our efforts to understand the symptoms and phenomenology of emotional and behavioral difficulties more accurately will evolve. With that reality, we should be humble in the assumptions we make about today's disorders. Much like the errors made in past generations of mental health professionals, it is likely that valid critiques of our practices will be evident in the coming years.

Finally, the concept of "Diagnosis by Response" is one you may encounter if medications are involved in the treatment. Quite simply, the idea here is that a clinician may feel more certain of a diagnosis based on the response to a given medication. For example, if a child focuses more on a stimulant, the appropriate diagnosis is likely ADHD. If they calm down being prescribed an antipsychotic medication, their condition may be disruptive mood dysregulation disorder (DMDD). If they feel a bit more upbeat and energetic being placed on an antidepressant, they were likely suffering from a depressive disorder. As we'll explore throughout the book, this is faulty reasoning and should not be accepted as a reliable diagnostic practice.

Walk Away Message

In the early iterations of the DSM, concerns were raised about the reliability and validity of psychiatric disorders. These concerns remain today, despite decades research and numerous new editions of the Diagnostic and Statistical Manual. Diagnoses are derived from clinical interviews and observations. These interactions are reflective of training the clinicians have received in completion of their degrees or experiences thereafter. There are no tests for psychiatric disorders; no blood tests, no brain scans, no definitive psychological tests can be used to confirm a diagnosis.

References

Allsopp, K., Read, J., Corcoran, R., & Kinderman, P. (2019). Heterogeneity in psychiatric diagnostic classification. *Psychiatry Research*. https://doi.org/10.1016/j.psychres.2019.07.005

American Psychiatric Association. (1952). *Diagnostic and statistical manual of mental disorders* (1st ed.).

American Psychiatric Association. (1968). *Diagnostic and statistical manual of mental disorders* (2nd ed.).

American Psychiatric Association. (1980). *Diagnostic and statistical manual of mental disorders* (3rd ed.).

American Psychiatric Association. (1987). *Diagnostic and statistical manual of mental disorders* (3rd ed., rev.).

American Psychiatric Association. (1994). *Diagnostic and statistical manual of mental disorders* (4th ed.).

American Psychiatric Association. (2000). *Diagnostic and statistical manual of mental disorders* (4th ed., text rev.).

American Psychiatric Association. (2013). *Diagnostic and statistical manual of mental disorders* (5th ed.).

American Psychiatric Association. (2022). *Diagnostic and statistical manual of mental disorders* (5th ed., text rev.).

Axelson, D., Birmaher, B., Findling, R., Fristad, M., Kowatch, R., Youngstrom, E., . . . Diler, R. (2011). Concerns regarding the inclusion of temper dysregulation disorder with dysphoria in the *Diagnostic and statistical manual of mental disorders* (5th ed.). *The Journal of Clinical Psychiatry, 72*(09): 1257–1262.

Cloitre, M. (2020). ICD-11 complex post-traumatic stress disorder: Simplifying diagnosis in trauma populations. *The British Journal of Psychiatry, 216*(3): 129–131. https://doi.org/10.1192/bjp.2020.43

Faust, D. (2011). *Coping with psychiatric and psychological testimony* (6th ed.). Oxford University Press.

Foltz, R., & Kupchan, J. (in press, 2025). Our diagnostic dilemma: A critical review of the DSM Framework. *Ethical Human Psychology and Psychiatry*, October.

Frances, A. (2012, May 8). Newsflash from APA meeting: DSM-5 has flunked its reliability tests. *HuffPost*. https://www.huffpost.com/entry/dsm-5-reliability-tests_b_1490857

Freedman, R., Lewis, D. A., Michels, R., Pine, D. S., Schultz, S. K., Tamminga, C. A., . . . Yager, J. (2013). The initial field trials of DSM-5: New blooms and old thorns. *American Journal of Psychiatry, 170*(1): 1–5. https://doi.org/10.1176/appi.ajp.2012.12091189

Kawa, S., & Giordano, J. (2012). A brief historicity of the diagnostic and statistical manual of mental disorders: Issues and implications for the future of psychiatric canon and practice. *Philosophy, Ethics, and Humanities in Medicine, 7*(2).

Moreno, C. (2007). National trends in the outpatient diagnosis and treatment of bipolar disorders in youth. *Archives of General Psychiatry, 64*.

Myers, B. E. (2014). *"Drapetomania": Rebellion, defiance and free Black insanity in the antebellum United States* [Dissertation, University of California, Los Angeles]. https://escholarship.org/uc/item/9dc055h5

Whitaker, R. (2011). *Anatomy of an epidemic: Magic bullets, psychiatric drugs, and the astonishing rise of mental illness in America*. Crown Books.

Whitaker, R. (2019). *Mad in America: Bad science, bad medicine, and the enduring mistreatment of the mentally ill*. Basic Books.

3
The Role of Trauma

Thousands of young people experience abuse and adversity every year, some experiencing it every day, for extended periods. Many can recover from those events and return to a healthy daily life. For others, however, the experiences of trauma and adversity can have profound, lasting effects that can continue for a lifetime.

We now know that traumatic experiences can negatively affect psychological, physical, interpersonal, educational, and occupational outcomes. Remarkably, our ability to quickly address the occurrence and impact of trauma is still woefully inadequate. Children and teens are dependent on us to keep them safe. When we fail, the immense costs—for both youth and society—can last decades. And with our often-perfunctory use of medications in response to distress, it has been established that there is a graded relationship between the number/extent of traumatic experiences and likelihood of being medicated (Anda et al., 2007).

Responding to Trauma

You have heard of the diagnosis posttraumatic stress disorder (PTSD). This condition reflects a specific set of symptoms that emerge following the experience of (or witness to) a life-threatening situation. There may be a delay in the presentation of these symptoms, but once they begin, it can be long-lasting. Unfortunately, the diagnosis of PTSD does not account for many different forms of adversity such as poverty, racism, community violence, parental divorce, having a mentally ill caregiver, etcetera. There are wide-ranging life events that are considered traumatic enough to disrupt functioning for many years. Especially for children, our diagnostic criterion for identifying trauma is sorely lacking. In fact, in one study of over fourteen hundred youth, researchers noted that 68 percent reported at least one traumatic event, over a third having more than one, and over 13 percent were presenting symptoms of PTSD, yet only 0.5 percent of these youth met sufficient criteria for the PTSD diagnosis (AHRQ, 2012). This is problematic on several levels.

Diagnostic criteria must be specific enough to capture the occurrence of a disorder. Although, as we see in the chapter on diagnosing, we continue to struggle to reliably identify disorders. An abundance of research has established that traumatic experiences can set many processes in motion that can lead to negative mental and physical health outcomes. If our ability to identify trauma's initial impact fails to activate a response to intervene and improve short- and long-term outcomes, we need to aggressively modify this approach. As a result, all those able to identify the first indicators of a youth struggling to manage their reaction to a traumatic event must be able to mobilize stakeholders to support the child. Quite simply, we should err on the side of caution, buffering a young person from the potential impact of trauma rather than waiting for their stress to evolve to the point of a diagnosable condition.

There is a clear flaw in our system of accessing care. Almost all those struggling with emotional and behavioral challenges need to pay for their treatment. To have services paid for, a diagnosis is required. It's part of the billing process. In my many years of providing therapy services, I could only bill insurance companies for those interventions if I provided a diagnosis. In fact, some insurance companies won't pay for therapy services if the diagnosis isn't severe enough. Or, therapy services may be restricted to limited sessions based on a diagnosis, or limitations within an insurance plan. Herein lies the problem. The symptoms of trauma exposure may start small, building insidiously into something larger, more debilitating. We know symptoms begin to emerge well before the criteria for a diagnosis can be fulfilled. This gap in time reveals a dramatic failure in our system to intervene early, which could potentially avoid unknown pain, distress, financial burden, stretched systems, and loss.

Another example of this failure is within our continuum of care. I spent many years as a clinician and administrator in residential treatment centers. Most of the youth placed in these facilities were being funded with Medicaid. These children and adolescents were troubled, trauma-exposed, and in need of intensive care. Many services were available to them within these facilities. But in my early efforts to explore treatments without the emphatic use of medications I was explicitly told, "If they [the youth] need residential treatment, they need to be on medication." This is not true, but it is our standard of care. Even today, it is indeed rare that a youth receives these intensive services without a necessary component being psychotropic medication.

Many providers and systems of care purport to be *trauma-informed*. This term suggests that they approach addressing the needs of their clients through the lens of trauma, understanding its effects, and are trained to utilize strategies to effectively mitigate the impact of these experiences. But being trauma-informed must also be supported at all levels of the system of care. It's not enough to have clinicians trained without an infrastructure to support their work. It requires administrative leadership with a vision for change, the resources to facilitate and support their clients, flexibility in service delivery based on the needs of their clients, support and self-care for the providers, and robust strategies to measure and monitor the strengths and challenges in the treatments offered.

My goal here is not to provide a comprehensive overview of trauma, adversity, and the most effective strategies to treat it. However, it is well established that adversity and trauma can have a lifelong impact on one's ability to achieve mental, emotional, physical, interpersonal, and functional health. Over the course of my own development as a psychologist, important contributions to the understanding of trauma and adversity have allowed the field to take dramatic strides in appreciating the impact and treatment of trauma. Important works by Bruce Perry, MD, PhD, Bessel van der Kolk, MD, Dante Cicchetti, PhD, Judith Herman, MD, Peter Levine, PhD, are among many other influential contributors who have devoted their careers to expanding our knowledge and practice and influenced my work. Despite the invaluable research and clinical work focused on trauma, it remains one of the costliest public health issues in the United States (van der Kolk, 2016).

As my work in the field has evolved, I've become particularly interested in Perry's Neurosequential Model of Therapeutics (NMT). Developmentally informed, tailored to understand the impact of trauma as well as the neurological underpinnings of self-regulation and interpersonal connection, this approach provides pragmatic intervention strategies that can be utilized across all levels of care. Educators, clinicians, direct care staff, and others can take this sophisticated information and develop methods to increase self-regulation skills, improve resilient responses to stress, and enhance interpersonal relationships.

Much of our thinking around "trauma" is rooted in the diagnosis of posttraumatic stress disorder (PTSD). Decades ago, this diagnosis emerged based on experiences from catastrophic trauma like exposure to war. The DSM-5-TR now provides details related to the thoughts, emotions, and behaviors that a person may have after a traumatic experience. While this description is tucked within the discussion of PTSD (and often ignored after reading the list of diagnostic criteria), it illuminates the reality of the overall impact of trauma exposure, as well as how a reaction to trauma can quickly be confused with other psychiatric disorders. The following symptoms are included in the DSM-5-TR as potential reactions to trauma:

- *Quick tempered*—Being quick tempered is a component of many disorders. It may appear as reactive, irritable, quickly defiant of authority, or having a limited tolerance for frustrating experiences. Having a reaction that is disproportionate to the event may be common.
- *Physical and/or verbal aggression*—Physical and verbal aggression can be very disruptive and difficult to manage. These behaviors can take a toll on relationships in the person's life and make other systems (schools, extra-curricular activities, peer groups) very reluctant to include a child or teen if they are showing these symptoms. Depending on how it presents, aggression can be included in various diagnoses.
- *Reckless or self-destructive behavior*—These behaviors can be challenging to control. In many ways, these behaviors can be seen as signs of intense distress or pain in the person, as they can include substance use, self-injurious behaviors (e.g., cutting), or behaving in ways reflecting a lack of concern for the harm or consequences that may result.
- *Negative moods* (including anhedonia, dysphoria, negative thoughts)—Trauma exposure can change how we feel about ourselves, the world around us, and people in our lives. Often, the victim of trauma may see themselves as "broken," "dirty," "unlovable," etc. These negative feelings influence their overall emotional tone and can also impact their ability to enjoy positive experiences.
- *Persistent inability to feel positive emotions*—As noted, pervasive negative feelings begin to impact our ability to feel pleasure, derive positive feelings from activities, or express a wide range of affect. That is, one may appear to have a flat, or disengaged, emotional reaction to what may otherwise have been a positive experience.
- *Increased sensitivity to perceived threats/hypervigilance*—Increased sensitivity may appear as if the child is on a "hair trigger," quickly interpreting interactions as disrespectful, antagonizing, or attributing too much meaning to innocuous events or interactions. They may appear distractible, in part because they attend small, seemingly meaningless, events. This is, however, an effort to keep themselves safe in a world perceived as threatening or harmful.

- *Over-reactive to unexpected stimuli, jumpiness*—This over-reactivity may appear as agitation, anxiety, difficulty regulating themselves, or a sense of vulnerability, even to small, seemingly harmless events.
- *Difficulties concentrating and in remembering daily events or focusing*—Poor concentration, inability to focus, staring out the window, missing the details of a conversation, and forgetting instructions are examples of how the traumatic experiences may impact one's functioning through the day.
- *Sleep disturbances*—Sleep problems may appear as difficulty falling asleep, difficulty staying asleep, waking up too early, or problematic dreams or nightmares. It does not take long for sleep problems to begin affecting other factors throughout the day. Fatigue, irritability, poor concentration, etc., can quickly impact a youth's day-to-day functioning as a result of sleep difficulties.
- *Auditory "pseudo-hallucinations"*—Hallucinations may be feared as an indicator of psychosis. Indeed, they can be. However, hallucinations may emerge as a result of trauma. There are some questions about the "pseudo" nature of these symptoms. Pseudo-hallucinations are conceptualized as having the impression that the voices may be experienced as if they are one's own thoughts or coming from inside one's head. However, having worked for many years with individuals diagnosed with psychotic conditions, there is variability in how they experience voices. Simplifying hallucinations to feeling as though they exist within one's head is not unique to trauma exposure. They may also be considered "non-psychotic hallucinations" but for the experience of the client, the frightening, disorienting, and intrusive nature of these experiences must be prioritized and appreciated as a result of trauma rather than attributed to a psychotic condition, which would further distract treatment efforts away from the traumatic experiences. While less frequently discussed, there is literature exploring the phenomenon of pseudo-hallucination that concludes it has poor construct validity and is clinically ambiguous (van der Zwaard & Polak, 2001). Finally, the World Health Organization has introduced the diagnosis Complex PTSD (C-PTSD). In its description, the WHO notes that symptoms can include "psychotic symptoms" (WHO, 2024, p. 346), recognizing that hallucinations may be a part of a trauma response. Earlier research stablished the connection between childhood trauma and psychosis saying, "child abuse is a causal factor for psychosis and 'schizophrenia' and, more specifically, for hallucinations, particularly voices commenting and command hallucinations" (Read, van Os,

Morrison, & Ross, 2005, p. 330). To this point, individuals who had suffered five or more types of trauma were 198 times more likely to be diagnosed with a psychotic condition than non-abused individuals (Read et al., 2008).

- *Paranoid thoughts*—In combination with the hypervigilance, perceptual distortions, negative emotions, and diminished sense of self, it is expected that this may also manifest as paranoia. Feeling like others are against you, the world is threatening, and you are constantly vulnerable may indeed look like a paranoid stance toward those around the traumatized individual.
- *Difficulties regulating their emotions*—Anger, depression, anxiety, distress, loneliness, shame, guilt, and fear are some of the powerful emotions that can accompany traumatic experiences. These emotions are complicated, overwhelming, and difficult to manage. Moreover, if the traumatic events are unknown to others, these feelings may appear out of nowhere. As discussed in this book, these feelings should be seen as warning signs that something is wrong. Efforts should be made to understand and support the young person.
- *Difficulties maintaining stable relationships*—Relationships with parents, siblings, friends, teachers, coaches or anyone else that a young person interacts with can be impacted by the young person's reaction to trauma. The behaviors and feelings may be confusing to others and as challenging as they may be, people in their lives may begin to distance themselves. Even trusted, stable relationships may become volatile.
- *Depersonalization and/or Derealization*—Depersonalization, the feeling that you are disconnected from your experiences; as though you are observing your thoughts, feelings, and sensations from the outside is troubling, confusing, and frightening. Equally disconcerting is derealization, where the world around you seems unreal. These symptoms could be qualified as dissociative symptoms and further threaten a trauma victim's sense of safety and connectedness.

As a diagnostic evaluation is completed, every dimension of the client's psychological, emotional, interpersonal, and academic functioning must be filtered through a trauma lens. Even when these psychological factors have been reviewed, physical factors must also be considered. Physical conditions can also mimic symptoms of trauma. As the AACAP points out,

> Physical conditions that may present with PTSD-like symptoms include hyperthyroidism, caffeinism, migraine, asthma, seizure disorder, and catecholamine- or serotonin-secreting tumors. Prescription drugs with

side effects that may mimic aspects of PTSD include anti-asthmatics, sympathomimetics, steroids, selective serotonin reuptake inhibitors (SSRIs), antipsychotics (akathisia), and atypical antipsychotics. Nonprescription drugs with side effects that may mimic PTSD include diet pills, antihistamines, and cold medicines.

(AACAP, 2010, p. 420)

Prescribers should know these factors but may not. Therapists are less likely to be trained in these details. Collaboration across the multidisciplinary team is essential. Psychoeducation for the family/caregivers and youth is also a necessary component of trauma-informed care. When youth and caregivers are empowered with the knowledge of how traumatic experiences can affect their psychological and physical health, it can be another catalyst for change.

Rule Out Trauma and *Then* Do Your Diagnosing

I have been teaching graduate courses on psychological disorders for many years. Knowing the diagnostic criteria, differentiating one condition from another, and staying abreast of emerging clinical issues are imperative. However, as you can see from the list above, many common reactions to trauma can appear to represent other psychiatric and physical conditions. Yet if you arrive at the wrong diagnosis, neglecting the role of trauma, the client will receive the wrong care, resulting in frustration and poor outcomes. "A mislabeled patient is likely to become a mistreated patient" (van der Kolk, 2016, p. 268). Achieving diagnostic clarity is challenging. From the *DSM-IV* era of criteria, it was established that there are 1,750 symptom combinations to meet the diagnostic threshold of PTSD (Donnelly, 2003).

Many common diagnoses in young people can be confused with trauma reactions. Major depressive disorder, disruptive mood dysregulation disorder, anxiety, ADHD, oppositional defiant disorder, and even psychotic conditions can be manifestations of traumatic experiences. Failing to conduct a thorough (and ongoing) evaluation of trauma exposure can interfere with positive outcomes for these children and adolescents. And as we have seen for decades, many first-line interventions for these conditions are medications. Simply medicating and suppressing these symptoms is like taking the batteries out of a smoke detector. The symptoms making up these disorders are signals of distress and pain. Losing access to them clouds our ability to accurately understand their experience.

Providing education around this is important for youth and caregivers. Broadening one's understanding of the effects of trauma helps the young person better understand their own experience. Because a trauma-informed approach conceptualizes problematic behaviors and emotions differently, the strategy to intervene is also different. Too often, disruptive behaviors like aggression or mood instability are targeted with medications to contain them. In this method, it may be seen as an aberrant neurological sequela connected to a psychiatric disorder (e.g., DMDD, bipolar disorder, etc.). Indeed, "many structural and functional brain abnormalities hitherto thought to characterize various psychiatric diagnoses may, in fact, be the direct consequence of childhood maltreatment" (van der Kolk, 2016, p. 267). In contrast, a collaborative, trauma-informed intervention would work to understand the function of the behavior, emphasizing the importance of perceived safety, interpersonal attachments, and skill development.

Recognizing the effects of trauma also enhances a comprehensive approach to address the multi-systemic ramifications. Not only behaviors, emotions, and relationships, but educational and physical effects of traumatic experiences need to be incorporated into the intervention strategies. As we will see below, the Adverse Childhood Experiences (ACEs) study provided a foundation to understand the long-term complications of negative life experiences.

The ACEs Study

In the late 1990s, researchers surveyed thousands of patients in the Kaiser Permanente health care system in California. Through this data collection emerged a groundbreaking understanding of the profound impact of life's adversities on health outcomes. It was an effort to understand how Adverse Childhood Experiences can influence health outcomes. The results were staggering. These ACEs were categorized as:

- physical abuse
- emotional abuse
- sexual abuse
- physical neglect
- emotional neglect
- having a mentally ill caregiver
- having a substance abuser in the home

- witness to domestic violence
- loss of a parent due to divorce, separation, etc.
- having a family member go to prison

The study's survey was to determine if these events occurred (simply yes or no) before the age of 18. The study evaluated over seventeen thousand adults with the average age of 56, which means there were many years between the age of the trauma and the impact it had on health outcomes. But these sophisticated researchers were able to determine strong correlations between your experience of trauma and difficulties later in life. Not only did these trauma experiences relate to physical health complications, but they influenced lifestyle, emotional health, and even life expectancy.

Researchers later added additional categories of trauma exposure, called the Philadelphia ACEs. This expansion of the original ACEs includes categories of witnessing violence, experiencing discrimination, living in an unsafe neighborhood, experiencing bullying, and living in foster care (Cronholm et al., 2015). Their research has also confirmed these factors as negatively influencing emotional well-being and overall health.

ACEs tend to occur in clusters and as a result, much research has focused on the impact of four or more ACEs. This threshold is a tipping point in many ways for the onset of more severe presentations. For example, large scale reviews have revealed that individuals with four or more ACEs, compared to those with none, were much more likely to develop anxiety conditions and depression, and to attempt suicide (Sahle et al., 2021). Cognitive functioning, substance use patterns, and relational stability can all be affected. Here are outcomes across research:

> Compared with a person with no adverse childhood experiences, a person with an ACE score of 4 or higher is seven times more likely to be alcoholic and six times more likely to have had sex before age 15. This person is also twice as likely to have heart disease and twice as likely to have cancer ... forty-six times more likely to be depressed, and twelve times more likely to commit suicide. ... people with an ACE score of 6 or higher died nearly twenty years earlier than those with a score of 0. ... A boy with an ACE score of 6 or higher has a 4,600 percent increase in the likelihood of abusing intravenous drugs later.
>
> (Karr-Morse & Wiley, 2012, pp. 10–11)

Trauma research has also explored the behavioral and emotional outcomes of multiple traumatic experiences in adolescents. First, this study revealed that youth placed in residential treatment experienced higher levels of trauma. In measuring how these experiences influenced behaviors, researchers found that approximately 70 percent of those that had experienced five or more traumas presented with attachment problems, academic problems, criminal activity, self-injury, suicidality, and running-away behaviors (Briggs et al., 2012).

Allostatic load is a concept that helps tie the features of trauma and adversity to negative health outcomes. This idea conveys how multiple systems throughout the body work to maintain homeostasis or allostasis. When stress is experienced, our resources are mobilized to promote adaptation and minimize trauma's impact, to return to allostasis. Unfortunately, our resources are limited, and under repeated or chronic exposure to adversity and stress, the "wear-and-tear" on the body accumulates. This toll becomes evident in inflammatory, neuroendocrine, and metabolic dysregulation (Finlay et al., 2022). Related to the physiological influence of stress exposure, growing evidence places emphasis on the pro-inflammatory consequences. Indeed, children and teens exposed to adverse events were found to have high inflammation levels (Danese & Lewis, 2017). This is particularly concerning as inflammation has been associated with a cascade of pathophysiological processes for both mental and physical health.

Practice Parameters

Selecting appropriate intervention strategies is complicated. Across resources, however, emphasis is placed on supportive, positive interpersonal interventions. In fact, Practice Parameters recommend against using psychotropic medications as a frontline treatment, particularly in the absence of a trauma-informed psychotherapy strategy. This is true for children, adolescents, and adults (including the guidelines developed for veterans).

The American Academy of Child and Adolescent Psychiatry developed its Practice Parameters in 2010 (AACAP, 2010) and have not updated them as of this writing. Since their release, there have been many important, valuable studies to better understand the evaluation and intervention strategies for children and adolescents, but we remain challenged in finding reliably successful outcomes for young people. The 2010 AACAP Parameters concluded that SSRI antidepressants could offer some advantages in managing PTSD but cautioned against using them without psychotherapy. Moreover, the evidence provided to support SSRIs in those 2010 Parameters was difficult to generalize across populations or across trauma types. For example, to support the use of antidepressants, they cited small studies of participants, some of whom experienced earthquakes. No doubt traumatizing, but not generalizable to the trauma so often experienced by children in the United States.

In 2021, the American Academy of Pediatrics published recommendations for mitigating the effects of toxic stress (Garner et al., 2021). The foundation of these recommendations was SSNRs. Sounds like another type of antidepressant, right? In fact, the AAP emphasized the role of Safe, Stable, Nurturing Relationships to meet the needs of trauma-exposed youth. This essential framework guides any range of support for youth and their families recovering from trauma exposure. Not only do relationships buffer against the negative impact of trauma, but safe, nurturing relationships play a key role in one's recovery. Specifically, these authors note that these supportive relationships "turn off the body's stress machinery in a timely manner. Even more importantly, a strengths-based, relational health framework leverages those SSNRs to proactively promote the skills needed to respond to future adversity in a healthy, adaptive manner" (Garner et al., 2021, p. 2).

Researchers have recently examined psychotherapy strategies for pediatric posttraumatic stress disorder. Their review of seventy randomly controlled trials concluded that Trauma-Focused Cognitive Behavioral Therapy (TF-CBT) resulted in the most significant reduction in pediatric PTSD. These findings are most reflective of short-term outcomes, as the authors note that long-term research is needed (Hoppen et al., 2024). Clearly, we're on a path toward improving our treatments but much more work is necessary to fully understand and operationalize strategies that will ensure long-term success and happiness.

Most recently, an integrated framework was proposed to enhance our understanding of the impact of adversity on adolescents (Pollmann, Bates, & Fuhrmann, 2024). With appreciation for the developmental period of adolescence, this adverse adolescent experiences (AAEs) framework takes a systemic lens, based on Bronfenbrenner's ecological work, while outlining the role of intrapersonal adversity, interpersonal adversity, community adversity, and societal adversity.

Circle of Courage

Throughout *No Method to the Madness*, I weave in the thread of the Circle of Courage. A strength-based, relationally focused framework for interventions with youth. Creating a sense of *Belonging*, developing *Mastery*, building *Independence*, and cultivating *Generosity* (Brendtro, Brokenleg,

& VanBockern, 2019). Responding to these universal needs establishes a framework that appreciates the unique interests and abilities of the youth, while creating an environment that promotes resiliency and responds to needs rather than just reacting to problems. As so many youth have experienced traumatic experiences, understanding their needs through the Circle of Courage framework helps us pivot from a symptom-driven, deficit-based approach to the health-focused strategy recommended above.

Protective and Compensatory Experiences (PACEs)

In addition to identifying types of traumatic experiences that can negatively impact psychological and physical health, research has also emerged to further expand our understanding of those factors that can reduce the negative effects of these adversities. In 2020, Jennifer Hays-Grudo and Amanda Sheffield Morris provided an overview of these important areas of one's life provide the "antidote to the ACEs."

In reviewing these important activities, you will notice that they are also consistent with the core values of the Circle of Courage, as well as providing our young people safe, stable, nurturing relationships. The protective and compensatory experiences outlined in their work are:

- unconditional love from a parent/caregiver
- spending time with a best friend
- volunteering or helping others
- being an active member in a social group
- having a mentor outside of the family
- living in a clean, safe home with enough food
- having opportunities to learn
- having/enjoying a hobby
- having routines and fair rules at home (Hays-Grudo & Sheffield Morris, 2020)

This important work related to PACEs should emphasize the value of supportive relationships and how focusing on strengths can elevate our young people in their efforts to recover from adversity and behavioral and emotional challenges. In the chapter on Child Welfare and Intensive Services, the discussion includes a therapeutic milieu, which creates an environment of support for our troubled young people. Every point of service should include a trauma-informed, strength-based strategy, rather than just focusing on a disorder-driven model.

References

Agency for Healthcare Research and Quality. (2012). Evidence-based practice center systematic review protocol, interventions addressing children exposed to trauma: Part 2—Trauma other than child maltreatment and family violence. https://www.effectivehealthcare.ahrq.gov

American Academy of Child & Adolescent Psychiatry. (2010). Practice parameter for the assessment and treatment of children and adolescents with posttraumatic stress disorder. *J. Am. Acad. Child Adolesc. Psychiatry*, *49*(4): 414–430.

Anda, R., Brown, D., Felitti, V., Bremner, J. D., Dube, S., & Giles, W. (2007). Adverse childhood experiences and prescribed psychotropic medications in adults. *American Journal of Preventative Medicine*, *32*(5): 389–394.

Brendtro, L., Brokenleg, M., & VanBockern, S. (2019). *Reclaiming youth at risk: Futures of promise* (3rd ed.). Solution Tree Press.

Briggs, E., Greeson, J., Layne, C., Fairbank, J., Knoverek, A., & Pynoos, R. (2012). Trauma exposure, psychosocial functioning, and treatment needs of youth in residential care: Preliminary findings from the NCTSN core data set. *Journal of Child & Adolescent Trauma*, *5*(1):1–15.

Cronholm, P., Forke, C., Wade, R., Bair-Merritt, M., Davis, M., Harkins-Schwarz, M., Pachter, L., & Fein, J. (2015). Adverse childhood experiences: Expanding the concept of adversity. *American Journal of Preventive Medicine*, *15*. https://doi.org/10.1016/j.amepre.2015.02.001

Danese, A., & Lewis, S. (2017). Psychoneuroimmunology of early-life stress: The hidden wounds of childhood trauma? *Neuropsychopharmacology*, *42*: 99–114.

Donnelly, C. L. (2003). Pharmacologic treatment approaches for children and adolescents with posttraumatic stress disorder. *Child and Adolescent Psychiatric Clinics of North America*, *12*(2): 251–269. https://doi.org/10.1016/s1056-4993(02)00102-5

Finlay, S., Roth, C., Zimsen, T., Bridson, T., Sarnyai, Z., & McDermott, B. (2022). Adverse childhood experiences and allostatic load: A systematic review. *Neuroscience & Biobehavioral Reviews*, *136*. https://doi.org/10.1016/j.neubiorev.2022.104605

Garner A., Yogman M., & Committee on Psychosocial Aspects of Child and Family Health, Section on Developmental and Behavioral Pediatrics, Council on Early Childhood. (2021). Preventing childhood toxic stress: Partnering with families and communities to promote relational health. *Pediatrics*, *148*(2):e2021052582

Hays-Grudo, J., & Sheffield Morris, A. (2020). *Adverse and protective childhood experiences: A developmental perspective*. American Psychological Association.

Hoppen, T., Wessarges, L., Jehn, M., Mutz, J., Kip, A., Schlecter, P., . . . Morina, N. (2024). Psychological interventions for pediatric posttraumatic stress disorder: A systematic review and network meta-analysis. *JAMA Psychiatry,* December. https://doi.org/10.1001/jamapsychiatry.2024.3908

Karr-Morse, R., & Wiley, M. (2012). *Scared sick: The role of childhood trauma in adult disease.* Basic Books.

Pollmann, A., Bates, K., & Fuhrmann, D. (2024). A framework for understanding adverse adolescent experiences. *Nature Human Behavior, 9*: 450–463. https://doi.org/10.1038/s41562-024 02098-x

Read, J., Fink, P., Rudegeair, T., Felitti, V., & Whitfield, C. (2008). Child maltreatment and psychosis: A return to a genuinely integrated bio-psycho-social model. *Clinical Schizophrenia & Related Psychosis,* October: 235–254.

Read, J., van Os, J., Morrison, A. P., & Ross, C. A. (2005). Childhood trauma, psychosis and schizophrenia: A literature review with theoretical and clinical implications. *Acta Psychiatr. Scand., 112*: 330–350.

Sahle, B., Reavley, N., Li, W., Morgan, A., Yap, M., Reupert, A., & Jorm, A. (2021). The association between adverse childhood experiences and common mental disorders and suicidality: An umbrella review of systematic review and meta-analyses. *European Child & Adolescent Psychiatry.* https://doi.org/10.1007/s00787-021-01745-2

van der Kolk, B. (2016). The devastating effects of ignoring child maltreatment in psychiatry: A commentary on Teicher and Samson 2016. *Journal of Child Psychology and Psychiatry, 57*(3): 267–270.

van der Zwaard, R., & Polak, M. A. (2001). Pseudohallucinations: A pseudoconcept? A review of the validity of the concept, related to associate symptomatology. *Compr. Psychiatry, 42*(1):42–50. https://doi.org/10.1053/comp.2001.19752. PMID: 11154715.

World Health Organization. (2024). *Clinical descriptions and diagnostic requirements for ICD: 11 mental, behavioural and neurodevelopmental disorders.* World Health Organization.

4
Medicating Attention Deficit Hyperactivity Disorder (ADHD)

> There simply is not sufficient empirical evidence to have confidence that the mental health field in the United States has the ADHD diagnosis correct.
>
> (Mallet, Natarajan, & Hoy, 2014)

It is true that attention deficit hyperactivity disorder (ADHD) is one of the most common psychiatric disorders in children and adolescents. As such, the disorder has been the focus of many research studies in hopes of better understanding the causes and treatment. The American Academy of Pediatrics (2019) notes that almost 10 percent of children and adolescents have received a diagnosis of ADHD, equating to over 5 million youth (Wolraich et al., 2019). But despite massive efforts through many years, we are still left with many unanswered questions. We have no clear ideas of the cause (or causes) of ADHD. The vast range of clinical presentations offered in our current diagnostic framework is a dramatic oversimplification. And the lack of sustained benefits from treatment leaves many children and families frustrated.

As of 2013 in the DSM-5, the American Psychiatric Association has designated ADHD as a "neurodevelopmental disorder." Prior to that, ADHD was more simply considered a "Disorder Usually First Diagnosed in Infancy, Childhood, or Adolescence" in the DSM-IV. One would reasonably presume that this change in categorization is firmly rooted in scientific research, particularly as the most current conceptualization is that of "neuro" (brain-based) "developmental" (based within an observed progression of development through childhood/adolescence). We'll discuss this new designation below. The symptoms used to identify ADHD did not change despite the category transition.

How Common Is Common?

Even in the early conceptualizations of hyperactivity, there has been controversy. Prior to "ADHD," the cluster of symptoms was called Hyperkinetic Reaction of Childhood. But research during this time highlighted dramatic disparity between the use of this diagnosis in the United States versus Great Britain. For example, in 1984, Thorley summarized, "The diagnosis of hyperkinetic syndrome is rarely used in the UK, in marked contrast to its counterpart in the USA. Most of the work on hyperkinesis is concerned with the North American concept and relatively little attention has been paid to the British approach," further noting that in thirteen years of data collection from a clinical setting, it only occurred in 1.2 percent of patients (Thorley, 1984, p. 16).

In the DSM-III (1980) the American Psychiatric Association described attention deficit disorder as "common" occurring in 3 percent of U.S. children. In 1980, this would translate to approximately 1.9 million diagnosed youth under the age of 18. Recent reports suggest the disorder occurs in over 10 percent of those under the age of 18 which, at the time of this writing, equating to over 7.3 million youth. It's a disorder that occurs more frequently in males. Remarkably, while the prevalence of ADHD has continued to increase since 2013, the costs for treating children and adolescents in that year surpassed the costs for treating depression, anxiety, and asthma, combined (Piper et al., 2018).

While arguments are made to imply that ADHD occurs across different cultures at similar rates, the United States uses the vast majority of stimulant medications (approximately 80 percent of the global methylphenidate consumption) to treat this condition (*The Pharmaceutical Journal*, 2015). This rate of medication use has been relatively consistent over many years, despite an increasing amount of medication being produced. That's right: even though more methylphenidate and amphetamine have been produced each year, the United States continues to use the overwhelming majority of that supply. In fact, as of this writing, there is a shortage of stimulant medication in the United States (McPhillips, 2023).

The disproportionately high use of stimulants in the United States has always been stunning to me, particularly as the field of psychiatric research attempts to establish a genetic and/or neurological problem as the basis of the disorder. If genetic and/or neurological abnormalities were confirmed as a basis for ADHD, it would speak to an epidemic affecting millions of youth, centered within the United States. Indeed, stimulant medications are available in other countries. So even if the incidence of ADHD is consistent internationally, others appear more able to effectively manage the condition with far less reliance on medications. This will be discussed more later.

Another often neglected consideration for ADHD is the role of a child's sensory functioning. To that point, the word "sensory" does not occur within the American Academy of Pediatrics' 2019 Guidelines for ADHD. However, Dr. Sophia Odeh (2019) completed a study examining sensory symptoms in children with an ADHD diagnosis. The goal of the study was to determine if sensory differences occurred in children with ADHD. These differences could be related to tactile (touch), proprioceptive (pressure on muscles and joints), vestibular (movement), interoception (internal sensations), auditory (sound), visual, and gustatory/olfactory (taste and smell). While a relatively small sample (sixty-two participants recruited from CHADD's website and CHADD's parent support blog), the findings were important. Sensory symptoms were reported across diagnostic types of ADHD, but the Combined Type (which is the most common form) had consistently higher rates of sensory symptom endorsement. The implication is clear: a child struggling with attention problems and impulse control must be evaluated holistically, as sensory issues will further jeopardize a successful outcome, or worsen symptoms. Moreover, sensory issues may require additional interventions (such as occupational therapy services) and influence the decision for specific medications as they may exacerbate a sensory issue.

Trauma and ADHD

ADHD may present in a wide range of symptom configurations. As we'll discuss, there are many ways that the symptoms of ADHD can be combined to reach the threshold of the diagnosis. However, if a young person experiences trauma or adverse life experiences, they may also manifest symptoms that would be easily confused with ADHD.

When a child experiences adversity or a traumatic experience, they go through a range of responses. Please review the chapter focused on trauma and its impact for more details. Reactions to trauma and adversity can impact a child's physiology, their cognitive processes, their emotional life, and their interpersonal experiences.

Hallmark signs of ADHD may include:

- poor concentration (having difficulty staying focused on a task);
- dysregulated or impulsive behaviors (jittery, high energy, quick disruptive actions);
- exaggerated reactions to external stimuli (easily distracted when someone walks past the classroom, overly focused on the activities of other students);

- emotional outbursts (quick to get frustrated, angered by feedback from peers); and
- poor compliance with adult expectations (despite clear instruction, child may not follow expectations, rules, norms).

While these symptoms could easily prompt adults to be concerned with ADHD as a clinical issue, if the child has been exposed to trauma or adversity, the above "symptoms" could all be responses to these difficult life experiences. For example, outwardly, a child may appear to have poor concentration but internally, they may not be focusing on their work because they are ruminating about what has happened to them—or what may happen when they are not at school. Quick, abrupt behaviors may also be rooted in anxiety or fear as the child is (maladaptively) trying to influence the outcome of an interaction to gain a sense of control. Exaggerated reactions or appearing startled by seemingly insignificant events also highlight a more hypervigilant approach to the world, reacting to it as if there may be threats around any corner. Emotional outbursts are tied to many psychiatric diagnoses but are common in ADHD and trauma exposure. Possibly appearing as frustration (from a failed assignment or being corrected in class) may be simple enough. Still, the outburst may also be rooted in their fear of a response *as a result* of that failed assignment or getting in trouble at school.

Given the disturbingly high prevalence of adversity and trauma exposure, I always recommend that the presenting "symptoms" of any troubled child first be examined through the lens of trauma exposure, and then do your diagnosing. If the above behaviors are mistakenly labeled as ADHD but are expressions of traumatic exposure, the child will receive insufficient care resulting in continued frustration of parents, teachers, and the child.

Marketing ADHD

The prevalence of ADHD is not an accident. As far back as the mid-1990s, pharmaceutical companies began offering training to teachers and school nurses. Knowing they are at the "front lines" of identifying problematic behaviors, they have quickly become a receptive audience to this information about understanding and improving these difficult behaviors in the educational setting. These staff also have regular contact with the parents of these difficult children. With a new campaign to educate school staff about ADHD, this information can quickly influence conversations with parents about "what" the difficulty is, and how to treat it. Keep in mind, neither teachers nor school nurses have the training nor the credentials to diagnose the condition of ADHD. This pharmaceutical industry "education" of ADHD also reached mental health professionals. While it was a nationwide effort, it is quite likely that this amplified the attention paid to disruptive and inattentive behaviors in the classroom. The marketing of ADHD in the 1990s worked. As seen in this chart (Public Broadcasting Service, n.d.), the dark lines represent the United States' use of methylphenidate (Ritalin). The light-colored line is the rest of the world.

With these educational programs, the pharmaceutical company, Shire, was aggressively marketing Adderall. However, there was eventually a cost to exaggerating their claims of effectiveness for Adderall and Vyvanse. In 2014, Shire Pharmaceuticals was ordered to pay a penalty of $56.5 million for making unsupported claims between 2004 and 2007 that Adderall XR was clinically superior to other ADHD drugs, and it would "normalize" people taking it and prevent poor academic performance, among other things. The penalty also involved claims that Vyvanse was less of a liability for abuse (United States Department of Justice). This financial penalty, however, was a small price given how much they had earned with Adderall. Shire had made a fortune on these medications, even before the period of false claims. For

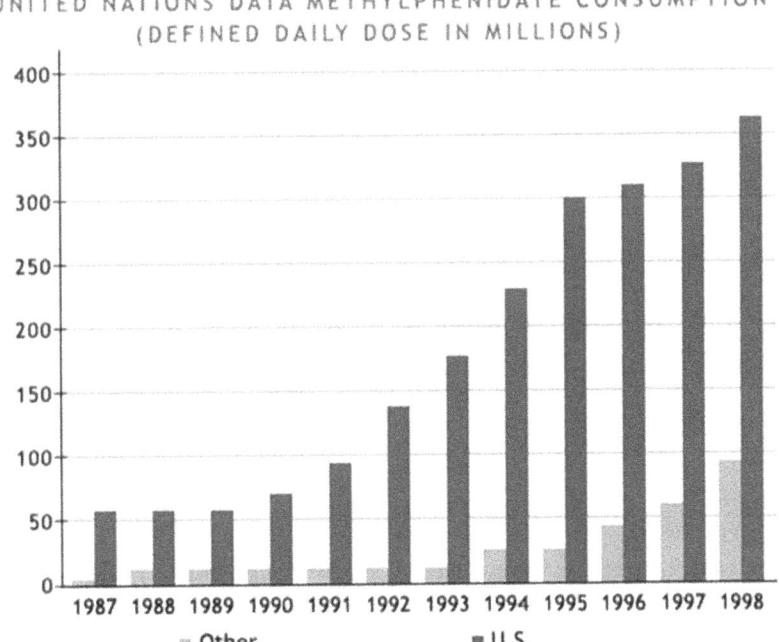

example, in just the *first three months* of 2003, Adderall produced revenue of over $115 million (*Pharmaletter*, 2003). Moreover, the paradigm had now been established to support the belief that Adderall was more effective than it actually was. Indeed, sales continued to soar. In 2015, Shire earned $1.7 billion with Vyvanse and $365 million with Adderall XR (Dabney, 2016). Of course, Shire wasn't required to go back and "re-educate" all those who attended their training to correct the exaggerated efficacy, so without the public being readily exposed to the disposition of lawsuits related to stimulant medications, the machine was in motion.

A more recent analysis of the marketing of stimulants raises additional concerns. Hadland and colleagues (2020) reviewed "industry-physician marketing interactions" between 2014 and 2018. These "interactions" were specific pharmaceutical efforts promoting stimulants directly to physicians. Payments included meals, travel, speaking fees, etc. During this period, one in eighteen physicians received marketing for stimulant medications, totaling over $20 million. Pediatricians, psychiatrists, and family physicians represented the largest portions of the marketing efforts. These authors note that "use of prescription stimulants doubled from 2006 to 2016 in the United States and, as of 2013, it resulted in more pharmaceutical expenditures for children than any other medication class" (Hadland et al., 2020, p. 385). Use of stimulants has continued to increase since that time.

Something is happening. Over recent decades, the rate of diagnosing ADHD and prescribing stimulants for its treatment has continued to increase. Now classified as a Neurodevelopmental Disorder, new efforts have been to highlight the existence of Adult ADHD. Indeed, some literature suggests that ADHD in childhood continues well into adulthood. More people are being diagnosed, more people are receiving medication to treat it, and now the field of mental health is saying the condition extends into adulthood.

The ADHD Diagnosis

The DSM-III

Beginning a discussion of attention deficit hyperactivity disorder must start with an overview of the diagnostic criteria. Early conceptualizations of these difficulties in children were labeled as "Minimal Brain Dysfunction" or Hyperkinetic Reaction of Childhood (or adolescence) in the DSM-II, but in 1980, the *Diagnostic and Statistical Manual, Third Edition*, was published. This reconceptualized the disorder as attention deficit disorder. To meet the threshold of attention deficit disorder *with hyperactivity* in the DSM-III, a child was required to meet:

- three of five symptoms in the Inattention category,
- three of six in the Impulsivity category,
- and two of five in the Hyperactivity category.

For ADD without hyperactivity, a child was just required to meet the same conditions, while not meeting the symptom threshold for the hyperactivity category.

DSM-III-R

There were changes to the diagnosis in the DSM-III-R (revised) in 1987. The disorder was now called attention deficit hyperactivity disorder, and a child was required to meet eight of fourteen symptoms. The word "often" begins eight of the fourteen criteria (we'll come back to this later). The symptoms had to be present before the age of 7, and the DSM-III-R introduced mild, moderate, and severe ratings, based on how many symptoms (beyond the required eight) a child presented.

DSM-IV

In the DSM-IV, the symptom list was expanded to eighteen, while now requiring just six symptoms to meet the condition. The qualifier "often" now begins every diagnostic criterion in this diagnosis. In the DSM-IV, "impairment" was required in at least two settings as a result of the symptoms. In the DSM-5, this was simplified to symptoms being "present" in at least two settings. Otherwise, the diagnostic criteria in the DSM-IV and DSM-5 (and DSM-5-TR) are virtually identical (with the reintroduction of the mild, moderate, and severe in the DSM-5).

The DSM-5-TR and ICD have significant overlap. Here are the descriptions of ADHD categories from the International Classification of Disease, 11th Edition (World Health Organization, 2024):

Inattention
Several symptoms of inattention that are persistent and sufficiently severe that they have a direct negative impact on academic, occupational or social functioning are among the essential components. Symptoms are typically from the following clusters:
• having difficulty sustaining attention on tasks that do not provide a high level of stimulation or reward or require sustained mental effort;

lacking attention to detail; making careless mistakes in school or work assignments; not completing tasks;
• being easily distracted by extraneous stimuli or thoughts not related to the task at hand; often seeming not to listen when spoken to directly; frequently appearing to be daydreaming or to have their mind elsewhere;
• losing things; being forgetful in daily activities; having difficulty remembering to complete upcoming daily tasks or activities; having difficulty planning, managing and organizing schoolwork, tasks and other activities (p. 143).

Hyperactivity-Impulsivity

Several symptoms of hyperactivity-impulsivity that are persistent and sufficiently severe that they have a direct negative impact on academic, occupational or social functioning are among the essential components. These tend to be most evident in structured situations that require behavioural self-control. Symptoms are typically from the following clusters:
• showing excessive motor activity; leaving their seat when expected to sit still; often running about; having difficulty sitting still without fidgeting (younger children); displaying feelings of physical restlessness and a sense of discomfort with being quiet or sitting still (adolescents and adults);
• having difficulty engaging in activities quietly; talking too much;
• blurting out answers in school or comments at work; having difficulty waiting their turn in conversation, games or activities; interrupting or intruding on others' conversations or games;
• having a tendency to act in response to immediate stimuli without deliberation or consideration of risks and consequences (e.g., engaging in behaviours with potential for physical injury; impulsive decisions; reckless driving) (p. 143).

Combined Presentation

All diagnostic requirements for attention deficit hyperactivity disorder are met, and both hyperactive-impulsive and inattentive symptoms are clinically significant aspects of the current clinical presentation, with neither clearly predominating. (p. 144)

DSM-5-TR

In the *Diagnostic and Statistical Manual of Mental Disorders, Fifth Edition, Text Revision* (APA, 2022) there are three types of ADHD consistent with the ICD-11: Inattentive, Hyperactive/Impulsive, and Combined Type. There are nine criteria under each Inattentive and Hyperactive types, and a child only needs to meet six of these nine criteria to have the disorder. If a child meets six criteria across both forms, they meet the criteria for Combined Type, which is the most common diagnosis of ADHD. The DSM-5-TR notes "symptoms are present in two or more settings" and "there is clear evidence that the symptoms interfere with, or reduce the quality of, social, academic, or occupational functioning" (p. 69). The modified language in the DSM-5-TR loosens the criteria because it contextualizes it with more subjective evaluation. Symptoms being "often" present and leading to "reduced quality" of work seems highly contingent on the context in which they're occurring.

But, as simple as the diagnostic process sounds, there are over eighteen thousand different symptom combinations that could establish an "ADHD, Combined Type" diagnosis. When put in those terms, rather than simple, it sounds problematic. Over eighteen thousand presentations of the same "thing" should raise questions about the validity of this diagnostic construct.

To highlight this point, in 1998, the National Institutes of Health (NIH) commented on the diagnostic integrity of ADHD. As they examined the diagnosis of ADHD, they concluded, "as of yet, there is no independent valid test for ADHD. . . . Further research is necessary to firmly establish ADHD as a brain disorder. . . . Additional efforts to validate the disorder are needed" (NIH, 1998, p. 7). Finally, "after years of clinical research and experience with ADHD, our knowledge about the cause or causes of ADHD remains speculative" (p. 21). The diagnostic criteria have remained the same since this statement and I don't believe this is by accident. Despite being criticized as problematic and overly subjective, the specific criteria have been unchanged for decades. Many intelligent, well-trained, insightful scientists have had the opportunity to improve the specificity of the diagnosis over several decades, yet here we are.

How Often is Often?

A major concern about the diagnostic criteria within the DSM is that the word "often" begins each criterion across both hyperactive and inattentive categories, for example, "often interrupts." This vague indicator of frequency will likely be different depending on who is describing the behavior (and challenges the reliability of the observation). For example, as a psychologist, if I meet with a child weekly, and he acts impulsively during each meeting, I could report that the child is "often" impulsive. Yet this may only represent my experience of him on a weekly basis. In contrast, a parent may see the child acting impulsively many times within an hour, which is a very different measure of "often." A soccer coach would define "often" in yet another way. The presence of symptoms must create distress and impair functioning *in multiple settings*. In other words, a child that only presents symptoms at school does not warrant a diagnosis of ADHD. These behaviors must show themselves at home, with friends, during activities, and/or at school.

The symptoms of ADHD must also negatively impact the child's functioning. Now, I am going to step carefully here, but people and events in the child's environment also influence the extent of the impact of ADHD symptoms on a child's functioning. ADHD is a disorder that is typically first identified in the school setting. No doubt, teachers and school staff are overburdened with responsibilities; with too few resources, they provide countless supportive duties in addition to their role as educators. Managing a classroom of children with competing needs can quickly become overwhelming. And those children with more pronounced needs place undue demands on a system that is already hanging on by a thread. Of course, there is always a range of "well-behaved" to "challenging" kids in a classroom. That is developmentally expected and normal. But those kids who strain the resources of the classroom or are unmanageable to the point that they're impacting the educational experience of others can quickly become the focus of concern.

Questioning the Cause

In considering causal factors for ADHD, we need to first acknowledge, as mentioned earlier, that the brain is involved in everything we do. Simply identifying activity in the brain when symptoms occur in any disorder is a correlation. The two events are related, but one may not cause the other. As we explored earlier, establishing a causal relationship is a much more demanding endeavor.

As a "Neurodevelopmental Disorder" as labeled by the DSM, it assumes a neurological foundation and developmental course to the disorder. There have also been assumptions regarding the genetic components of ADHD. There are many studies examining all these domains, so we will review some of the most compelling findings rather than an exhaustive summary.

Neurological Basis

As ADHD is classified as a *neuro*developmental disorder, it is important to note the neurological foundation, or lack thereof. As stated, the brain is involved in everything we do, but the American Psychiatric Association (2022) highlights:

> No biological marker is diagnostic for ADHD. Although ADHD has been associated with elevated power of slow waves (4–7 Hz 'theta') as well as decreased power of fast waves (14–30 Hz 'beta'), a later review found no differences in theta or beta power in either children or adults with ADHD relative to control subjects.
>
> Although some neuroimaging studies have shown differences in children with ADHD compared with control subjects, meta-analysis of *all* neuroimaging studies do not show differences between individuals with ADHD and control subjects. . . . No form of neuroimaging can be used for diagnosis of ADHD.
>
> (p. 72)

In summary of that passage, when using advanced technologies to measure the physical characteristics and/or activity in the brain, the American Psychiatric Association could not report any reliable differences in the brains of ADHD-diagnosed individuals compared to controls. It is fair to assume that if reliable data existed to identify the pathognomonic neurological foundation for this disorder, it would have been presented in the most recent edition of the DSM-5-TR. In its absence, and with the acknowledgment that our current neuroimaging cannot be used to diagnose the condition, clinicians should be cautious about making such claims.

To further complicate our assumptions about the neurological foundation of ADHD, the influential journal *Lancet Psychiatry* published an article purporting to identify specific neurological differences between ADHD and "normal" youth (Hoogman et al., 2017). Upon further scrutiny by Corrigan and Whitaker, the neurological differences were dubious, and the ADHD children had higher IQ scores than controls at sixteen of twenty sites in the study (Corrigan & Whitaker, 2017). Many efforts have been made to determine reliably identified differences in the brains of those with—and without—ADHD, yet these differences remain elusive.

The DSM claims that under certain circumstances, the symptoms of this neurologically based disorder may become "minimal or absent." Indeed, this raises questions. For many neurological disorders (consider dementia), one would not expect changes to their environment capable of eliminating the symptoms. But as the APA (2022) notes in the DSM, specific interventions can make the symptoms of ADHD virtually disappear:

- frequent rewards for appropriate behavior,
- close supervision

- novel settings
- especially interesting activities
- consistent external stimulation
- interacting in one-to-one situations

Remarkably, while determining ADHD to be a *neuro*developmental disorder, the American Psychiatric Association provides no supportive evidence for a *neuro* foundation for the condition but highlights that through interactions with others, the disorder may be minimal or absent. Given this list of interventions capable of minimizing or eliminating the symptoms, one may wonder why psychotropic medications are so commonly used as a first-line treatment.

There have been decades of research attempting to understand the neurological underpinnings of ADHD. Without substantive information in the latest DSM, and without conclusions of any causal findings in published research, a neurological foundation—while plausible—remains unproven.

Genetic Findings

Despite considerable discussion of the role of genes in the development of ADHD, the American Psychiatric Association is less confident about their influence. In fact, with the DSM-5, it was concluded, "while specific genes have been correlated with ADHD, they are neither necessary nor sufficient causal factors" (APA, 2013, p. 62). Most recently, DSM-5-TR considers recent genetic research, but ultimately states that "there is no single gene for ADHD" (APA, 2022, p. 71). Again, the most recent DSM provides an opportunity to establish the most recent and relevant scientific foundations for these disorders. In their absence, we must remain careful about making assumptions about the genetic underpinnings of the condition. Moreover, given the complexity that the emerging field of epigenetics offers, it is not surprising that deciphering the genetic influences of any psychiatric disorder has remained so elusive. I would not expect such genetic summaries anytime soon.

ADHD is considered to have acceptable inter-rater reliability. Some use that as evidence that it is a "real" psychiatric disorder. In contrast, there are many very intelligent people that believe ADHD is just a socially constructed disorder to identify children that are problematic in the classroom and difficult to manage at home. My own position is that ADHD can represent the symptoms listed in the DSM-5-TR. We could call it whatever we want. Many of those symptoms do represent frustrating behaviors that occur in classrooms and other settings. Those are, in fact, societal standards that are deemed problematic. Those behaviors can also be very challenging for a child to manage and will interfere with their learning and socializing. If the child doesn't develop strategies to manage these behaviors, in hopes of improving their functioning, problems can persist into adulthood. My concern is about making genetic and neurological assumptions related to this diagnosis. Currently, science does not provide sufficient evidence to draw any conclusions about an identified neurological basis or a genetic foundation. However, we use these assumptions to drive decision-making around treatment recommendations, heavily emphasizing medication use.

ADHD Medication Treatment

The U.S. Food and Drug Association (FDA) evaluates the efficacy of medications before they are approved for use in children and adolescents. The FDA requires that a medication outperform a placebo in two studies to receive approval. Most people assume that these medications have been studied for months, if not years, before recommending them for use in children. However, this is not the case. Table 4.1 is compiled from the "package inserts" of popular medications and summarizes studies that were completed in order to receive FDA approval.

You may be surprised to learn that the studies conducted to receive FDA approval occur over just weeks, not months or years. As these are all short-term studies, the results can only be generalized to short-term use. Obviously, practice guidelines and typical care offered by prescribers expect long-term adherence to these medications. Another factor to consider is the "sample size"—that is, how many children participate in the studies to establish their effectiveness. Given that millions of children are prescribed these medications, research studies including only between 27 and 584 children, lasting only two to eight weeks, seem insufficient to adequately inform our typical patterns of use once the medications are approved.

Measuring "Effectiveness"

In medication trials, a variety of tools are used to measure "success" or "effectiveness." One of the most popular tools is called the SKAMP (Swanson, Kotkin, Agler, M-Flynn, and Pelham Scale). The SKAMP is designed for clinicians to document their observations of ADHD symptoms. The reliability and validity of the SKAMP tool were established in 1992 (Murray et al., 2009).

Table 4.1 Trials Used to Establish Efficacy in the Management of ADHD Symptoms

Drug Name	Generic	Details
Adderall XR	Dextroamphetamine Sulf-Saccharate	1. N = 584 3 weeks 2. N = 327 4 weeks
Aptensio XR	Methylphenidate HCL	1. N = 27 2 weeks option to join 21-month open label 2. N = 230 1 week, then 11-week open label
Concerta	Methylphenidate HCL	1. N = 416 3 weeks 2. N = 177 4 weeks (adolescents)
Evekeo	Amphetamine Sulfate	1. N = 105 8 weeks open, 2. N = 97 2 weeks crossover
Focalin XR	Dexmethylphenidate HCL	1. N = 103 5 weeks open optimization, then 2 weeks crossover 2. Two additional studies—minimal details
Ritalin LA	Methylphenidate HCL	1. N = 134 2 weeks
Quillivant XR	Methylphenidate HCL	1. N = 45 4 to 6 weeks open optimization, then 2 weeks crossover
Vyvanse	Lisdexamfetamine Dimesylate	1. N = 290 4 weeks 2. N = 52 3 weeks open optimization, then 2 weeks crossover 3. N = 129 4 weeks open optimization, then 2 weeks crossover

There are additional forms available, such as the T-SKAMP, designed for teachers. And the SKAMP-D represents items 5 through 8 on SKAMP.

> The SKAMP is a 10-item scale designed to assess impairment associated with specific context-bound ADHD classroom behaviors. Teachers rate the severity of 10 items (6 for attention, such as "difficulty getting started on classroom assignments"; and 4 for deportment, such as "difficulty remaining quiet according to classroom rules") on a 4-point scale: 0 = *not at all*, 1 = *just a little*, 2 = *pretty much*, to 3 = *very much*. It should be noted that subsequent versions of the SKAMP have been developed, including one with a 7-point scale and the addition of an individualized write-in item.
>
> (Murray et al., 2009, p. 196)

There are ways to analyze the scores. Some research summarizes the entire score across items, while as noted, the SKAMP-D looks at items 5 through 8.

The ten-item SKAMP is published in Murray et al. (2009). As noted above, concerns around the use of "often" in the ADHD diagnostic criteria persist. And the SKAMP, in its measure of medication effectiveness, also utilizes a continuum of frequency descriptors that may be of concern. For example, if you imagine the range of behaviors in classrooms across the country, quantifying them with these anchors may be problematic. How consistent is a measurement of "Pretty Much" across classrooms? (See Table 4.2.)

For a medication to be determined "effective," scores on the SKAMP would demonstrate improved scores, compared to placebo. As noted in the DSM, other strategies can minimize, if not make disappear, the symptoms of ADHD. The SKAMP has been in use for approximately thirty years and remains one of the primary measures of medication effectiveness. While this remains the "gold standard" for medication trials, it is worth considering why the field has not been able to improve the precision in measuring treatment effectiveness.

The American Academy of Pediatrics released the most recent Clinical Practice Guidelines for ADHD in 2019. These guidelines are often used as reflective of the best research, expertise, and clinical guidance. Table 4.3 represents a concise summary of the recommendations (Wolraich et al., 2019):

Given the discussion to follow, as a psychologist, I am surprised by the confidence with which these recommendations are given. The outcomes shown for AAP recommendations are weaker than I would expect. Yet most physicians/clinicians are not going to check the references of their cited research, nor will they be aware of what studies were omitted from their review and recommendations. We'll discuss this below.

Table 4.2 A Sample of Items from the SKAMP Scale Used to Evaluate Symptom Presentations in ADHD

Sample SKAMP item	Not at All	Just a Little	Pretty Much	Very Much
Difficulty staying on task for a classroom period	0	1	2	3
Problems in completion or work on classroom assignments	0	1	2	3
Difficulty attending to an activity or discussion of the class	0	1	2	3

Table 4.3 Intervention Recommendations from the American Academy of Pediatrics in the Treatment of ADHD

Age	Primary Recommendation	Secondary Recommendation
4–6	Parent Training in Behavior Management (PTBM)	Methylphenidate if PTBM does not yield sufficient improvement, or if behavioral strategies are unavailable.
6–12	FDA-approved ADHD medications	Behavioral interventions should be offered in conjunction with medication
12–18	FDA-approved ADHD medications	Consider the use of behavioral strategies

The first-line treatments for ADHD are central nervous system stimulants. There are many medications to choose from, but we will examine the primary forms as types of amphetamine and methylphenidate. These medications have been available for decades and can provide specific effects, whether one has ADHD or not, but it has been hypothesized that the effects of stimulants compensate for many challenges experienced in those with an ADHD diagnosis. And as they belong to the large family of CNS stimulants, let's start with a general discussion.

The CNS Stimulants—From Caffeine to Cocaine

Most of those reading this have used stimulants of some kind. A majority of adults enjoy a cup of coffee or tea in the morning to get going, or a cup during the day to stay going. These beverages, as well as some soft drinks and energy drinks, rely on caffeine as the ingredient to give that boost or focus. Over the years, I have had students as well as parents of clients ask about using coffee instead of medication to help focus and stay on task. It's a reasonable question. As adults, we use caffeine regularly without any obvious side effects.

As ADHD is broadly theorized to involve the neurotransmitters dopamine and norepinephrine, the following summaries will focus on the influence of various stimulants on those chemicals.

Caffeine

As caffeine is likely the most consumed CNS stimulant in humans, there is wide-ranging research as it relates to the behaviors associated with ADHD. Surprisingly, the results of this research are ambiguous because of the variability in response that people have to caffeine. Of course, most of the studies have been conducted on animals or adults, so information on caffeine in the treatment of ADHD in children is lacking. Moreover, much of the research is fairly outdated, so it is difficult to arrive at any clear conclusions.

There are a variety of observations of how caffeine works in the brain, but the primary mechanism of action seems to be "antagonism" (reducing the availability) of adenosine. As an example, adenosine is a chemical occurring in the body that acts as a neurotransmitter in the brain. So, when adenosine increases, it promotes a person's need for sleep. Some medications influence adenosine to lower blood pressure. But when caffeine reduces the availability of adenosine, it decreases our need for sleep—prolongs wakefulness—and can also increase your blood pressure. In high doses, it can give you heart palpitations. In those ways, it has a stimulating effect. It is not, however, as powerful a stimulant as popular ADHD medications.

Blocking the availability of adenosine (specifically, at the adenosine A_1 receptor) increases levels of dopamine and glutamate (Solinas et al., 2002). More recently, caffeine was observed to significantly increase dopamine availability (at the D_2 and D_3 receptors) (Volkow et al., 2015). It is these effects that raise questions about caffeine's usefulness in the treatment of ADHD. However, the degree to which caffeine increases dopamine is less than that of prescription medications. That being said, recent research based on animal studies raises new questions about the value of caffeine in the management of many ADHD symptoms.

In 2022, researchers completed a meta-analysis of studies related to the effects of caffeine on ADHD symptoms in animals (Vazquez et al., 2022). As it turns out, there is an established and validated animal model for ADHD to be used in research like this. These researchers examined thirteen studies and arrived at interesting conclusions. Admittedly, there are limitations to what you can apply to children from animal studies, but this practice is regularly done in the development of medications. They found that "overall, the reviewed results show that caffeine treatment increases attention and improves learning, memory" (p. 18), although it did not seem to offer an advantage in hyperactive behaviors. They conclude, "Our results are supported at the neuronal/molecular level, and strengthen the hypothesis that the cognitive effects of caffeine found in animal models of ADHD could be translated to humans diagnosed with the disorder, particularly during adolescence. Nonetheless, caution is needed when extrapolating potential effects identified in animal studies to human patients" (Vazquez et al., 2022, p. 20).

The goal here is not to make the argument that caffeine should be used to replace methylphenidate or amphetamine in managing ADHD symptoms, although caffeine brings a much lower side effect profile. This dilemma has already been evaluated by the American Academy of Pediatrics over a decade ago. When reviewing the use and misuse of energy drinks for children and adolescents, these experts arrived at a clear conclusion: "Rigorous review and analysis of the literature reveal that caffeine and other stimulant substances contained in energy drinks have no place in the diet of children and adolescents . . . [and that] regular intake (of caffeine) has many noted negative health effects" (American Academy of Pediatrics, 2011, pp. 1182 and 1185). This review of caffeine's effects includes increased heart rate, blood pressure, motor activity, attentiveness, gastric secretion, sleep disturbances, increased anxiety, and "concerns regarding . . . its effects on the developing neurological and cardiovascular systems" (p. 1185).

These conclusions likely raise additional questions for you:

- If caffeine should be avoided, how is it that drugs that are much more powerful (ADHD medications) are recommended by doctors to millions of children and adolescents?
- Even if ADHD medications are more potent, are they safer than caffeine, since they are being prescribed by my physician/pediatrician/psychiatrist?
- Even if ADHD medications have risks, do the benefits outweigh those risks?

Methylphenidate (Ritalin)

Methylphenidate is a medication that has been used for decades. First created in 1944 and later patented in 1954, its first applications were for conditions such as fatigue, lethargy, and depression, among others (Morton & Stockton, 2000). Consistent with changes to our diagnostic framework (transitioning from Hyperkinetic Disorder to Attention Deficit Disorder) in the 1980s, methylphenidate saw dramatic increases in use in the 1990s and has continued since.

Over the years, many forms of methylphenidate have been developed. They include Ritalin, Concerta, Quillivant, Aptensio, and Jornay, among others. Derivatives of methylphenidate include drugs like Daytrana and Focalin. While all of these are forms of methylphenidate, differences may be in their form (pill versus liquid) and duration (short- or long-acting). Given these different forms, dosing levels may also be different. For these reasons, these medications must be taken as prescribed. Moreover, sensitivity to these medications can vary across individuals, so even at a "standard" dose it is important to communicate with the prescriber immediately upon experiencing side effects or unpleasant reactions.

In reviewing the information provided by drug makers, the way methylphenidate "works" is described as: "methylphenidate is thought to block the reuptake of norepinephrine and dopamine into the presynaptic neuron and increase the release of these monoamines into the extraneuronal space" (Alza Corporation). Let's unpack that. The overall effect of methylphenidate is to increase the availability of dopamine and norepinephrine. In normal circumstances, once these chemicals are released into the spaces between the cells (synapse), if they go unused, they are reabsorbed by the presynaptic neuron. This process of reuptake is blocked with the use of methylphenidate thereby allowing more dopamine and norepinephrine to remain available. In addition, methylphenidate promotes the release of these chemicals. So, the net result is that more dopamine and norepinephrine are released and rather than the unused chemicals being reabsorbed, it remains in the synapse.

The action of methylphenidate is substantial. At a "therapeutic dose" (the dose administered to achieve the intended effect), the drug blocks 70 percent of those "transporters" that would return dopamine to the presynaptic cell. As a result, it has a major impact across the dopaminergic system (Whitaker, 2011).

Of concern, methylphenidate has a wide range of side effects. In its use as an oral medication, a long list of side effects has been documented that can further complicate the presentation of ADHD. Moreover, these side effects can create more discomfort in the day-to-day functioning of a child while they are maintained on the medication.

While this is not a complete summary (Elbe et al., 2023), the following list shows an overview of side effects that may occur with use of stimulants in the treatment of ADHD.

- Restlessness
- Irritability
- Anxiety
- Insomnia
- Anorexia

- Aggression
- Hostility
- Tics
- Stomach ache
- Headache
- Hyperactive rebound
- Dysphoria
- May exacerbate psychotic symptoms
- Increased blood pressure

Of course, whenever these effects occur, the child's physician/psychiatrist should be contacted and notified so they can address these concerns.

Animal studies have suggested that early exposure to methylphenidate can increase the likelihood of complications into adulthood. While making them less responsive to natural rewards (such as sugar, novel environments, fun), methylphenidate exposure also made them more sensitive to stressful situations (Higgins, 2009). Additional animal research has revealed that ongoing exposure to stimulants can impair "working memory" and this impairment persisted for years after the medication exposure was terminated (Higgins, 2009).

As stimulants are prescribed by physicians, these medications are typically assumed to be safe. The discussion here of side effects may raise concerns. Further, research in 2009 demonstrated "cocaine-like structural and chemical alterations in the brains of mice given methylphenidate" (Higgins, 2009, p. 41). "Intranasal [methylphenidate] abuse produces effects rapidly that are similar to the effects of cocaine in both onset and type" (Morton & Stockton, 2000, p. 159).

Cocaine Considerations

Mentioning cocaine in any discussion about ADHD medications and youth may raise eyebrows. But there are significant similarities between the way methylphenidate, amphetamines, and cocaine influence activities in the brain. "Cocaine's central nervous system effects are mediated primarily through dopamine, norepinephrine, and serotonin. . . . Cocaine primarily blocks the dopamine 'transporter' or uptake pump, thus impairing the reuptake of dopamine into presynaptic neurons. As a consequence, dopamine accumulates in the synaptic clefts and produces sustained stimulation of dopaminergic receptors" (Boghadi & Henning, 1997, p. 469). And even though stimulants are thought to be short-acting, that is, their effects dissipate after the medication leaves the system, "repetitive cocaine use gradually depletes dopamine stores in the presynaptic neurons of the brain by inhibiting the dopamine reuptake mechanism" (p. 469).

The U.S. Drug Enforcement Agency (DEA) also draws parallels between the drugs. Of course, the concern of the DEA is the misuse of these drugs, but they note: "the effects of amphetamines are similar to cocaine, but their onset is slower and their duration is longer. . . . Chronic abuse produces a psychosis that resembles schizophrenia and is characterized by paranoia, picking at the skin, preoccupation with one's own thoughts, and auditory and visual hallucinations" (U.S. Drug Enforcement Agency, 2020).

My goal in identifying this comparison is to highlight the strength of medications that we are giving to millions of children and teens every day. It should be said that methylphenidate and amphetamines are not cocaine but the dramatic similarities of how they affect the central nervous system should be carefully considered when deciding to use these medications; and using them for extending periods of time.

Amphetamine

Adderall is one of the most popular amphetamines in the treatment of ADHD. The way these medications "work" has been described as: "amphetamines are thought to block the reuptake of norepinephrine and dopamine into the presynaptic neuron and increase the release of these monoamines into the extraneuronal space" (Shire). This description is identical to that of methylphenidate.

Like methylphenidate, amphetamines are marketed with a variety of names and also differ in their delivery (e.g., extended release or pill, capsule, etc.). You are likely familiar with Adderall, Dyanavel XR, Evekeo, Mydayis, etcetera, which are all forms of amphetamine. There are additional derivatives of amphetamine (such as dextroamphetamine and lisdexamfetamine) which include drugs like Dexedrine and Vyvanse, respectively.

Years ago, when Vyvanse was new to the market, I was working with an adolescent diagnosed with ADHD. While we had been meeting for several months, his psychiatrist had recently switched his medication to Vyvanse—just a week before our session. In this particular meeting, he arrived on time but was a bit disheveled. It was a Saturday mid-morning, so I didn't think much of it at first. In starting our discussion, I asked how the week had been. "Not good," he said, "I've had some problems with other kids at school this week." "Really," I responded. This was uncharacteristic as he was typically pleasant and well-received by his peers. "Tell me what's been going on." He started describing some interactions with his peers and then said that kids were talking about him. He paused and said, "they're talking about me right now . . . out in the hallway," pointing to the door to my office. I clarified, "the kids that were talking about you at school are out in the hallway talking about you again?" He nodded, tilting his head as if trying to listen more carefully, and said, "Yes, that's them." Knowing his mom was in the waiting room, I told him I was going to get her, and I brought her into the office to describe what was going on. I recommended to her that while I continued meeting with her son she call the psychiatrist's office and let them know what was going on. He was experiencing auditory hallucinations. We finished our session and set up a plan with his mom to keep an eye on things. The next week, he came in for our scheduled session. His psychiatrist had discontinued the Vyvanse. In reviewing what had occurred, he described a disturbing experience. He said, "I knew what I was saying was crazy, but I could not *not* say it."

Erratic, disorganized, or even psychotic symptoms are not typical reactions to stimulant medications, but they can occur. When they do, rather than misdiagnosing them as "breakthrough psychotic symptoms" or trying to suggest they are indicative of an emerging psychotic diagnosis, they should be evaluated as the psychiatrist did in this situation. Any potential contributing factors to the symptom should be reduced/eliminated and then reevaluated once this occurs.

Stimulants as "Treatment"

As stimulants have been around for decades, there is a vast library of research related to their use. The goal here is to examine the biggest, most applicable studies, rather than a complete review of all studies. Small studies may have exaggerated outcomes and a limited ability to generalize to a larger population. As a result, large, longer-term studies provide the best reference points in terms of treatment outcome expectations.

The MTA Study

The Multimodal Treatment Study of Children with ADHD (MTA) study is the largest, and longest, project to understand the effects of treatment strategies (The MTA Cooperative Group, 1999). The study included 579 children with ADHD Combined Type (which is the most common form). At the beginning of the study, these children were aged between 7 and 10 years old. Approximately 20 percent of participants were female. Not only is the MTA study one of the largest, but it has also followed these children for many years, even into young adulthood.

There were four arms of treatment in the MTA study:

- Medication: A total of 289 children were assigned to receive medication. Nearly 90 percent (256) of these youth received methylphenidate while just 26 children were titrated to dextroamphetamine. Following titration to an optimal dose, these medicated children were then separated into the Medication Management group (144) and 145 were assigned to the Combined Treatment group.
- Behavioral Treatment: This group of 144 children received services including Parent Training, Child-Focused Treatment, and school-based strategies. The Parent Training component included twenty-seven group sessions and eight individual sessions per family. The Child-Focused Treatment was an eight-week, five-days-per-week Summer Treatment Program. The program involved a point system, skill development, problem solving, and modeling, among others. School interventions included consultation with teachers, behavioral monitoring, and reward strategies. The components of Behavioral Treatment gradually reduced until they terminated at the end of the study period. In fact, contacts with therapists were typically reduced to once monthly three to six months before the end of the study.
- Combined Treatment: This group of 145 children received both methylphenidate (or a small number receiving dextroamphetamine) and Behavioral Treatment described above. The researchers note that children in this group were maintained on lower doses of methylphenidate than the Medication Management group.
- Community Care: This group of 146 children received standard treatment within the community as a naturalistic comparison group. Data were collected on these subjects at the intervals of other participants. The majority of these subjects were receiving stimulant medications (most prescribed methylphenidate). Some children in this group also received additional medications, such as antidepressants.

As shown in Table 4.4, the MTA study evaluated these youth across seven domains. These domains were measured across nineteen different outcome data points, indicated by topic and those providing a rating.

At the conclusion of the first phase of the MTA study (fourteen months), researchers found that all four groups showed "marked reductions" in

Table 4.4 A Summary of Outcome Domains and Evaluators in the MTA Study

Domain	Category	Rater
ADHD Symptoms	Inattention	Teacher and Parent
	Hyperactivity/Impulsivity	Teacher, Parent, and Observer
Aggression-ODD	Oppositional Defiant Aggression	Teacher, Parent, and Observer
Internalizing Symptoms	Social Skills Rating System,	Teacher and Parent
	Internalizing Symptoms	Teacher and Parent
	Multidimensional Anxiety Scale	Child
Social Skills	Social Skills Rating System	Teacher and Parent
Parent-Child Relations	Power Assertion	Parent
	Personal Closeness	Parent
Academic Achievement	Reading	Child scores
	Mathematics	Child scores
	Spelling	Child scores

symptoms. In further analysis, Medication Management outperformed Behavioral Treatment for ADHD symptoms. However, these benefits were limited to *just three* of nineteen data points. That's right, daily medication only outperformed Behavioral Treatment on the Parent rating of inattention, Teacher rating of inattention, and Teacher rating of hyperactivity. On all other measures, there was no significant difference. Behavioral Treatment was reduced to monthly visits three to six months before the study ended, while medication was taken regularly.

Combined Treatment strategies are typically touted as being more powerful and effective. MTA researchers compared the results for the Combined Treatment group to the Behavioral Treatment group. Remarkably, Combined Treatment only outperformed Behavioral Treatment on six of nineteen outcome measures. In the initial phase of the MTA study, the advantage of Combined Treatment over Behavioral Treatment included:

- inattention rated by the teacher and the parent;
- hyperactivity-impulsivity rated by the parent;

- oppositional-aggressive behaviors rated by the parent; and
- internalized symptoms rated by the parent.

Reading scores were also improved in the Combined Treatment group compared to the Behavioral Treatment. There were no significant differences between the Combined Treatment and Medication Management groups.

Subsequent analysis of this first MTA phase revealed that even though the Behavioral Treatment had been reduced in frequency by the study's end, maintenance procedures were successful in sustaining Behavioral benefits to twenty-four months. In contrast, researchers observed that medication advantages diminished over time, noting that children and families may only achieve maximum medication benefit when it is accompanied by intensive support and regular contact with their doctor (MTA Cooperative Group, 2004). Researchers admit that the benefits of medication were reduced by half at twenty-four months (Jensen et al., 2007).

MTA at Three Years

The MTA Cooperative Group continued to follow the children in their study for years following the initial phase. Simply put, "by 36 months, none of the randomly assigned treatment groups differed significantly on any of the five clinical and functional outcomes" (Jensen et al., 2007, p. 993). In their effort to understand the loss of benefit from medications, researchers identified that there was some reduction in medication adherence in the Combined and Medication Management groups, although fully accounting for the diminished medication benefits is dubious as medication compliance was approximately 90 percent down to 71 percent at the three-year follow-up. Moreover, it's fair to assume that some of the reduced medication adherence was due to a lack of observed benefit, possibly already captured in earlier data collection. In other words, if patients were experiencing benefits, it increases the likelihood of adherence. Those not experiencing benefit are more likely to discontinue the treatment. However, researchers also discovered that "participants using medication in the twenty-four- to thirty-six-month period actually showed increased symptomatology during that interval relative to those not taking medication" (Jensen et al., 2007, p. 996). Researchers speculate that children doing well may have discontinued their medications. At the three-year analysis, MTA researchers concluded, "medication use variables during the year from 24 to 36 months did not reveal any advantage on 36-month outcomes and instead showed a tendency toward disadvantage" (Jensen et al., 2007, p. 998).

MTA at Eight Years

Long-term effects were observed for the children participating in the MTA study. Again, "there were no statistically significant effects of original randomized treatment group assignment on any of the 24 outcome variables tested" (Molina et al., 2009, p. 488). The researchers determined that "the MTA group as a whole was functioning significantly less well than the non-ADHD classmate sample recruited at 24 months" and "initial clinical presentation in childhood, including severity of ADHD symptoms, conduct problems, intellect, and social advantage, and strength of ADHD symptom response to any treatment, are better predictors of later adolescent functioning than the type of treatment received in childhood for 14 months" (Molina et al., 2009, p. 494). As they conclude, "Although the MTA data provided strong support for the acute reduction of symptoms with intensive medication management, these long-term follow-up data fail to provide support for long-term advantage beyond 2 years for the majority of children" (Molina et al., 2009, p. 497).

The MTA—Young Adult Outcomes

In 2017, MTA researchers conducted additional analysis of the outcomes for youth (now young adults) participating in the study. This review occurred twelve years after the initial enrollment in the study. Data collected at this point reveals significant persistence of the disorder due to higher levels of symptom severity and of concern:

> comparisons of ADHD-treated and ADHD-untreated groups suggests that in the long-term, symptom-related benefit of treatment with medication may dissipate and not remain significant but growth-related cost may remain statistically significant in adulthood.
>
> (Swanson et al., 2017, p. 671)

The MTA Study has been recognized as the most rigorous, well-funded, and most sustained project examining our best treatments for ADHD. Despite our best efforts, our outcomes are woefully inadequate.

As noted, the MTA study is the largest and longest, examining the effectiveness of ADHD treatments. It is true, however, that it is just one study in a sea of dozens. In 2018, researchers completed a systematic review and meta-analysis examining medication treatments for ADHD (Cortese et al., 2018). Their analysis included eighty-one studies including over ten thousand children and adolescents. It is touted as "the most comprehensive available evidence base to inform patients, families, clinicians, guideline developers, and policymakers on the choice of ADHD medications across age groups" (Cortese et al., 2018, p. 1). Consistent with the MTA study, these authors note short-term benefits from the use of stimulant medications. While both methylphenidate and amphetamines demonstrated short-term symptom improvement, side effects eliminated amphetamines as a first choice in their recommendations. Remarkably, they could only support these benefits for three months of treatment. In their effort to examine longer-term outcomes, they determined the data available for twenty-six-week and fifty-two-week analysis was insufficient. After decades of commonly using stimulant drugs in the treatment of ADHD, it is very concerning that the available research only supports the effectiveness of medications in the short-term (twelve weeks) (Cortese et al., 2018).

Medication Must Improve Academic Performance, *Right*?

Children are often prescribed stimulant medications after behavioral, or performance problems are identified in their academic settings. Indeed, a child's full-time job is being a student. While the value of stimulant medications on academic performance is of interest, research on this topic is curiously lacking. For example, if a pharmaceutical company could demonstrate medication to improve academic performance, we would all take it. Imagine a medication that could take a D student to C, a C student to B, a B student to A, and an A student to Honors. It would be a global phenomenon.

In 2006, the American Psychological Association released a report on psychotropic medications (APA Working Group on Psychoactive Medications for Children and Adolescents). Related to stimulant use, they pointedly noted, "stimulants have no effect on academic achievement in the short-term. No long-term effects have been reliably reported on any outcome measure" (APA Working Group, 2006, p. 43). In 2010, Canadian researchers examined interventions to determine their value in the classroom:

> Based on the correlational analyses, a disassociation was found between the impact of medication objective (i.e., standardized assessment) and subjective (i.e., questionnaire) measures of academic achievement. The results indicate that teacher and parent ratings of children's academic achievement were more positive when the child was receiving medication. However, there was no significant improvement found in the performance of these same children on a standardized measure of

achievement. . . . These results are consistent with the conclusions of previous research, which indicated that medication has little to no impact on long-term academic achievement.

(Corkum, McGonnell, & Schachar, 2010, p. 10)

Most recently, researchers released their findings exploring the impact of stimulants on learning (Pelham et al., 2022). In their sample of 173 children between 7 and 12 years old, these researchers found that while medication improved productivity it did not translate to learning. Specifically, ADHD medication was seen to have an improvement in "seatwork productivity and classroom behavior" but "there was no detectable effect of medication on learning the material taught during instruction" (Pelham et al., 2022, p. 367). In other words, medications were associated with behavioral control, but this did not enable improved accuracy on work products or the overall learning outcomes.

Stimulant Use as a Disorder

The DSM-5-TR includes the diagnosis of Stimulant Use Disorder. The criteria for this condition are designed to capture those individuals who are abusing stimulant medications and include patterns of abuse but also tolerance. As it is relevant to this discussion, information provided within the DSM-5-TR provides keen insights into the negative effects of stimulants. While it is focused on those abusing stimulants, it is important to recognize that the negative effects of stimulants observed here may also be impacting youth, possibly just to a lesser degree.

So, what has the American Psychiatric Association recognized about stimulants? First, they acknowledge that the effects of amphetamine-type substances are similar to those of cocaine, which provides justification for them to classify the condition as "stimulant use disorder." Specifically, they say "both are potent central nervous system stimulants with similar psychoactive and sympathomimetic effects. Amphetamine-type substances are longer acting than cocaine" (APA, 2022, p. 635). In the criteria for the disorder, they differentiate these behaviors from individuals taking stimulants under appropriate medical supervision (e.g., for ADHD).

The APA has also acknowledged that when these substances are abused, they can result in negative changes in mood (e.g., irritability, depression, aggression), can create psychotic conditions, and a host of complicated physical effects.

As stimulants are used as a treatment for inattention and impulse-control problems, it is fascinating to know that when stimulants are abused, neurocognitive impairment is common. The APA highlights that this impairment includes "deficits related to attention, impulsivity, verbal learning/memory, working memory, and executive functioning" (APA, 2022, p. 639). Further, "there is some evidence that chronic use causes neuroinflammation and neurotoxicity in dopaminergic neurons" (p. 639). The APA does not provide parameters (e.g., dosing amounts) for what constitutes abuse, yet I am sure many of you working in the field with children prescribed stimulants have seen their doses progressively increase when their response to being medicated diminishes. While stimulant prescriptions are under the supervision of medical professionals, these iatrogenic complications (that is, negative effects caused by the treatment) should be closely monitored.

As a clinician, how should we evaluate the negative effects of excessive stimulant use? The effects are exactly those that are symptoms of the disorder for which they're used to treat. Indeed, this could be an issue of dose, but many children remain on stimulants for years and dosing regularly increases due to a diminished positive benefit from these medications. Future research could explore the trends of Adult ADHD as our stimulant use increased. In a way, increasing use of stimulants could be correlated to a growing population of adults with ADHD, simply as a result of the negative effects of long-term, increasing doses of stimulant exposure.

Walk Away Message

Diagnostic Dilemma: The diagnosis of ADHD has been problematic for decades. Using the criteria essentially established in 1994 (the DSM-IV), in 1998, the National Institute of Mental Health noted that because of these problems, the validity of the disorder continues to be a problem. In other words, for the last thirty years, even though the diagnosis of ADHD leads to diagnostic confusion, inaccuracy, and other complications, no changes have been made. In fact, in 2013 the American Psychiatric Association has actually made the diagnostic criteria *less* stringent rather than more specific. Is this an accident? Is it a lack of attention to the issue? Or is it intentional?

Treatment Dilemma: Despite our best treatments, as examined by the MTA study and meta-analyses, our outcomes in the treatment of ADHD are still painfully poor. For decades, the primary treatment has been to emphasize the use of stimulants to control the symptoms of ADHD. Yet long-term, highly funded research demonstrates that the advantage of medication use is short-term, diminishes fairly quickly, and does not lead to long-term functional improvement. The U.S. has continued to consume approximately 70 percent of the global stimulant supply over the last thirty years; and this has been maintained even with increasing production each year. However, behavioral treatments offer comparable outcomes, albeit still insufficient, and are generally less recommended than medications. Is this an accident? Is it a lack of attention to the issue? Or is it intentional?

References

Alza Corporation. Concerta (methylphenidate HCI) package insert. https://www.accessdata.fda.gov/drugsatfda_docs/label/2007/021121s014lbl.pdf

American Academy of Pediatrics, Committee on Nutrition and the Council on Sports Medicine and Fitness. (2011). Clinical reports—sports drinks and energy drinks for children and adolescents: Are they Appropriate? *Pediatrics, 127*: 1182–1189.

American Psychiatric Association. (1980). *Diagnostic and statistical manual of mental disorders* (3rd ed.).

American Psychiatric Association. (1987). *Diagnostic and statistical manual of mental disorders* (3rd ed., rev.).

American Psychiatric Association. (1994). *Diagnostic and statistical manual of mental disorders* (4th ed.).

American Psychiatric Association. (2013). *Diagnostic and statistical manual of mental disorders* (5th ed.).

American Psychiatric Association. (2022). *Diagnostic and statistical manual of mental disorders* (5th ed., text rev.).

American Psychological Association Working Group on Psychoactive Medications for Children and Adolescents. (2006). *Report of the working group on psychoactive medications for children and adolescents. Psychopharmacological, psychosocial, and combined interventions for childhood disorders: Evidence base, contextual factors, and future directions.* https://www.apa.org/pi/families/resources/child-medications.pdf

Boghadi, M., & Henning, R. (1997). Cocaine: Pathophysiology and clinical toxicology. *Heart & Lung: The Journal of Acute Critical Care, 26*(6): 466–483. https://doi.org/10.1016/s0147-9563(97)90040-6

Corkum, P., McGonnell, M., & Schachar, R. (2010). Factors affecting academic achievement in children with ADHD. *Journal of Applied Research on Learning, 3*(9).

Corrigan, M., & Whitaker, R. (2017). *Lancet Psychiatry* needs to retract the ADHD-Enigma Study. MIA report: Authors' conclusion that individuals with ADHD have smaller brains is belied by their own data. https://www.madinamerica.com/2017/04/lancet-psychiatry-needs-to-retract-the-adhd-enigma-study

Cortese, S., et al. (2018). Comparative efficacy and tolerability of medications for attention-deficit hyperactivity disorder in children, adolescents, and adults: A systematic review and network meta-analysis. *Lancet Psychiatry*, August. https://doi.org/10.1016/52215-0366(18)30269-4

Dabney, J. (2016). How Vyvanse could fuel Shire's ADHD portfolio sales. https://www.yahoo.com/news/vyvanse-could-fuel-shire-adhd-150656111.html

Elbe, D., Black, T., McGrane, I., & Choi, S. (2023). *Clinical handbook of psychotropic drugs for children and adolescents*. Hogrefe Publishers.

Hadland, S., Cerda, M., Earlywine, J., Krieger, M., Anderson, T., & Marshall, B. (2020). Analysis of pharmaceutical industry marketing of stimulants, 2014 through 2018. *JAMA Pediatrics*, *174*(4): 385.

Higgins, E. (2009). Do ADHD drugs take a toll on the brain? *Scientific American Mind*, July / August.

Hoogman, M., Bralten, J., Hibar, D., Mennes, M., Zwiers, M., Schweren, L., et al. (2017). Subcortical brain volume differences in participants with attention deficit hyperactivity disorder in children and adults: a cross-sectional mega-analysis. *Lancet Psychiatry*, *4*(4): 310–319.

Jensen, P. et al. (2007). 3-year follow-up of the NIMH MTA study. *Journal of the American Academy of Child and Adolescent Psychiatry*, *46*(8): 989–1002.

Mallett, C., Natarajan, A., & Hoy, J. (2014). Attention deficit/hyperactivity disorder: A DSM timeline review. *International Journal of Mental Health*, *43*: 36–60.

McPhillips, D. (2023). FDA, DEA call on drugmakers to boost manufacturing amid ongoing shortage of prescription stimulants. *CNN*, August 1. https://www.cnn.com/2023/08/01/health/adderall-shortage-fda-dea-letter/index.html

Molina, B. et al. (2009). The MTA at 8 years: Prospective follow-up of children treated for combined-type ADHD in a multisite study. *Journal of American Academy of Child and Adolescent Psychiatry*, *48*(5): 484–500.

Morton, W., & Stockton, G. (2000). Methylphenidate abuse and psychiatric side effects: Primary care companion. *Journal of Clinical Psychiatry*, October, *2*(5): 159–164.

MTA Cooperative Group. (1999). A 14-month randomized clinical trial of treatment strategies for attention-deficit/hyperactivity disorder. *Archives of General Psychiatry*, *56*: 1073–1086.

MTA Cooperative Group. (2004). National Institute of Mental Health multimodal treatment study of ADHD follow-up: 24-month outcomes of treatment strategies for attention-deficit/hyperactivity disorder. *Pediatrics*, *113*(4):754–761.

Murray, D., Bussing, R., Fernandez, M., Hou, W., Garvan, C., Swanson, J., & Eyberg, S. (2009). Psychometric properties of teacher SKAMP ratings from a community sample. *Assessment*, *16*(2): 193–208.

National Institutes of Health. (1998). Diagnosis and treatment of attention deficit hyperactivity disorder (ADHD). *NIH Consensus Statement*, *16*(2): 1–37.

Odeh, S. (2019). *Sensory processing within attention-deficit/hyperactivity disorder in children and adolescents* [Doctoral Dissertation]. Chicago School of Professional Psychology.

Pelham, W. et al. (2022). The effect of stimulant medication on the learning of academic curricula in children with ADHD: A randomized crossover study. *Journal of Consulting Clinical Psychology*, *90*(5): 367–380.

Pharmaceutical Journal. (2015). Narcotics monitoring board reports 66% increase in global consumption of methylphenidate. *294*(7853). https://doi.org/10.1211/PJ.2015.20068042

Pharmaletter. (2003). Adderall drives growth at Shire in 1st quarter. https://www.thepharmaletter.com/article/adderall-drives-growth-at-shire-in-1st-quarter

Piper, B., Ogden, C., Simoyan, O., Chung, D., Caggiano, J., Nichols, S., et al. (2018). Trends in use of prescription stimulants in the United States and Territories, 2006 to 2016. *PLoS ONE 1*(11): e0206100. https://doi.org/10.1371/journal.pone.0206100

Public Broadcasting Service. (n.d.). *Frontline*: Statistics on stimulant use. https://www.pbs.org/wgbh/pages/frontline/shows/medicating/drugs/stats.html

Shire, U.S. Adderall XR full prescribing information (package insert). https://www.accessdata.fda.gov/drugsatfda_docs/label/2013/021303s026lbl.pdf

Solinas, M., Ferré, S., You, Z., Karcz-Kubicha, M., Popoli, P., & Goldberg, S. (2002). Caffeine induces dopamine and glutamate release in the shell of the nucleus accumbens. *Journal of Neuroscience*, *22*(15): 6321–6324.

Swanson, J. et al. (2017). Young adult outcomes in the follow-up of the multimodal treatment study of attention-deficit / hyperactivity disorder: Symptom persistence, source discrepancy, and height suppression. *Journal of Child Psychology and Psychiatry*, *58*(6): 663–678.

Thorley, G. (1984). Hyperkinetic syndrome of childhood: Clinical characteristics. *British Journal of Psychiatry*, *141*(1): 16–24. https://doi.org/10.1192/bjp.144.1.16

United States Department of Justice. (2014). Shire Pharmaceuticals LLC to pay $56.5 million to resolve False Claims Act allegations relating to drug marketing and promotion practices. Retrieved July 27, 2025, from: https://www.justice.gov/archives/opa/pr/shire-pharmaceuticals-llc-pay-565-million-resolve-false-claims-act-allegations-relating-drug

United States Drug Enforcement Agency. (2020). Amphetamine drug fact sheet. https://www.dea.gov/sites/default/files/2020-06/Amphetamines-2020_0.pdf

Vazquez, J., Martin de la Torre, O., Palomé, J., & Redolar-Ripoll, D. (2022). Effects of caffeine consumption on attention deficit hyperactivity disorder (ADHD) treatment: A systematic review of animal studies. *Nutrients*, *14*. https://doi.org/10.3390/nu14040739

Volkow, N., Wang, G., Logan, J., Alexoff, D., Fowler, J., Thanos, P., . . . Tomasi, D. (2015). Caffeine increases striatal dopamine d2/d3 receptor availability in the human brain. *Translational Psychiatry*, *5*(4). https://doi.org/10.1038/tp.2015.46

Whitaker, R. (2011). *Anatomy of an epidemic: Magic bullets, psychiatric drugs, and the astonishing rise of mental illness in America*. Crown Publishers.

Wolraich, M. L., Hagan, J. F., & Allan, C., et al; (2019). Subcommittee on children and adolescents with attention-deficit/hyperactive disorder. clinical practice guideline for the diagnosis, evaluation, and treatment of attention-deficit/hyperactivity disorder in children and adolescents. *Pediatrics*, *144*(4): e20192528.

World Health Organization. (2024). *Clinical descriptions and diagnostic requirements for ICD: 11 mental, behavioural and neurodevelopmental disorders*. World Health Organization; License: CC BY-NC-ND 3.0 IGO.

5
Rethinking the Treatment of Adolescent Depression

A crisis of depression is occurring across the United States. It is having a deep impact on our young people. More young people have psychiatric diagnoses than ever before. Suicide rates are alarmingly high. We are seeing some of the highest rates of youth presenting at hospital emergency departments for depression, anxiety, and suicidal ideation. A primary treatment to address this distress is antidepressant medication. This chapter closely examines the scientific studies for antidepressants. And the research just doesn't support the scale of our use or how much we rely on them to provide relief. But you be the judge. I believe our youth deserve better. I also believe that when a teen "fails to respond" to antidepressants, rather than labeling them "treatment resistant," we need to recognize that this is what the research tells us will happen.

The following chapter will address the diagnosis and treatment of depression and associated behaviors and feelings. I should give you a word of warning. What you are about to read will likely conflict with what you assume to be true, or what you have actually seen as accepted treatment. One of the surprising facts you will learn is that the vast amount of research and testing on antidepressants has not identified any substantial benefit for children and adolescents with depressive conditions. To expand this point, despite potential side effects of worsening depression or suicidal ideation, there is actually much more evidence that fluoxetine (the preferred antidepressant for youth) does *not* work in teens compared to the evidence that supports its use. A recent critique of adult antidepressant studies further emphasizes:

> Rising antidepressant prescribing is not associated with an improvement in mental health outcomes at the population level, which, according to some measures, have worsened as antidepressants have risen. . . . Multiple meta-analyses have shown antidepressants to have no clinically meaningful benefit beyond placebo for all patients but those with the most severe depression.
>
> (Davies et al., 2023, p. 1)

I have been a clinical psychologist for decades and teaching clinical psychology at the graduate level for fifteen years. Rest assured, the evidence and information cited within this chapter is well-researched, emanates from the highest-quality sources, and may challenge your ideas—whether you are a student studying mental health, a clinician in the field, or a parent struggling to find the best treatment for your child. With my own students, clients, and colleagues I always encourage them to be critical consumers of information. Check my sources. But most importantly, be an advocate for transparent, reliable, replicated science in mental health treatment.

This chapter will begin by reviewing depressive disorder diagnoses and their prevalence in youth. From there, the goal is to examine our currently suggested best treatments, largely focusing on medication treatments. This will lead us to the fundamental assumptions that drive medication use, raising questions related to chemical imbalances, the meaning of symptoms, and most effective treatments. Regarding depressive disorders, as disruptive mood dysregulation disorder (DMDD) is considered a depressive condition within the DSM diagnostic manual, the treatment of this condition will also be discussed in the chapter exploring antipsychotic medication. Following an overview of diagnostic criteria, medication treatments will be explored. Finally, common assumptions regarding depression, causes, and treatment expectations will be discussed.

The Current Problem

The Diagnostic Framework

The DSM-5-TR (*Diagnostic and Statistical Manual of Mental Disorders, Fifth Edition, Text Revision*) was released in 2022 and has several different conditions within the category of depressive disorders. These diagnoses are generally based on the severity and duration of the presenting symptoms. However, it is important to know that while children and adolescents experience depressed feelings as a normal part of life experiences, considering them to be a psychiatric disorder was quite rare before the release of the DSM-IV (APA, 1994) and DSM-IV-TR (APA, 2000). Interestingly enough, an increase in diagnosing youth with depression coincided with the release of the blockbuster antidepressant medication Prozac (which received its FDA approval in 1987 and was approved for children aged 7 to 17 in 2003).

In that earlier DSM-IV and DSM-IV-TR era, the observed prevalence of major depression in youth was 2 percent for children and 5–8 percent for adolescents (Son & Kirchner, 2000), whereas now over a third of adolescents globally are at risk for depression (Shorey, Ng, & Wong, 2021). And those data were collected before the global COVID-19 pandemic, which accelerated the experiences of distress, isolation, unpredictability, loss, and fear. Recent research also notes the sustained increases in the use of antidepressants in adolescents in the early phase of the pandemic (Amill-Rosario, Lee, Zhang, & dosReis, 2022).

Increases in the diagnosis of depression could be reflective of *finally* having a blockbuster medication treatment. The marketing of Prozac, and subsequent SSRI medications, was aggressive and sought to explain depression as a "chemical imbalance." And we remember the commercials of the bouncing little Zoloft pill, assuring us that "depression may be related to an imbalance of natural chemicals between nerve cells in the brain. Zoloft works to correct this imbalance" (Pfizer, original Zoloft commercial). With the increase in published articles, reports of fewer side effects, and this apparent newfound ability of antidepressants to target a chemical imbalance, the identification of depression and use of these medications soared.

The rates of depression in youth, however, are not simply by-products of our diagnostic manuals and drug marketing. The stress on young people is undeniable. Such challenges are connected to the need for a sense of belonging, wanting to feel capable, the desire for responsibility and independence, managing relationships, and the wide-ranging effects of society, technology, social media, their education, family dynamics, etcetera. Also, with young brains still developing their capacities for impulse control, rational decision-making, interconnectedness, and other developmental and maturational issues, the list of factors related to depression goes on and on.

Without a doubt, feelings of sadness, helplessness, frustration, hopelessness, anger, uncertainty, are likely in teens and when these feelings begin to emerge, they can also be very confusing and frightening. As a developmental period, adolescence increases access to a broader range of emotions, and relationships become more complicated. These new and complex experiences may be difficult to manage. Moreover, young people have much less influence over the events in their lives compared to adults. This lack of control can amplify the intensity of these depression-related feelings.

Traumatic experiences will be discussed in another chapter. It is essential to recognize that exposure to traumatic or adverse experiences are also powerful contributors to feelings of depression, hopelessness, despair, and isolation. When adversity has occurred, clinical priority must be directed toward addressing those issues. Simply identifying symptoms of depression and assuming medication will provide relief is short-sighted. Many of the effects of trauma can look like depression and without addressing the experiences of trauma, symptoms will likely persist. Books like *What Happened to You?* and *The Boy Who Was Raised as a Dog* highlight the wide-ranging impact of trauma. They are must-reads for mental health professionals to understand the wide-ranging, systemic implications of traumatic and adverse experiences. Consistent with this important work, in 2021, the American Academy of Pediatrics recommended SSNRs to address trauma. Sounds like a medication, right? They are recommending Safe, Stable, Nurturing Relationships (Forkey et al., 2021).

Reactions to depressive thoughts and feelings can vary. As you know, some people become withdrawn when they are feeling depressed, while others may lash out and be angry and aggressive (which could include efforts to harm themselves or others). But this continuum of reaction makes our understanding of "treatment response" more complicated. If a treatment works for someone who is shut down or withdrawn with their depression, the same treatment may not have any benefit if the depression results in aggressive, angry behavior. In fact, some medication treatments for depression can *worsen* symptoms at each end of this continuum. Conversely, antidepressants are often reported to create an "emotional blunting" (Langley et al., 2023). That is, while depressive feelings are lessened, so are pleasurable ones.

From the DSM-5-TR, the disorders that reflect feelings of depression to be discussed here include major depressive disorder, persistent depressive disorder, and disruptive mood dysregulation disorder. There are several others, but more likely to occur in adults. As we review the symptoms, understanding that these emerge from unmet needs is equally important. Historically, symptoms were understood to be signs of distress, of frustration, of despair, etc.

Unfortunately, our contemporary models of diagnosing don't really concern themselves with "cause" but intend to simply identify the symptoms and in what combination they occur. If they meet the established threshold for a disorder, a diagnosis is given. Yet all of this ignores the reasons, function, or catalyzing factors for the symptoms. Relying on the diagnosis to drive our decision-making may actually move us further away from understanding the pains, distress, losses, and fears that are being experienced. When treatments simply aim to reduce symptoms, we are only offering temporary gains.

Major Depressive Disorder

Symptoms for a major depressive disorder only need to occur for a period of two weeks. While five symptoms are required to meet the diagnosis, one of the symptoms must be either a "depressed mood" and/or "loss of interest or pleasure" (APA, 2022). These symptoms must be persistent over the two-week period and be observed by others. The criteria also note that in children and teens, a depressed mood may also manifest as irritability. Other symptoms that are included may be:

- an increase or decrease in weight (or significant changes in appetite);
- noticeable changes in sleep (sleeping much more or much less);
- increased behavioral activity (called psychomotor agitation) or decreased activity (psychomotor retardation);
- a noticeable loss of energy;
- a sense of worthlessness or inappropriate guilt;
- poor concentration, difficulty making decisions, or difficulty thinking; and
- thoughts of death or thinking about suicide (with or without a plan) (APA, 2022).

As with other diagnoses, these symptoms must cause distress and negatively influence how the child or adolescent is functioning across settings, such as home, school, or with peers. In an extreme form, major depressive disorder can also include psychotic symptoms (such as hallucinations or bizarre, disorganized behaviors) although this is much less common in youth.

Here is some bad news: The diagnostic criteria are difficult to accurately apply in identifying the disorder. Of concern, the inter-rater reliability for major depressive disorder in the DSM-5 is just 0.28, falling into the "questionable" category of agreement. In other words, when multiple trained clinicians evaluated the psychiatric conditions of specific individuals showing symptoms for depression, there was fairly poor agreement that it was, indeed, depression (American Journal of Psychiatry, Editorial, 2013). Think of it this way, based on our current diagnostic criteria, there was only fair agreement, barely better than chance. "This is the reason that many texts recommend 80 percent agreement as the minimum acceptable inter-rater agreement. . . . Any Kappa below 0.60 indicates inadequate agreement among the raters and little confidence should be placed in the study results" (McHugh, 2012, p. 277). Those criteria are unchanged in the DSM-5-TR. Contributing to this lack of reliability is the fact that "40% to 90% of youth with depressive disorders have psychiatric comorbidities" (Walter et al., 2022, p. 6). Indeed, most youth presenting with depressive symptoms will also show symptoms that meet the criteria for other disorders, quickly leading to confusing clinical presentations.

I believe simply focusing on the diagnosis of major depression misses the point. The required symptoms for the diagnosis speak to distress. Unmet needs create distress, and indeed, symptoms. Honestly, being unable to effectively cope with unmet needs should not always equate to, or be considered, a mental disorder, chemical imbalance, or brain problem. These symptoms can take many forms, but as depression has been a part of the human experience since our beginning, our goal should be to understand what needs are unmet, frustrated, or defeated. We also need to appreciate the reality that distress—in all its forms—affects our physiology, our relationships, our sense of self, our goals, and our perception of the world around us. When our needs continue to go unmet, our reactions can become more desperate, more intense, or more self-defeating.

The Impact of Depression

Depression is very real. Feelings of depression are taking their toll on our children and adolescents. In the past twenty years, suicide rates for children have increased by more than 50 percent (Curtin, 2020). As of 2021, suicide was the second leading cause of death among those aged 10–14 and the third leading cause of death for those 15–24 years old (Heron, 2023). Within 2021–2022, 40 percent of high school students reported feelings of sadness or hopelessness in the last year, with 20 percent seriously considering attempting suicide (U.S. CDC, 2024).

In 2021, the U.S. Centers for Disease Control and Prevention (CDC) reported that 20 percent of high school students seriously considered attempting suicide (U.S. CDC, 2023). Most recently, in their initial review of data, the CDC has projected a decrease in suicide for 10- to 14-year-old, as well as 15- to 24-year-old individuals between 2021 and 2022. They note this to be statistically significant, but these numbers continue to represent disturbing rates of young people dying from suicide. Specifically, in those aged 10–14 years, suicide dropped from 3.2 in 2021 to 2.8 (per 100,000) in 2022. In the 15- to 24-year-old group, the decrease was from 23.8 to 21.6 (per

100,000). For the adolescent/young adult group, this translates to 8,868.3 deaths in 2021 to 8,198.7 deaths in 2022 (Curtin, Garnett, & Ahmad, 2023).

When I entered the field, "evidence-based treatments" were expected to provide the best interventions, thereby resulting in the best outcomes. Over recent decades, the fields of psychology and psychiatry have been immersed in studying and providing these "evidence-based treatments." No doubt, many valuable studies have been completed, people have been helped, and our understanding of certain treatments and conditions has improved. However, the rates of depression and suicide in young people have been going in the wrong direction. Despite our vast investments in these research and training pursuits, our outcomes are inadequate. As Tom Insel, MD (former head of NIMH) highlights, this national dilemma needs our urgent attention:

> There are over 47,000 suicide deaths in the U.S. each year, the equivalent of a mass shooting of 129 people each day, every day. That is a suicide every 11 minutes. . . . Suicide in the United States has been trending up, not down, over the past few decades . . . from 1999 through 2018 increasing by over 33 percent.
>
> (Insel, 2022, p. 9)

Recent data show the continued problem. Researchers in Illinois observed that the rate of emergency department (ED) visits with youth aged 5 to 19, presenting with suicidal ideation, rose 59 percent when comparing visits between 2016–2017 to those in 2019–2021 (Brewer et al., 2022). Those suffering with these distressing thoughts and feelings deserve better. The many hurdles in this challenge are beyond the scope of the discussion here, but suffice to say, the field of mental health has many more questions than answers.

Over these recent decades, we have become increasingly comfortable with using psychiatric medications, designed for adults, in young people. Some medications are FDA-approved for use in youth, but the growing use of psychiatric medications is not without scrutiny. To offer a bit of historical perspective, in 2004, the United States House of Representatives examined the efficacy of antidepressants in children and adolescents. The initial statement of this report was stunning:

> In reviewing this issue, the subcommittee will be focused on the 15 placebo-controlled randomized studies submitted to the FDA for an indication in children with depression. The FDA found that in 12 out of the 15 studies, there was no efficacy that was shown (U.S. House of Representatives, Committee on Energy and Commerce, 2004, p. 1).

In other words, 80 percent of the studies in their review on antidepressants resulted in no benefit over a placebo for youth. And this was known twenty years ago. As we'll see below, the research that shows antidepressants outperforming placebos may be statistically significant, but not clinically significant. So how have we arrived at this point? Decades later, after realizing that the preponderance of the evidence demonstrates SSRI antidepressants offer no advantage over a placebo in the treatment of pediatric depression, these medications remain some of the most commonly prescribed psychotropic medications to young people. The congressional hearing noted that Prozac was the only antidepressant that demonstrated superiority over placebo. But as we'll see below, even this is dubious when examining a wider range of research.

Medication Treatment: The Current Guidelines

The American Academy of Child and Adolescent Psychiatry (AACAP) revised its *Clinical Practice Guidelines for the Assessment and Treatment of Children and Adolescents with Major and Persistent Depressive Disorders* in 2022 (Walter et al., 2022). As these were recently published, they can be seen as the latest representation of AACAP's "best evidence" in their assessment and treatment guidelines. AACAP is seen as an authoritative body in making recommendations for the use of psychiatric medications in youth, so these Practice Guidelines are widely accessed to guide treatment decisions.

The authors of the AACAP Practice Guidelines conducted a thorough and thoughtful review of the available research on antidepressants, the use of psychotherapy, and their combination. The guidelines evaluated dozens of studies and based their findings on an SOE (strength of evidence) grade. For example, a "High SOE reflected high confidence that the evidence reflects the true effect. Further research is very unlikely to change confidence in the estimate or effect." In contrast, a "Low SOE indicates low confidence that the evidence reflects the true effect. Further research is likely to change confidence in the estimate of the effect and is likely to change the estimate" (Walter et al., 2022, p. 10). There were four ratings of Strength used: High, Moderate, Low, and Insufficient.

Regarding psychotherapy, the AACAP Guidelines reviewed twenty-five studies and of these, only six were utilizing CBT and just three of IP. They also reviewed five studies of Family Therapies, parent-child interaction, short-term psychoanalytic therapy, and others. Based on their review, the AACAP concluded that cognitive behavioral therapy (CBT) and interpersonal therapy

(IP) improved depressive symptoms from a clinician perspective and self-report measures. However, for both psychotherapy strategies, the strength of the evidence was determined to be *low*. The American Psychological Association released its guidelines for adolescent depression as well. Their 2019 report recommends cognitive behavioral therapy or interpersonal therapy. Furthermore, they identify fluoxetine as the first-line medication treatment. Revealing the dilemma within the field, "there was insufficient evidence to recommend either treatment (psychotherapy or fluoxetine) over the other for major depressive disorder" (American Psychological Association Guideline Development Panel, 2019, p. 8).

Reviewing antidepressants, however, the AACAP Guidelines examined twenty-seven studies which included fourteen trials of selective serotonin reuptake inhibitors (SSRIs) which are by far the most commonly prescribed antidepressants. These fourteen trials included eight focused on fluoxetine (Prozac), with the remaining trials including escitalopram (Lexapro), citalopram (Celexa), vilazodone (Viibryd), and paroxetine (Paxil). The guidelines concluded that *only* fluoxetine outperformed placebo for *clinician-reported* depressive symptoms. It was *low* strength of evidence, meaning that confidence was low that the effect observed was a true effect. The other SSRI medications were deemed insufficient in their ability to demonstrate benefit. The review also noted that there are three meta-analyses that support the use of fluoxetine over placebo. It's important to reiterate that the strength of evidence for fluoxetine was *low* when compared to a placebo (an inactive pill resembling medication).

The AACAP Guidelines "suggest that selective serotonin reuptake inhibitor medication (except paroxetine), preferably fluoxetine, could be offered to adolescents and children with major depressive disorder" and while the SSRI escitalopram is an FDA-approved medication, the guidelines note "no statistically significant improvements in depression in children and adolescents were found for escitalopram versus placebo" (Walter et al., 2022, pp. 13–14). We're going to examine the data a bit further.

In my years of practice and teaching, I've found that many people scan research, but many don't drill down on the details. Seeing an article entitled, "Antidepressants Shown Safe and Effective" leads one to feel assured that if they're working with someone on the medication, they should be getting better. I get it. People are busy, new articles come out every day, and you can't be an expert in everything. But failing to *read* the research leads to faulty assumptions, as we'll see below.

In the AACAP Guidelines, placebos were found to be as effective as all of the SSRIs, except for one: fluoxetine (Prozac). Fluoxetine was only found to have a low strength of evidence. With the failures of active medications to outperform a placebo, and very weak evidence to support the use of fluoxetine, one may wonder as to why they are so commonly prescribed to young people; why do prescribers believe they will be beneficial?

Prozac Proof: As It Turns Out, Size *Does* Matter

Sample size and effect size matter. A larger sample size—meaning more participants in a study—provides a better representation of how the intervention affects a larger portion of the population. If you're looking at the outcomes of an intervention applied to four people, and three respond positively, you can claim a 75 percent effectiveness rate. But this has little applicability to a larger population. Many people assume that antidepressant medications have been tested on thousands of youth, even before being marketed. This is far from the reality. Effect size refers to the amount of difference in outcomes between the treatment group and placebo group. Small differences between those groups reduce one's confidence that the treatment is truly making a practical, clinically meaningful difference. For example, a large effect size of 0.8 indicates that 79 percent of the control group (or a placebo group) have outcome scores below the average of the experimental (or active medication) group. In other words, the active treatment outperformed the control group in 80 percent of cases. But let me be very clear: an effect size of this magnitude is not demonstrated in antidepressant studies.

In reviewing the studies used to support AACAP's Practice Guideline conclusions for fluoxetine, one of the meta-analyses cited highlights that "fluoxetine (alone or in combination with CBT) seems to be the best choice for the acute treatment of moderate-to-severe depressive disorder in children and adolescents but *the quality of evidence is low*" (Zhou et al., 2020, p. 582, italics added).

Zhou and colleagues (2020) examined seventy-one medication trials and these researchers also acknowledge that previous meta-analyses have found that antidepressants, except for fluoxetine, have not demonstrated any benefit for children and adolescents with depressive conditions. Further, earlier studies only demonstrate a "Hedges g" of 0.21 (the Hedges g is a statistical measurement for effectiveness and 0.20 is a low effect. As noted above, results of 0.80 and above are large effects). Having a low effect size provides little confidence that the gains achieved are of any clinical significance or benefit for clients.

Zhou and colleagues' meta-analysis of antidepressants was referenced within the AACAP Guidelines and concluded that among antidepressants, fluoxetine demonstrated a small benefit over placebo. But, as shown in Table 5.1, the specific details of those fluoxetine studies reviewed deserve additional discussion.

In the largest study above (Emslie, 2002), the primary depression outcome measure was collected using the Children's Depression Rating Scare-Revised (CDRS-R). The CDRS-R is a seventeen-item scale, with scores ranging from 1 to 5 and 1 to 7, with the highest number representing a more severe symptom presentation. The scoring range of the CDRS-R is 17 to 113. Obtaining a score greater than or equal to 40 indicates depression and a score of less than or equal to 28 indicates remission. Scores under 40 may suggest mild symptoms of depression, but not enough to meet the diagnostic criteria for the disorder. Youth entering the study averaged a CDRS-R score of 57.1 and

Table 5.1 Placebo-controlled Fluoxetine (Prozac) Studies in the Treatment of Major Depression in Youth

Source	Treatments	Number of Youth in the Study	Duration of Study	Overall effect
Almeida-Montes et al. (2005)	Fluoxetine vs. placebo	12 vs. 11	6 weeks	Unavailable
Eli Lilly et al. (1986)	Fluoxetine vs. placebo	21 vs. 19	6 weeks	Unpublished trial
Emslie et al. (1997)	Fluoxetine vs. placebo	48 vs. 48	8 weeks	A 10-point average advantage in the CDRS-R for fluoxetine
Emslie et al. (2002)	Fluoxetine vs. placebo	109 vs. 110	9 weeks	Effect size 0.51 (moderate)
Findling et al. (2009)	Fluoxetine vs. placebo	18 vs. 16	8 weeks	Placebo outperformed fluoxetine
	Total on Fluoxetine	208 youth on Fluoxetine	~8 weeks	

Adapted from the Zhou et al. (2020) meta-analysis.

55.1 (fluoxetine and placebo, respectively). At the study endpoint, the average CDRS-R scores were 35.1 and 40.2 (fluoxetine and placebo, respectively).

It is true that on average, fluoxetine outperformed placebo over nine weeks with an average reduction of the CDRS-R score by 22 points. However, and importantly, the placebo achieved an average reduction of 14.9 points, bringing the youth in the placebo group to the threshold where a depression diagnosis may not be indicated. As the CDRS-R has seventeen items, differing by an average of 7 points may mean just a 1-point difference on less than half of the items. The difference may be statistically significant, but it does not appear to be a clinically significant difference (Emslie et al., 2002).

The Emslie et al. (1997) study included forty-eight youth in each treatment group. The CDRS-R was also used as a primary outcome measure. The authors noted that no statistically significant differences (between fluoxetine and placebo) occurred until week five. The average CDRS-R baseline scores were 58.5 and 57.6 (fluoxetine and placebo, respectively). The average scores at week eight were 38.4 and 47.1, representing a 20.1-point and 10.5-point decrease for fluoxetine and placebo. This was a small sample, so generalizing this to the larger population is difficult (Emslie et al., 1997).

Findling et al. (2009) explored the effectiveness of fluoxetine in depressed teens with alcohol and cannabis use disorders. These additional diagnoses would be considered comorbid conditions, further complicating the results of this study to be generalized to the adolescent population at large (although alcohol and cannabis use is not uncommon). Moreover, this was a small sample, only comparing eighteen teens on fluoxetine to sixteen receiving placebo. The CDRS-R was the primary outcome measure. Authors noted that "placebo-treated patients experienced a greater mean reduction in CDRS-R score than fluoxetine-treated patients at the end of study participation" (Findling et al., 2009, p. 7). In other words, placebo was *more effective* than fluoxetine.

To summarize the Zhou et al. (2020) meta-analysis of studies comparing fluoxetine to placebo, there were indications that fluoxetine did outperform placebo. Overall, these differences appear statistically significant but not clinically significant. Moreover, some results demonstrated that placebo outperformed fluoxetine. One small trial found no differences between fluoxetine versus placebo (Almeida-Montes & Friederichsen, 2005). The Eli Lilly trial was unpublished. As it is unpublished, one may wonder why. Having it would further support the use of their medication unless the results were not favorable. The total number of youth tried on fluoxetine in these trials was 208. Of these, 178 outperformed the placebo (it may be as low as 157 if the abovementioned unpublished Eli Lilly trial showed no differences). Keep these numbers in mind.

You may feel a bit surprised to realize that the data supporting the use of fluoxetine are simply based on just under two hundred teens. But I suspect that you may be even more stunned by the number of youth that have not benefited from fluoxetine when compared to placebo. Integrating these data into our perspective is important. And here's how we get it: When a new antidepressant is being proposed, the FDA expects it to perform as well—or outperform—the approved medication. So, when new antidepressants are trying to achieve FDA approval, they have to compare themselves to fluoxetine and placebo. As shown in Table 5.2, the Zhou et al. (2020) meta-analysis included these comparative trials between novel antidepressants versus fluoxetine versus placebo.

In the Emslie et al. (2014) study, the authors indicated that the trial was "inconclusive." However, what *was* concluded was that neither duloxetine nor fluoxetine was more effective than a placebo. All participants averaged the same level of improvement. The study used the CDRS-R as a primary outcome

Table 5.2 Antidepressant vs. Fluoxetine vs. Placebo Studies in the Treatment of Major Depression in Youth

Source	Treatments	Number of Youth in the Study	Duration of Study	Overall Effect
Emslie et al. (2014) Two doses of duloxetine were included in the trial	Duloxetine vs. Fluoxetine vs. placebo	108/116 vs. 117 vs. 122	10 weeks	Active medications *did not* outperform placebo
Atkinson et al. (2014)	Duloxetine vs. Fluoxetine vs. placebo	117 vs. 117 vs. 103	10 weeks	Active medications *did not* outperform placebo
Weihs, K. et al. (2018)	Desvenlafaxine vs. Fluoxetine vs. placebo	115 vs. 112 vs. 112	8 weeks	Active medications *did not* outperform placebo
	Total on Fluoxetine	*346 youth on Fluoxetine*	10 weeks	

Adapted from the Zhou et al. (2020) meta-analysis.

measure. Within the first two weeks, results indicated a statistically significant difference between active medications and placebo, but these differences disappeared in the subsequent weeks of the study (Emslie et al., 2014).

Atkinson et al. (2014) conducted a similar comparison between duloxetine, fluoxetine, and placebo. Using the CDRS-R for ten weeks, they too found no differences between duloxetine, fluoxetine, and placebo. This trial showed no significant differences between active medications and placebo throughout the duration of the study, while all groups averaged the same improvement (Atkinson et al., 2014).

A third, large study was conducted comparing desvenlafaxine, fluoxetine, and placebo. The CDRS-R was also used as the primary outcome measure and, yet again, the active medications did not significantly differ from placebo at the ten-week endpoint. Averages of CDRS-R across all treatment groups showed improvement at the conclusion of the trial (Weihs et al., 2018).

In these comparative studies, over 340 youth were tried on fluoxetine, none of whom outperformed placebo. Simply put, there is essentially twice as much data to indicate that fluoxetine is no better than a placebo compared to the available research to support its use. The irony is unavoidable. We are supposed to be using evidence to guide our practice.

A meta-analysis study in 2016 by Cipriani et al. offered additional analysis of some of the studies already mentioned here, specifically those related to fluoxetine. While this study was used in a review to support the use of fluoxetine, these authors were less than confident about its effectiveness. "The findings of this comprehensive network meta-analysis provide *some* evidence that fluoxetine *might* reduce depressive symptoms in children and adolescents with major depressive disorder and the extent to which this reduction is clinically meaningful is *still uncertain*" (Cipriani et al., 2016, p. 9, italics added).

The Cochrane Collaboration is well-respected and generates substantial research contributions to the field. In 2021, they conducted an extensive network meta-analysis review regarding antidepressant treatment for children and adolescents. Their findings, adding to Cipriani (2016) above, indicate:

> Overall, the results of our review are consistent with Cipriani 2016, the previous version of this review, and other reviews, in that it highlights the **lack of robust evidence** on which clinicians can base their treatment of young people with depressive disorders. We rated most comparisons of antidepressants to be of **very low-certainty evidence**. . . . There remain important questions about the clinical effectiveness of these treatments and, even though they may reduce depression symptoms in comparison to placebo, **the effects are small and unimportant**" (Hetrick et al., 2021, p. 68, italics added).

In summary of the review above, just 178 (possibly 157) youth on fluoxetine outperformed youth on placebo, but it is questionable whether this was a clinically significant difference. In contrast, there were almost 350 youth on fluoxetine and 456 on other antidepressants that *did not* outperform placebo in other studies. Despite the preponderance of evidence indicating little if any advantage for fluoxetine, it remains a frontline treatment for teens. In fact, a study guide that closely follows the American Board of Psychiatry and Neurology standards for recertification examination asks the question: "Which of the following antidepressants has the greatest body of evidence for efficacy in treating major depressive disorder in children and adolescents?" (Hales & Rapaport, 2014, p. 73). Of course, the answer is fluoxetine. This is factually correct because other antidepressants have consistently failed. But practice should be guided by the preponderance of the evidence. So, what *is* claimed to be the convincing evidence for fluoxetine?

The Treatment for Adolescents with Depression Study (TADS)

The TADS study is often cited as the foundation for evidence demonstrating that fluoxetine is an effective treatment for adolescent depression. One strength of this study was that it extended beyond the typical four- to eight-week trials most often used to test SSRI effectiveness, and they followed these youth for a long time. A noteworthy weakness was that while the TADS study included a combined therapy and medication component, it failed to include a combined therapy and placebo component for comparison.

In 2004, TADS researchers published their findings from a twelve-week study comparing fluoxetine alone, cognitive behavioral therapy (CBT), or combined treatment across a sample of 439 adolescents (TADS Team, 2004). Across treatment groups, 109 youth received fluoxetine alone, 111 received CBT alone, and 107 received combined treatment. In the first phase of the TADS study, there were also 112 youth assigned to placebo. The CDRS-R was used as a primary outcome measure.

Table 5.3 represents the observed, average CDRS-R outcomes across treatment groups at baseline, six weeks, and twelve weeks.

As shown, at six weeks and at twelve weeks, combined fluoxetine and CBT resulted in the most significant point reduction on the CDRS-R (27 total points). Most of that change was seen in the first six weeks of any treatment, representing approximately 84–85 percent of the total improvement. All treatment conditions (including placebo) resulted in symptom improvement that brought the CDRS-R scores very close to or below the threshold for

Table 5.3 CDRS-R Scores for TADS Treatment Groups at Baseline, 6 Weeks, 12 Weeks, and Study Endpoint

Treatment Condition	CDRS-R Baseline Average	CDRS-R at 6 Weeks Average	CDRS-R Average Score Difference at 6 Weeks	CDRS-R at 12 Weeks Average	Additional Average Benefit at Endpoint
Combined Treatment	60.79	38.10	-22.69 points	33.79	-4.31 points
Fluoxetine alone	58.94	39.80	-19.14 points	36.30	-3.5 points
CBT alone	59.64	44.63	-15 points	42.06	-2.57 points
Placebo	61.18	44.90	-16.28 points	41.77	-3.13 points

identifying depression (a CDRS-R score of 40) with combined treatment reaching 33.79. Additional benefit between six and twelve weeks is negligible, particularly on a measurement tool of seventeen categories. Authors note that while combined treatment was statistically superior to placebo, fluoxetine alone and CBT alone did not outperform placebo (TADS Team, 2004, p. 813). It is also interesting that scores on a self-report measure of depressive symptoms (Reynolds Adolescent Depression Scale) showed the most significant differences at the six-week point, followed by insignificant subsequent improvement at twelve weeks.

Regarding the CBT intervention: Within the first twelve weeks of the TADS study, those assigned to the CBT treatment received fifteen sessions focusing on cognitive restructuring, behavioral activation, and behavioral family therapy. "Partial responders were then given 6 additional weeks of weekly CBT; full responders were given biweekly CBT during the same interval. After week 18, CBT was provided every 6 weeks on a maintenance visit schedule" (TADS Team, 2007, p. 1133). This diminished provision of psychotherapy has implications as researchers continued to follow clients in subsequent months.

Providing CBT in this way underscores my point of how we are failing to meet the needs of troubled youth. These depressed youth received several months of cognitive behavioral therapy. Simply put, this approach is designed to reframe our maladaptive thoughts, look at how our thoughts and beliefs influence our choices and behaviors, and how those behaviors influence different events in our life. It is a structured therapy process, focused on reducing the intensity of symptoms and hoping to create more effective strategies in the future. Sounds great. But having provided therapy for decades, I appreciate the difficulty in changing long-standing behaviors, reframing entrenched thoughts, and committing to new behaviors. In my experience, several months of therapy is rarely sufficient for durable change.

The TADS Team continued to collect data on 327 participants who remained engaged in the protocol. At nine months, they collected data again. All treatment groups continued to improve and were nearing the CDRS-R score of remission (28). Average CDRS-R scores were 29.2 (combined), 30.4 (fluoxetine alone), and 32.0 (CBT alone). Subsequent follow-up at twelve months reveals that all treatment groups converge at essentially the same average CDRS-R score (26.6, 26.4, and 25.7 for combined, fluoxetine, and CBT, respectively), achieving remission in over two-thirds of participants across treatment arms (TADS Team, 2009). This means that all treatment groups ended up being equally effective.

Remarkably, while CBT was reduced to a session every six weeks for maintenance, this group achieved the lowest average CDRS-R score (25.7). As the CBT alone group averaged a 20-point reduction in CDRS-R score at the end of twelve weeks (weekly CBT sessions), they achieved an additional 15-point reduction in the subsequent months with maintenance sessions every six weeks (TADS Team, 2009). These results also highlight the diminished returns with long-term exposure to antidepressants. Small reductions in their outcome scores occurred, but as we'll see below, these medications come with concerning side effects. The TADS study is often used as proof of success for antidepressants. This more thorough review raises questions about the continued justifications to use these medications and demonstrates that CBT ends up being just as effective, with virtually no side effects.

After the TADS project was completed, a different team of researchers wanted to examine the combination of medications and psychotherapy. In this experiment, adolescents and young adults were assigned to a CBT and Prozac group or a CBT and placebo group (seventy-six and seventy-seven participants, respectively). The participants were between 15 and 25 years old. It was a twelve-week trial and a multisite study (Davey et al., 2019). This comparison would offer the opportunity to examine the "placebo effect," which was not offered within the TADS methodology. Using the Montgomery and Asberg Depression Rating Scale (MADRS), results revealed no significant difference between groups. Nor were there differences for self-reported depressive symptoms.

Additional Considerations

Escitalopram (Lexapro) is also an antidepressant with FDA approval for kids 12 and older. In order to obtain FDA approval, the medication outperformed placebo (using the CDRS-R) in two eight-week trials. However, the drug maker also reported two additional trials (one using Lexapro in 7- to 17-year-olds and one in adolescents) that did not outperform placebo (AbbVie, n.d.).

As many medications are approved for adults, and then prescribed for youth, there is an influential study that deserves consideration. In the mid-2000s, many articles were published touting the effectiveness of antidepressants in adults for depression. A large, expensive, naturalistic study was developed called the Sequenced Treatment Alternatives to Relieve Depression (STAR*D). It was funded by the National Institute of Mental Health and included over four thousand adults. The purported benefits of this trial indicate that "over the course of all four treatment levels, almost 70 percent of those who did not withdraw from the study became symptom-free" (NIMH, 2006). This robust outcome was questioned several years later (Insel & Wang, 2009), but a recent re-analysis of the data reveals that "conclusions" about antidepressant effectiveness, as reflected in the STAR*D, are dramatically overrated. Reviewers have concluded that original STAR*D researchers violated established protocols in their data analysis, resulting in inflated outcomes. A re-analysis, in compliance with evaluation protocol, determined a cumulative remission rate of just 35 percent (Pigott et al., 2023). In summary, initial reports from the multimillion-dollar STAR*D study indicated that over two-thirds of participants could achieve remission. In reality, it was about one-third, leaving two-thirds with inadequate symptom control.

Persistent Depressive Disorder

Persistent depressive disorder (formerly known as dysthymia) is considered a less severe but longer-lasting experience of depressive thoughts, feelings, and behaviors. For children and adolescents, the time requirement for symptoms is one year (and two years for adults). As such, a diagnosis of persistent depressive disorder requires a depressed mood for most of the day, for more days than not. In addition, two or more of the following must be present during periods of depression: increased or decreased appetite, too much or too little sleep, decreased energy, poor self-esteem, difficulty with concentration or decision-making, and/or feelings of hopelessness (APA, 2022). Of course, these symptoms can worsen, meeting the criteria for a major depressive disorder during this time period. In those cases, the youth would have the combined diagnosis. Generally, persistent depressive disorder is considered more chronic (but less severe) and less responsive to interventions. However, the popular intervention strategies are consistent with efforts to manage a major depressive disorder.

Given the longer-term nature of persistent depressive disorder, the clinical approach may be less aligned with specific evidence-based strategies. For example, in the TADS study discussed above, the cognitive behavioral strategy was used for twelve weeks, possibly extended six more weeks, but then only provided in maintenance sessions very six weeks thereafter. However, for a young person struggling with chronic, low-grade feelings of depression, it would be common for the psychotherapy experience to be prolonged. This would not be derived from a specific proven approach, but simply the effort to provide ongoing support, skill development, build coping strategies, and work to avoid potentially more severe symptoms. And let's not forget: chronic feelings of depression are not proven to emerge from a brain problem or chemical imbalance. The focus of psychotherapy must be directed at the unmet needs, fears, relationships, and distress in the young person's life.

Disruptive Mood Dysregulation Disorder (DMDD)

The DMDD diagnosis was created for the DSM-5, published in 2013. The DSM-5-TR notes that this diagnosis was added to the diagnostic manual due to concerns about over-diagnosing (and overmedicating) bipolar disorder in young people. Remarkably, with the availability of the DMDD diagnosis, the prevalence of pediatric bipolar disorder is vanishing (Mojtabai & Olfson, 2024). This is noteworthy as bipolar disorder is commonly considered to be driven by genetic predispositions resulting in neurological problems. Yet, simply with the introduction of a new diagnosis, its presence across pediatric populations is being reduced. The point here is that due to diagnostic inaccuracies, the American Psychiatric Association created a new diagnosis. The invention of this new DMDD diagnosis, already afflicting millions of young people, is not without controversy.

Before the publication of the DSM-5, the newly invented diagnosis of DMDD was called temper dysregulation disorder with dysphoria (TDD). In the development of criteria to identify this condition, prominent mental health professionals expressed concern in a summary released before the release of the DSM-5. Their article highlighted a variety of problems with the diagnosis, and they argued that the diagnosis should not be included in that soon-to-be-released update to the diagnostic manual (Axelson et al., 2011). These clinicians, researchers, educators, and authors—seen as leading experts in the field—summarized their concerns with the following:

- There is insufficient scientific support to include TDD as a unique diagnostic entity.
- Inclusion of the diagnosis in the DSM-5 will have a negative impact on:
  - patient care
  - research
  - public perception of child psychiatry
- Instead of reducing the use of antipsychotics in youth . . . it is quite possible that it will serve as a justification for expanding antipsychotic use to a much broader range of children.

These authors did not believe there was enough information to uniquely differentiate TDD (now DMDD) from other disorders. As a result, children and teens would receive interventions that did not effectively meet their needs. This lack of accuracy and effectiveness, in turn, would lead to a negative impression of psychiatry. Finally, DMDD was created in hopes of correcting the inappropriate diagnosing of bipolar disorder in youth which resulted in skyrocketing rates of antipsychotic prescriptions. Yet these authors feared the new diagnosis would only become another target for these powerful medications. While their concerns went unheeded, they have come to fruition.

In the DSM-5-TR, the criteria to establish the DMDD diagnosis are characterized by severe, disruptive verbal or behavioral outbursts. These outbursts are determined to be out of proportion to the triggering event, and developmentally inappropriate (recognizing that there are developmentally appropriate outbursts). Moreover, these outbursts must occur three or more times a week and must continue at this pace before a diagnosis can be established. The condition requires that an irritable or angry mood be present nearly every day between outbursts. Consistent with other diagnoses discussed here, the condition must create distress and/or impaired functioning and be observed in multiple settings—and occur for at least twelve months before the diagnosis is established and is not given before the age of 6 years (but given before the age of 10).

When field trials were conducted to measure the inter-rater reliability for disruptive mood dysregulation disorder, it achieved a kappa score of 0.25 (Freedman et al., 2013). A score of 0.25 can be interpreted as only "fair." Again, a kappa of 0.60 is the accepted threshold of reliability. A measure of 0.25 is quite low, in fact. As noted in the discussion of major depression, this score means that when trained clinicians were using the DMDD diagnostic criteria proposed for the DSM-5, there was low agreement in accurately identifying this condition. In other words, it is diagnostic confusion.

The lack of clarity in the DMDD diagnosis is well established. A 2019 review of the literature highlights that the most common comorbid disorders with DMDD (those conditions that also present during the diagnosis of DMDD) include oppositional defiant disorder (up to 96%), ADHD (81%), and conduct disorder (13%) (Bruno et al., 2019). And despite the dramatic overlap between DMDD and oppositional defiant disorder, "even for children in whom criteria for both disorders are met, only the diagnosis of disruptive mood dysregulation disorder should be made" (APA, 2022, p. 182).

While the American Psychiatric Association has determined that this is a "common" disorder, "prevalence estimates of the disorder in the community are unclear" (APA, 2022, p. 179). This apparent confusion over the diagnostic rates may also be complicated by the difficulty in differentiating this condition from others or separating from other diagnoses in complicated clinical presentations. These complications, however, speak to the poor specificity of the diagnosis. That is, if many symptoms of one diagnosis can be confused with another, or one condition can also include symptoms of DMDD making its clear identification challenging, our understanding of the condition itself is incomplete. To this point, the American Psychiatric Association admits that many of the youth with DMDD "have symptoms that also meet criteria for attention-deficit / hyperactivity disorder (ADHD) and for an anxiety disorder" (APA, 2022, p. 180). Further, the DSM-5-TR notes "rates of comorbidity in DMDD are extremely high. It is rare to find individuals whose symptoms meet criteria for DMDD alone" (APA, 2022, p. 182). Indeed, a study by Findling and colleagues in 2022 revealed a comorbidity rate of 97 percent (Findling et al., 2022).

This comorbidity creates a major problem in creating a treatment plan. If an angry youth is also presenting with poor concentration, impulsivity, and feelings of sadness and failure, it is not at all uncommon that a prescriber may use several medications to address these issues. An antipsychotic to manage anger and outbursts; a stimulant to suppress impulsivity; and an antidepressant to alleviate the sadness. In isolation, these efforts may follow their training. But in reality, this combination of medications creates many competing and overlapping "mechanisms of action." The ways these drugs work neurochemically begin to work against each other.

These problematic medication combinations are exactly what Findling and colleagues found. They confirm the earlier concerns about medicating DMDD: it would become an easy target for antipsychotic prescriptions (with 60% of the young people in the Findling et al. sample being prescribed an antipsychotic medication). Also concerning was that these young people were more likely to be prescribed multiple medications (polypharmacy) which included stimulants and antidepressants (Findling et al., 2022). As will be discussed throughout *No Method to the Madness*, medication combinations that include antipsychotics, stimulants, and antidepressants create unknown downstream effects in the developing central nervous system of youth, have unproven effectiveness, and significantly raise the likelihood of side effects.

Our understanding of DMDD is still quite limited despite its invention more than a decade ago. There are no biological markers that are considered diagnostic for the condition. Specifically, it is noted that physiological indications for the disorder are also observed in other diagnostic conditions, meaning they are not exclusive to DMDD (APA, 2022). Although the core feature of DMDD is irritability, some discussions of neurological underpinnings include neuroimaging studies focused on recognition of facial expressions, frustration tolerance, reward mechanisms, and amygdala activation. While interesting, these areas of exploration are not uncommon across psychiatric disorders and have not yet yielded any diagnostic specificity.

Aggressive medication strategies to manage DMDD were voiced as a concern before its introduction in the DSM-5. Now a reality, antipsychotic medications have become popular to manage the symptoms of DMDD. In the review from Bruno et al. (2019), they included a table of "published efficacy trials on pharmacological treatment of DMDD," a 2004 study utilizing the second-generation antipsychotic Risperdal, and a 2009 trial using the third-generation antipsychotic Abilify. The focus of these trials was to manage irritability in children.

The summary by Bruno and colleagues (2019) indicates that in seventy-nine children aged 5–12 years in the eight-week trial, there was a "greater decrease on the irritability compared with patients who were taking placebo" (p. 327). Unfortunately, a closer look at the study referenced indicates that only forty children were given Risperdal, and the children were diagnosed with *autism*. Moreover, 90 percent of the Risperdal group were receiving additional medications. While most of these were not psychotropic, there were some with side effects that could be considered sedating. This study was funded by the makers of Risperdal (Shea et al., 2004). The 2009 Abilify study was also eight weeks in duration, involving forty-seven children (aged 6–17) taking Abilify versus fifty-one on placebo. Again, these children were not diagnosed with DMDD; they were diagnosed with *autism* (Owen et al., 2009). Researchers in this study had numerous financial connections to pharmaceutical companies. The symptom targeted in these studies was irritability, although the phenomenology of irritability in autism must be carefully considered in order to simply generalize this symptom to DMDD, a depressive disorder, with markedly different manifestations compared to autism.

Persistent irritability, anger, and outbursts are characteristic of DMDD (and trauma exposure in young people). From a psychologist's point of view, the goal would be to understand what experiences (internal and external) in the youth's life are creating these feelings and behaviors. It's hard to imagine that feelings and behaviors of this intensity emerge without reason. Granted, children and teenagers see the world in very different ways than that of an adult, but it is quite likely that in the moment of an outburst, or feeling of anger, the child may describe their feeling or behavior just coming from nowhere. Even if an adult would not agree, the young person—from their vantage point—believe what they're doing makes sense. Another factor to consider in their experience is the lack of control or decision-making ability for these youth. Frustration, sadness, confusion, social exclusion, poor self-efficacy, academic challenges, etcetera can be significant triggers for outbursts. Over time, an angry reaction becomes more "efficient" in these children. Moreover, coping strategies for children are in their basic building blocks, and emotional regulation is one of the most complicated. So how can we intervene to help these youth and families to become more successful and happier?

DMDD is categorized within the depressive disorders in the DSM-5-TR. As noted, it was created to address the inaccuracies of a pediatric bipolar disorder, with irritability and outbursts as hallmark signs. As a depressive disorder, one may wonder about the use of antidepressants in this group of youth, as it is commonly occurring (Findling et al., 2022). But given its origins, we should tread carefully down this path. A study presented at the Fifth International Conference on Bipolar Disorder in 2003 highlights the risks of antidepressant use in youth diagnosed, at that time, with bipolar disorder. In this study, of a sample of 195 children and adolescents, 134 of them were administered an antidepressant.

> Within the first four months of antidepressant treatment, 75.4% experienced some adverse effects. Increased cycling starting within a day of initiation of antidepressants was experienced by 79%, 70.9% experienced increased aggression, and 23.1% experienced psychotic symptoms. . . . Increased aggressiveness, violence, and suicidal thoughts

and behaviors usually accompanied antidepressant exposure in this sample of bipolar juveniles.

(Vogin, 2003)

Providing effective care is the goal. One essential ingredient in this process is to understand the experience of the child and family from all perspectives. No one has a monopoly on the truth, and each family member has a valuable voice, even when it seems just one person in the family is struggling. The challenges may not just be within the home; they may exist at work, at school, among peers, be rooted in traumatic experiences, social media, and so on. Regardless of where it has emerged, there are many psychotherapy strategies that can help in addressing feelings of anger, and irritability, even when those feelings and behaviors are rooted in depression.

We must recognize that anger, disruptive behaviors, and outbursts, can be incredibly challenging for parents. Because of this, when parents bring their child to a clinician, efforts are made to quickly control these behaviors. Whether a therapist or psychiatrist, the goal is to help. But in crisis, people want to feel better quickly. And while the use of powerful antipsychotic medications can quickly suppress the behaviors that are associated with DMDD, they offer little in terms of cure. As experts accurately predicted early on, the use of antipsychotics has become quite popular. This is not because a scientific understanding of DMDD supports their use. Rather, while antipsychotics can be effective in sedating, or controlling, disruptive behaviors, containing a symptom is not treating the disorder.

Antidepressants and How They "Work"

Let's start by recognizing that there is no "location" of depression in the brain. To be explored here is that medications target chemicals in the brain called neurotransmitters and these chemicals have an expansive reach across different regions of the brain. In contrast to some precise, surgical-like targeting of a problem in the brain, these medications have wide-ranging effects. In the case of SSRI antidepressants, increasing the availability of serotonin has a cascade of effects across different chemicals and processes. These effects travel through different areas and networks of connectivity in the brain.

Without a depression target in the brain, how do pharmaceutical companies know what to pursue in their development of antidepressants? You'll be surprised to learn about the "forced swim test." As chemists and researchers are developing new medication products, one phase of that research is on lab rats. You've likely seen pictures of those little white rats in research stories. One challenge they give rats is called the forced swim test. Imagine having two groups of rats. One group will receive a placebo, an inactive substance. The other group will receive a new compound being developed by the researchers. The rats are then placed in clear plexiglass cylinders of water to watch their behavior and measure their persistence in swimming to stay afloat. If the rats on the new compound swim longer than those on the placebo, it may be concluded to have antidepressant potential.

Wait. Really? You probably think I'm making this up. The forced swim test is based on psychological concepts called "learned helplessness" or "behavioral despair." This idea suggests that if faced with challenging circumstances, some determine that despite their best efforts they cannot improve their situation, so they give up trying. They lose hope of escaping the situation. In the case of these unfortunate rats, if those on the experimental compound swim longer than those on the placebo, researchers believe it means that the compound reduces the likelihood of giving up, keeping them more motivated to continue swimming. The test typically lasts just six minutes (Can et al., 2012).

It is remarkable that the forced swim test is the initial benchmark to consider a compound an antidepressant. It is "one of the most commonly used assays for the study of depressive-like behavior in rodents. . . . Moreover, its sensitivity to a broad range of antidepressant drugs that make it a suitable screening test is one of the most important features leading to its high predictive validity" (Yankelevitch-Yahav et al., 2015, p. 1). Clearly, the behavioral despair experienced by rats during the experiment is vastly different from the factors that may precipitate the human experience of depression. Yet this first step in research has led to millions of youth and adults taking antidepressant medications.

The SSRIs

The most popular class of antidepressants are the selective serotonin reuptake inhibitors (SSRIs). This class of medications has a variety of FDA approvals, represented in Table 5.4.

As its name describes, this type of antidepressant works by inhibiting the reuptake of serotonin. Here is a simple example of this process: Imagine two neurons (brain cells) in the brain trying to communicate. The space in between them is called the synapse. The neuron sending the message is called the presynaptic neuron. It sends its message chemically, to the post-synaptic neuron. In this case, the chemical is serotonin, a neurotransmitter. To send the message, serotonin is released by the presynaptic neuron and received by the post-synaptic neuron. Any serotonin that is not initially used is typically

Table 5.4 FDA-Approved Indications for Antidepressant Medications in Youth

Generic Name	Brand Name	Class	Approvals
Fluoxetine	Prozac	SSRI	Approved for children and adolescents for depression (8–17 years old). Approved for OCD (7–17 years old).
Fluvoxamine	Luvox	SSRI	Approved for OCD (7+ years old).
Sertraline	Zoloft	SSRI	Approved for OCD (6+ years old).
Citalopram	Celexa	SSRI	*Not approved for children / adolescents*
Escitalopram	Lexapro	SSRI	Approved for children and adolescents (12–17 years old) for depression.
Paroxetine	Paxil	SSRI	*Not approved for children / adolescents*

returned to the presynaptic neuron to be used later. This process is called reuptake. SSRI antidepressants dramatically increase the availability of serotonin by inhibiting (or blocking) this reuptake process. So, after the initial message is sent, rather than serotonin being reabsorbed for later use, it remains in the synapse, being available for a sustained period.

As indicated in Table 5.5, SSRI antidepressants have a high potency related to inhibiting the reuptake of serotonin. The "+" signs indicate the strength of the receptor affinity. Those with more "+" signs represent higher potency, in that a much smaller dose can achieve 50 percent occupancy of the specific receptor (Simple and Practical Medical Education, 2022). Remarkably, 20 mg (the common starting dose) of fluoxetine achieves an 80 percent occupancy of serotonergic transporters (thereby blocking the vast majority of serotonin reuptake that would have been completed by those transporters) (Meyer et al., 2004). What is also revealed here is that antidepressants do more than inhibit the reuptake of serotonin. SSRIs also affect dopamine (often depending on the dose), norepinephrine, muscarinic acetylcholine, and histamine receptors. This matters because while they are purported to "work" by increasing the availability of serotonin, there are multiple impacts. Each one of these neurochemicals, of course, interacts with many other chemicals and functions throughout the body.

There are many side effects of SSRIs to be aware of, beyond what can be described here. Since the release of Prozac (fluoxetine) in 1987, SSRI

Table 5.5 Receptor Affinity for Popular Antidepressant Medications

	Fluoxetine Prozac	Citalopram Celexa	Escitalopram Lexapro	Sertraline Zoloft
Norepinephrine (NE) reuptake block	++	+	+	++
Serotonin (5-HT) reuptake block	++++	++++	++++	+++++
Dopamine (DA) reuptake block	+	-	-	+++
5-HT1a blockade	-	-	?	-
5HT2a blockade	++	+	?	+

Key: Ki (nM) > 10,000 = -; 1,000–10,000 = +; 100–1,000 = ++; 10–100 = +++; 1–10 = ++++; 0.1–1 = +++++ *Adapted from:* Elbe, D., Black, T., McGrane, I., and Choi, S. (Eds.). (2023). *Clinical Handbook of Psychotropic Drugs for Children and Adolescents.* Hogrefe Publishers.

antidepressants have become some of the most frequently prescribed medications in the United States. Not long after the FDA approval, antidepressant medications received a "Black Box" warning from the FDA indicating that they can increase suicidal ideations and behaviors in young people. Advocates argue that prescriptions should not be curtailed by this warning, as an overreaction to the Black Box warning may prevent those who "really need" antidepressants from receiving them. While occurring at a low frequency, there is little science to inform who will or will not have this response. As a result, whenever a young person is starting a prescription or changing the dose of their medication, they should be closely monitored by their prescriber and treatment team to monitor for this deterioration.

Other significant reactions can include increased agitation, restlessness (in as many as 32–46%), activation, hypomania (in over 10%), sleep disruptions, increased irritability, and social disinhibition (in up to 25%) (Elbe et al., 2019). Many different systems in the body can be impacted using SSRI antidepressants. The central nervous system (CNS) effects, cardiovascular system effects, hematologic (blood related) effects, endocrine effects, gastrointestinal effects, sexual side effects, and others. Clearly, close monitoring of a person's response is critical when starting, maintaining, or discontinuing a medication like this.

Little is understood about the impact of ongoing exposure to an SSRI in the developing central nervous system of a young person. But of concern, research has shown that these medications do, in fact, change neurochemistry, neurophysiology, and other systems in the body. The following passage provides an overview:

> For observable symptom improvement to arise, there must be a gradual shift in brain homeostasis and neurofunctioning over time, a shift away from a current depressive baseline, involving many different neuroanatomical areas and structures in the brain (e.g., receptors and enzymes). In this process, elevated serotonin may be, at first, biologically "interpreted" by neurons as locally toxic, causing certain cells to undergo stress-related changes in order to accommodate, or adapt to, higher than-baseline serotonin levels. Subsequently, the activity of certain neuronal enzymes (i.e., those involved in serotonin metabolism) will increase, while that of others will decrease; similarly, a subset of receptors will start to become desensitized or downregulated, while other receptors (i.e., those responsive to serotonin) will be more heavily synthesized and shuttled to the plasma membrane.
> (Santarsieri & Schwartz, 2015, p. 4)

Introducing medications into the central nervous system changes it physiologically and neurochemically. Let's be clear here. We currently have no clear understanding of the neurological and/or neurochemical foundations of depression. No abnormalities are reliable indicators of depression. A specific "depression target" does not exist to date. In considering a cost/benefit analysis of using antidepressants in youth, there is very little evidence to suggest they are helpful. Yet there is research that indicates that the use of these medications alters brain homeostasis and neurofunctioning (remember, we haven't identified any problems in these areas). The use of antidepressants then causes the brain to react to the increased serotonin as a toxin, causing stress on the neurons, and inducing changes in the otherwise normal sensitivity of the neurons. In the developing central nervous systems of young people, we have no idea whether these changes are permanent, return to normal, or something in between. Given the lack of evidence for antidepressant efficacy in adolescents, and the significant range of side effects that they can cause, how can we justify their use?

As noted here, the FDA approvals for SSRI antidepressants in young people are limited. However, you've probably seen children or teens prescribed those that are not approved. This is not uncommon. It is a practice called "off-label" prescribing. Once a medication receives approval for use, even if it's just for adults, physicians can prescribe it at their discretion. This flies in the face of "evidence-based practice," but it is rarely, if ever, challenged.

NDRIs

Another popular class of antidepressants is known as norepinephrine dopamine reuptake inhibitors. Using the same process of inhibiting/blocking reuptake described above, these medications focus on norepinephrine and dopamine. These neurotransmitters also affect wide-ranging areas and networks within the brain and have not been shown to be exclusively related to depression. Dopamine has been called a "pleasure chemical" and related to the "reward systems" in the brain but is involved in a multitude of our day-to-day activities and functions.

In this class, the most popular medication is bupropion (known as Wellbutrin). This class of antidepressants is not approved by the FDA for treatment in children or adolescents, but I have worked with many, many adolescents who have been prescribed this medication. Some thinking around this is that Wellbutrin, as it increases the availability of norepinephrine and dopamine, works in a similar fashion to stimulant medications like Ritalin or Adderall. As a result, some prescribers have justified this off-label use to treat depressive symptoms in children with a co-occurring ADHD diagnosis. However, this practice is occurring without the safety and effectiveness being sufficiently established for the pediatric population.

SNRIs

A newer class of antidepressants includes the Serotonin Norepinephrine Reuptake Inhibitors (SNRIs). They "work" through increasing the availability of serotonin and norepinephrine by blocking the reuptake process. This class includes medications like desvenlafaxine (Pristiq), duloxetine (Cymbalta), and venlafaxine (Effexor). None of these medications are approved by the FDA for children and adolescents. Moreover, as seen in the discussion above in their attempts for FDA approval (and being compared to fluoxetine in those trials), neither the SNRIs, nor fluoxetine, outperformed placebo.

The Chemical Imbalance—Serotonin?

Selective Serotonin Reuptake Inhibitor (SSRI) antidepressants have been exceptionally popular medications since their creation in the late 1980s, with the launch of Prozac. With billions of dollars in revenue and millions of people taking them, one could conclude they *must* be exceptionally effective.

Recognizing their success and knowing they "work" by dramatically increasing the availability of serotonin, is it accurate to conclude that serotonin deficiency is, indeed, the cause of depression?

We will examine that question from several angles. First, let us identify some basic challenges to that conclusion, and look more specifically at each one.

1. If increasing serotonin alleviates depression, then intentionally decreasing serotonin should induce depressive feelings.
2. If serotonin is the key to reducing depression, how would other antidepressants work when their primary target is not increasing the availability of serotonin?
3. Why are placebos so effective in treating depression when they do not affect serotonin?

Serotonin Depletion Studies

In 2007, researchers compiled and analyzed a collection of studies examining the effects of depleting serotonin (5-HT). There are specific chemicals that can be administered that deplete serotonin. Researchers can use these and then evaluate the results. Remarkably, there were forty-five such studies to examine the effects of serotonin depletion on symptoms of depression (Ruhé, Mason, & Schene, 2007). The results create a major problem when assuming SSRI antidepressants "work" because they correct serotonin deficiencies. In these forty-five studies, the results were as follows:

- 5-HT depletion did not lower mood in healthy individuals;
- 5-HT depletion in healthy individuals with a family history of Major Depressive Disorder experienced a "slightly lowered" mood;
- 5-HT depletion induced relapse in Major Depressive Disorder patients who used SSRI antidepressants.

Interestingly, those who had been taking SSRI antidepressants experienced the most problematic outcome of serotonin depletion. This likely reflects the compensatory neurological mechanisms resulting from SSRI exposure. The studies above were completed on adult subjects. The dynamic compensatory mechanisms that may occur in children and adolescents are not well understood but given the importance of a healthy neurodevelopmental trajectory to optimize healthy outcomes, these studies raise significant concerns about exposure to antidepressants in these formative years.

Other Antidepressants and Effectiveness

Even more than those noted above, there are a variety of antidepressants available, beyond the SSRIs. While limited research has been conducted on youth, many studies exist to demonstrate outcomes in adults of antidepressants across different classes. For example, Wellbutrin is a norepinephrine dopamine reuptake inhibitor (NDRI). As this medication increases the availability of norepinephrine and dopamine, a secondary effect of this dopamine elevation is a decrease of serotonin at certain receptor sites. As a result, it competes with the serotonin theory of depression. Another medication, mirtazapine (Remeron), focuses primarily on blocking serotonin and histamine. Again, *reducing* serotonin to achieve its effects.

As it turns out, in adult treatment, Remeron is one of the most commonly used antidepressants in Europe (Forns et al., 2019), while its use in the United States is far less common. This inconsistency in utilization may be an important indicator of marketing versus efficacy. If researchers and practitioners have access to the same data to drive their use of antidepressants, why is there such a discrepancy in use? You may assume that U.S. prescribers have simply realized that SSRI antidepressants like Prozac are simply more effective in head-to-head comparisons. However, this is not the case. Remeron has demonstrated equal (if not better, depending on the outcome measure) effectiveness in treating severe depression when compared to Prozac in a double-blind study of almost three hundred adults (Versiani et al., 2005) as just one example. Further, "mirtazapine has similar effect as fluoxetine in the treatment of adult depression, but works faster, with low incidence of adverse reactions. Thus, it is a safer and quicker antidepressant for clinical application" (Zhang, Long, & Xu, 2019, p. 135). Of course, the goal here is to point out that "evidence" may not be driving the choices that guide utilization of medication.

The Power of Placebos

There is a substantial body of literature highlighting the effectiveness of placebos in treating depression, even outperforming the active medications in certain trials with adults. Harvard Medical School research psychologist, Irving Kirsch, PhD, has published extensively on the powerful antidepressant effects of placebo. His early research revealed that 75 percent of the improvement achieved by antidepressants was also achieved by placebos (Kirsch, 2014). Dr. Kirsch soon after reviewed unpublished antidepressant trials, including data previously unavailable to the public. In this dataset, most of them failed to find a significant advantage of the medication over placebo (Kirsh, 2014). In fact, only 43 percent of the trials Dr. Kirsch and his colleagues reviewed showed an advantage of antidepressants over placebo. This revised review of the available research trials concluded that the placebos achieved 82 percent of that obtained by the active medication (Kirsch, 2014). And, as Dr. Kirsch and colleagues have concluded, and as noted above, published research often highlights a "statistically significant" difference between medication and placebo, although in the case of antidepressants, this is easier to achieve than "clinical significance." That is, achieving a meaningful difference in the life of the person taking it.

There are many resources that have demonstrated the strong placebo response in drug trials and antidepressants. What this suggests is that *our expectations* of improvement or achieving symptom remission can bring about effective results. And while this has been repeatedly demonstrated, understanding the full nature of "the placebo effect" remains elusive. Remarkably, this placebo effect extends beyond just antidepressant studies to include other classes of psychiatric medications.

A Definitive Conclusion on Serotonin—2022

In 2022, a "systematic umbrella review" was conducted to evaluate research studies that would reveal a connection between serotonin and depression. Dr. Joanna Moncrieff and her colleagues carefully examined studies that included *thousands* of participants, using various methods to identify and/or understand any interactions between serotonin and depressive conditions, including genetic–environment interaction studies. Through their exhaustive analysis of the data, these researchers concluded:

> Our comprehensive review of the major strands of research on serotonin shows there is no convincing evidence that depression is associated with, or cause by, lower serotonin concentrations or activity. Most studies found no evidence of reduced serotonin activity in people with depression compared to people without, and methods to reduce serotonin availability using tryptophan depletion do not consistently lower mood in volunteers. High quality, well-powered genetic studies effectively exclude an association between genotypes related to the serotonin system and depression, including a proposed interaction with stress.
>
> (Moncrieff et al., 2022, p. 11)

Remarkably, after decades of mental health professionals promoting an idea of "chemical imbalance," serotonin deficiencies, and offering antidepressants as a panacea to correct these neurochemical challenges, no evidence of neurochemical abnormality is identified in the latest edition (2022) of the *Diagnostic and Statistical Manual*. To underscore this point, a most recent examination of the available data shows no connection exists between serotonin and depression. These issues are troubling and should temper our expectations of antidepressant treatment.

Walk Away Message

For Clinicians

Diagnostic Dilemma: Rule out Trauma first, and then do your diagnosing. This will clarify what needs to be of focus in treatment. Depression, hopelessness, and loneliness are affecting children and adolescents at higher levels than ever before. These high rates of despair and suicide for adolescents have persisted throughout recent decades emphasizing the use of evidence-based conceptualizations and treatments. We know that there is "temporal instability" in the diagnoses in youth (meaning they change over time). This is particularly true for depressive conditions, as they can overlap with anxiety, anger, social withdrawal, etc. Clinicians should work with an awareness of this fact—and seek to collaborate with other providers to ensure clear diagnostic and treatment planning. Further, all of those involved in the care and support of a young person with depressive feelings should be mindful of the elevated risks of suicide. Understand their experience. Be curious about their fears, hopes, dreams, failures, and how they see life being unfair.

Treatment Dilemma: While antidepressant medications are commonly used in children and adolescents, I believe there is insufficient evidence to support the claims of effectiveness. Even if symptom improvement is observed initially, this is demonstrably temporary and raises the risk of side effects and unpredictable outcomes. The most popular forms of these medications (the SSRIs) "work" by dramatically increasing the availability of serotonin. However, a recent comprehensive review of the available research indicates no connection between serotonin and depression. Further, numerous studies demonstrate that placebos can outperform antidepressants in the treatment of adolescents. Efforts must be redirected to discover more effective methods to intervene. If antidepressants are chosen, discussions among collaborating providers should include the likelihood of diminished benefit and planning to prepare for that eventuality. If symptoms don't respond to treatment, it's not "treatment resistant." It's the treatment that failed. But we must renew our exploration of what needs are going unmet. Needs such as Belonging, Mastery, Independence, and Generosity (Brendtro, Brokenleg, & Van Bockern, 2019).

For Parents

As stated throughout *No Method to the Madness*, do not make any changes to your child's medication (change in dose, timing, starting/stopping) without the guidance of your prescriber. If your child is experiencing depression, it is essential that you seek out support for them. Being open and honest with the clinician and encouraging your child to actively participate in their treatment will yield the best results. In discussing the diagnosis and treatment plan with the clinician, ask questions. Ask about their impression of what has caused the depressive feelings, what is maintaining them, and what can be done to alleviate them.

If the decision is made to use medications, your child may initially experience a boost in mood or energy. Whether placebo effect or drug effect, I have seen this occur. But be cautious in assuming this will be a sustained benefit. It is a relief to see the distress in your child lessen, and we want to believe that they've finally found a "cure." But when your teen begins to express a loss of that benefit, don't conclude that their depression is "treatment resistant." Their symptoms are just following the trajectory that has occurred over and over in research.

When talking about treatment options with your provider(s), ask specifically: What symptom is expected to improve with the use of the medication? For example, "improving your child's depression" is a very vague answer. Will anger decrease? Will feelings of sadness disappear? Will periods of tearfulness diminish? Will they become increasingly social? Depression symptoms are wide-ranging and there are many ways to see progress. Moreover, how long is the benefit expected to last? What is the plan if those goals are not achieved? Open discussions with your treatment providers will further enhance your overall outcomes.

References

AbbVie, Inc. (n.d.). Lexapro package insert. https://www.accessdata.fda.gov/drugsatfda_docs/label/2017/021323s047lbl.pdf

Almeida-Montes, L., & Friederichsen, A. (2005). Treatment of major depressive disorder with fluoxetine in children and adolescents: A double-blind, placebo-controlled study. *Psiquiatria Biologica*, *12*(5): 198–205.

American Journal of Psychiatry. (2013). Editorial. The initial field trials of DSM-5: New blooms and old thorns. *American Journal of Psychiatry*, *170*(1).

American Psychiatric Association. (1994). *Diagnostic and statistical manual of mental disorders* (4th ed.).

American Psychiatric Association. (2000). *Diagnostic and statistical manual of mental disorders* (4th ed., text rev.).

American Psychiatric Association. (2022). *Diagnostic and statistical manual of mental disorders* (5th ed., text rev.).

American Psychological Association Guideline Development Panel for the Treatment of Depressive Disorders. (2019). APA clinical practice guideline for the treatment of depression across three age cohorts. https://www.apa.org/depression-guideline/guideline.pdf

Amill-Rosario, A., Lee, H., Zhang, C., & dosReis, S. (2022). Psychotropic prescriptions during the COVID-19 pandemic among U.S. children and adolescents receiving mental health services. *Journal of Child and Adolescent Psychopharmacology*, *32*(7). https://doi.org/10.1089/cap.2022.0037

Atkinson, S. et al. (2014). A double-blind efficacy and safety study of duloxetine flexible dosing in children and adolescents with major depressive disorder. *Journal of Child and Adolescent Psychopharmacology*, *24*(4): 180–189.

Axelson, D., Birmaher, B., Findling, R., Fristad, M., Kowatch, R. Youngstrom, E., . . . Diler, R. (2011). Concerns regarding the inclusion of temper dysregulation disorder with dysphoria in the *Diagnostic and statistical manual of mental disorders* (5th ed.). *Journal of Clinical Psychiatry*, *72*(9): 1257–1262.

Brendtro, L., Brokenleg, M., & Van Bockern, S. (2019). *Reclaiming youth at risk: Futures of promise* (3rd ed.). Solution Tree Press.

Brewer, A., Doss, W., Sheehan, K., Davis, M., & Feinglass, J. (2022). Trends in suicidal ideation-related emergency department visits for youth in Illinois: 2016–2021. *Pediatrics*, *150*(6).

Bruno, A. et al. (2019). Focus on disruptive mood dysregulation disorder: A review of the literature. *Psychiatry Research*, *279*: 323–330.

Can, A., Dao, D., Arad, M., Terrillion, C., Piantadosi, S., & Gould, T. (2012). The Mouse Forced Swim Test. *Journal of Visualized Experiments*, *59*. https://doi.org/10.3791/3638

Cipriani, A. et al. (2016). Comparative efficacy and tolerability of antidepressants for major depressive disorder in children and adolescents: A network meta-analysis. *The Lancet*. https://pubmed.ncbi.nlm.nih.gov/27289172/

Committee on Energy and Commerce, Subcommittee on Oversight and Investigations, United States House of Representatives. (2004). Publication and disclosure issues in antidepressant pediatric clinical trials.

Curtin, S. (2020). State suicide rates among adolescents and young adults aged 10–24: United States, 2000–2018. *Natl Vital Stat Rep., 69*(11).

Curtin, S., Garnett, M., & Ahmad, F. (2023). *Provisional estimates of suicide by demographic characteristics: United States, 2022*. Centers for Disease Control, Report No. 34, November. https://www.cdc.gov/nchs/data/vsrr/vsrr034.pdf

Davey, C. et al. (2019). The addition of fluoxetine to cognitive behavioural therapy for youth depression (YoDA-C): A randomized, double-blind, placebo-controlled, multicentre clinical trial. *The Lancet Psychiatry* (July). https://doi.org/10.1016/S2215-0366(19)30215-9

Davies, J. et al. (2023). Politicians, experts, and patient representatives call for the UK government to reverse the rate of antidepressant prescribing. *British Medical Journal, 383*. https://doi.org/10.1136/bmj.p2730

Elbe, D., Black, T., McGrane, I., & Choi, S. (Eds.). (2023). *Clinical handbook of psychotropic drugs for children and adolescents*. Hogrefe Publishers.

Elbe, D., Black, T., McGrane, I., & Procyshyn, R. (2019). *Clinical handbook of psychotropic drugs for children and adolescents*. Hogrefe Publishers.

Emslie, G. et al. (1997). A double-blind, randomized, placebo-controlled trial of fluoxetine in children and adolescents with depression. *Archives of General Psychiatry, 54*: 1031–1037.

Emslie, G. et al. (2002). Fluoxetine for acute treatment of depression in children and adolescents: A placebo-controlled, randomized clinical trial. *Journal of the American Academy of Child and Adolescent Psychiatry, 41*(10): 1205–1215.

Emslie, G. et al. (2014). A double-blind efficacy and safety study of duloxetine fixed doses in children and adolescents with major depressive disorder. *Journal of Child and Adolescent Psychopharmacology, 24*(4).

Findling, R. et al. (2009). The short-term safety and efficacy of fluoxetine in depressed adolescents with alcohol and cannabis use disorders: A pilot randomized placebo-controlled trial. *Child and Adolescent Psychiatry and Mental Health, 3*(11).

Findling, R., Zhou, X., George, P., & Chappell, P. (2022). Diagnostic trends and prescription patterns in disruptive mood dysregulation disorder and bipolar disorder. *Journal of the American Academy of Child and Adolescent Psychiatry, 63*(3): 434–445.

Forkey, H. et al. (2021). Trauma-informed care. *Pediatrics, 148*(2). https://doi.org/10.1542.peds.2021-052580

Forns, J., Pottegard, A., Reinders, T., et al. (2019). Antidepressant use in Denmark, Germany, Spain, and Sweden between 2009 and 2014: Incidence and comorbidities of antidepressant indicators. *Journal of Affective Disorders, 15*(249). https://doi.org/10.1016/j.jad.2019.02.010

Freedman, R., Lewis, D. A., Michels, R., Pine, D. S., Schultz, S. K., Tamminga, C. A., . . . Yager, J. (2013). The initial field trials of DSM-5: New blooms and old thorns. *American Journal of Psychiatry, 170*(1): 1–5. doi:10.1176/appi.ajp.2012.12091189

Hales, D., & Rapaport, M. (Eds.). (2014). *Psychiatric review, volume 2, DSM-5 edition*. American Psychiatric Association.

Heron, M. (2023). *Deaths: Leading causes for 2021: National vital statistics reports*. National Center for Health Statistics.

Hetrick, S. et al. (2021). New generation antidepressants for depression in children and adolescents: A network meta-analysis (Review). *Cochrane Database of Systematic Reviews*, Issue 5. Art. No.: CD013674

Insel, T. (2022). *Healing: Our path from mental illness to mental health.* Penguin Press.

Insel, T., & Wang, S. (2009). The STAR*D trial: Revealing the need for better treatments. *Psychiatric Services*, *60*(11). https://doi.org/10.1176/ps.2009.60.11.1466

Kirsch, I. (2014). Antidepressants and the placebo effect. *Z Psychol.*, *222*(3): 128–134.

Langley, C. et al. (2023). Chronic escitalopram in healthy volunteers has specific effects on reinforcement sensitivity: A double-blind, placebo controlled semi-randomized study. *Neuropsychopharmacology*, *48*: 664–670.

McHugh, M. (2012). Interrater reliability: The kappa statistic. *Biochemical Medicine*, *22*(3): 276–282.

Meyer, J., Wilson, A., Sagrati, S., Hussey, D., Carella, A., Potter, W., . . . Houle, S. (2004). Serotonin transporter occupancy of five selective serotonin reuptake inhibitors at different doses: An (11C) DASB position emission tomography study. *American Journal of Psychiatry*, *161*(5): 826–835.

Moncrieff, J., Cooper, R., Stockmann, T., Amendola, S., Hengartner, M., & Horowitz, M. (2022). The serotonin theory of depression: A systematic umbrella review of the evidence. *Molecular Psychiatry*. https://doi.org/10.1038/s41380-022-01661-0

Mojtabai, R., & Olfson, M. (2024). Trends in mental disorders in children and adolescents receiving treatment in the state mental health system. *Journal of the American Academy of Child and Adolescent Psychiatry*, August. https://doi.org/10.1016/j.jaac.2024.08.008

National Institute of Mental Health. (2006). Questions and answers about NIMH sequenced treatment alternatives to relieve depression (STAR*D) study—All medication levels. https://www.nimh.nih.gov/funding/clinical-research/practical/stard/allmedicationlevels

Owen, R. et al. (2009). Aripiprazole in the treatment of irritability in children and adolescents with autistic disorder. *Pediatrics*, *124*(6). https://doi.org/10.1542/peds.2008-3782

Perry, B., & Szalavitz, M. (2017). *The boy who was raised as a dog.* Basic Books.

Pfizer original Zoloft commercial. https://www.youtube.com/watch?v=twhvtzd6gXA

Pigott, H., Kim, T., Xu, C., Kirsch, I., & Amsterdam, J. (2023). What are the treatment remission, response, and extend of improvement rates after up to four trials of antidepressant therapies in real-world depressed patients? A reanalysis of the STAR*D study's patient-level data with fidelity to the original research protocol. *BMJ Open*, *13*:e063095. https://doi.org/10.1136/bmjopen-2022-063095

Ruhé, H., Mason, N., & Schene, A. (2007). Mood is indirectly related to serotonin, norepinephrine, and dopamine levels in humans: A meta-analysis of monoamine depletion studies. *Molecular Psychiatry*, *12*(4): 331–359. https://doi.org/10.1039/sj.mp.4001949

Santarsieri, D., & Schwartz, T. (2015). Antidepressant efficacy and side-effect burden: A quick guide for clinicians. *Drugs in Context*, *4*: 212290. https://doi.org/10.7573/dic.21229

Shea, S. et al. (2004). Risperidone in the treatment of disruptive behavioral symptoms in children with autistic and other pervasive developmental disorders. *Pediatrics*, *114*(5). https://doi.org/10.1542/peds.2003-0264-F

Simple and Practical Medical Education. (2022). What does the ki (inhibition constant) for a drug mean? https://simpleandpractical.com/ki-inhibition-constant-receptor-binding-affinity

Son, S., & Kirchner, J. (2000). Depression in children and adolescents. *American Family Physician, 62*(10).

Shorey, S., Ng, E., & Wong, C. (2021). Global prevalence of depression and elevated depressive symptoms among adolescents: A systematic review and meta-analysis. *British Journal of Clinical Psychology, 61*(2).

TADS Team. (2004). Fluoxetine, cognitive-behavioral therapy, and their combination for adolescents with depression. Treatment for adolescents with depression study (TADS) randomized controlled trial. *Journal of the American Medical Association (JAMA), 292*(7).

TADS Team. (2007). The treatment for adolescents with depression study (TADS): Long-term effectiveness and safety outcomes. *Archives of General Psychiatry, 64*(10): 1132–1144.

TADS Team (2009). The treatment for adolescents with depression study (TADS): Outcomes over 1 year of naturalistic follow-up. *American Journal of Psychiatry, 166*: 1141–1149.

U.S. Centers for Disease Control. (2024). Data and statistics on children's mental health. https://www.cdc.gov/children-mental-health/data-research/?CDC_AAref_Val=https://www.cdc.gov/childrensmentalhealth/data.html

U.S. Centers for Disease Control and Prevention. (2023). *Youth risk behavior survey: Data summary & trends report, 2011–2021.* https://www.cdc.gov/healthyyouth/data/yrbs/pdf/YRBS_Data-Summary-Trends_Report2023_508.pdf

Versiani, M., Moreno, R., Ramakers-van Moorsel, C., et al. (2005). Comparison of the effects of mirtazapine and fluoxetine in severely depressed patients. *CNS Drugs, 19*(2): 137–146. https://doi.org/10.2165/00023210-200519020-0004

Vogin, G. (2003). Adverse effects from antidepressants for bipolar treatment are common in children. *Medscape,* June 16. https://www.medscape.com/viewarticle/457339

Walter, H., et al. (2022). Clinical practice guidelines for the assessment and treatment of children and adolescents with major and persistent depressive disorders. *Journal of the American Academy of Child and Adolescent Psychiatry, 62*(5): 479–502.

Weihs, K. et al. (2018). Desvenlafaxine versus placebo in a fluoxetine-referenced study of children and adolescents with major depressive disorder. *Journal of Child and Adolescent Psychopharmacology, 28*(1).

Winfrey, O., & Perry, B. (2021). *What happened to you?* Flatiron Books.

Yankelevitch-Yahav, R., Franko, M., Huly, A., & Doron, R. (2015). The forced swim test as a model of depressive-like behavior. *Journal of Visualized Experiments, 97.*

Zhang, L., Long, M., & Xu, L. (2019). Comparative studies on the therapeutic and adverse effects of mirtazapine and fluoxetine in the treatment of adult depression. *Tropical Journal of Pharmaceutical Research, 18*(1): 135–139.

Zhou, X. et al. (2020). Comparative efficacy and acceptability of antidepressants, psychotherapies, and their combination for acute treatment of children and adolescents with depressive disorder: A systematic review and network meta-analysis. *The Lancet Psychiatry, 7*: 581–601.

6
Containment vs. Treatment: The Use of Antipsychotic Medications

Antipsychotic medications have been in use for decades. As they've evolved, so have the terms to describe them, such as major tranquilizers, neuroleptics, antipsychotics, and now mood stabilizers to augment antidepressant treatment. The goal of the discussion here is not to provide an exhaustive review of their use, but to raise questions that will help us temper our expectations of treatment outcomes. You may be surprised by some of the findings here, but I've tried to select studies or reviews that have larger sample sizes, include placebos, and have relevance to the use of these medications in young people.

The use of antipsychotic medications is complicated. Not only because antipsychotic medications influence many neurochemicals, but because they are used to manage so many different conditions. Even though they are designed and developed to "treat" symptoms of psychosis, they are used to control many other behaviors and emotions, often characterized as disruptive or dysregulated. In fact, to highlight the complexity of these medications, it's worth quoting a renowned expert in psychopharmacology:

> The atypical antipsychotics as a class have perhaps the most complicated pattern of binding to neurotransmitter receptors of any drug class in psychopharmacology and no two agents have an identical portfolio of these additional properties.
>
> (Stahl, 2013, p. 169)

Antipsychotic medications are used for many symptoms that can be found across a variety of diagnoses. Psychotic symptoms, unstable moods (e.g., bipolar diagnoses, DMDD), impulsivity, aggression, autistic conditions, anxiety, or as a supplement to ineffective antidepressant treatment to name just a few. The fact that they are used for such varying conditions speaks more to their suppressive effects than any targeted approach based on an understanding of neurochemical etiology.

I've been a professor of clinical psychology for many years, and with decades of experience across clinical settings. With that as a foundation for this review, I often emphasize to my students that they should focus on research from within the last five years, or so. I use that as a guidepost because ongoing research tends to add to our body of knowledge, without needing to "reinvent the wheel" with each step of scientific study. However, antipsychotic medications have been studied for decades. Some of what was realized many years ago has been abandoned or forgotten, not because it was incorrect, but because we are inundated with a flood of ongoing research. In this discussion, I am going to revisit some of that earlier research, as it created a foundation of understanding and significantly influenced my approach to working with those prescribed these medications.

The antipsychotic class of medications first emerged with the original release of Thorazine in the early 1950s. When Thorazine was released, it was seen as a bit of a miracle drug, recommended for conditions such as "mental anguish from cancer," emotionality in the "menopausal patient," and "control of nausea and vomiting in children" (Smith Kline & French Laboratories advertisements). In a similar fashion, in 1937, the *New York Times* reported that lobotomies could relieve tension, apprehension, anxiety, depression, insomnia, delusions, hallucinations, crying spells, panic, and nervous indigestion, among other conditions (Whitaker, 2019). Remarkable, indeed. But I digress.

With Thorazine's antagonism of dopamine, theoretical models of etiology emerged called the "dopamine hypothesis." In this formulation, it was hypothesized that schizophrenia and psychosis were caused by excessive dopamine. As Thorazine could be used to reduce its availability, it was considered an "antipsychotic" function. This was further supported by evidence that stimulant or amphetamine intoxication (dramatically increasing the availability of dopamine) could also mimic a psychotic condition. Subsequent research looked to confirm this dopamine dysregulation, with less-than-compelling results. At first, postmortem analysis (in small samples) seemed to suggest increased dopamine receptor density, but most of the subjects involved had received antipsychotic medication. Thus, this increased dopamine receptor density revealed the compensatory mechanism at work when patients received these potent medications. But in drug-naive patients, these differences were not reliably found across subjects. Ultimately, an international effort concluded that any differences in dopamine receptors were "entirely iatrogenic" (caused by the treatment) (Valenstein, 1998, p. 113). This reaction of the brain reflects the concept of "neuroplasticity," in that the brain changes with our experience. "When antipsychotic drugs such as Risperdal, Zyprexa, or Haldol reduce reactivity in the dopaminergic system, the brain compensates, producing hyperactivity in the same system by increasing the number and sensitivity of dopamine receptors" (Breggin, 2008, p. 9).

The use, and continued evolution, of the antipsychotic class of medications has been lauded as revolutionary, enabling patients to be released from institutions, enhancing their functioning and well-being, and leading to more productive lives. No doubt, this is true in some cases. But the increasing use of these medications has raised serious concerns across clinicians and policymakers. In addition, families have also expressed concern about using antipsychotic medications (SAMHSA, 2019). And with their use, there have indeed been setbacks, which we will discuss below.

The original class of antipsychotics are now classified as "first generation" (typical), the next phase called "second generation" (atypical), and the most recent, "third generation." Some examples are shown in Table 6.1.

Table 6.1 Popular Antipsychotic Medications

	Generic Name	Trade Name
First Generation	Haloperidol	Haldol
	Chlorpromazine	Thorazine
	Fluphenazine	Prolixin
Second Generation	Risperidone	Risperdal
	Paliperidone	Invega
	Lurasidone	Latuda
	Ziprasidone	Geodon
	Quetiapine	Seroquel
	Olanzapine	Zyprexa
Third Generation	Aripiprazole	Abilify
	Cariprazine	Vraylar
	Brexpiprazole	Rexulti
	Lumateperone	Caplyta

As we'll explore in this chapter, the "mechanism of action" across these medications varies. In the first generation, the therapeutic effects were presumed to be from the significant dopamine antagonism. These medications could potently reduce the availability and reception of dopamine. This was believed to be primarily at the dopamine type 2 receptors. The second generation emerged on the market and their action was blocking both dopamine and serotonin availability. The newest, third generation medications increase dopamine availability at certain sites while blocking it at others. They also influence serotonin differently.

First generation antipsychotics were believed to achieve their therapeutic effect when they could occupy at least 60 percent of the dopaminergic receptors. However, occupancy of 80 percent of the receptors could result in extrapyramidal side effects (Stahl, 2013), which are very problematic. Not only are they difficult to treat, but they may also evolve into permanent tardive dyskinesia, and lead to noncompliance.

The original formulations of antipsychotic effectiveness don't hold up well over time. If 60 percent dopamine receptor occupancy was required to achieve a therapeutic effect, newer antipsychotics aren't likely to achieve that level, at least across the dopaminergic system. This is in part due to the relationship between dopamine and serotonin. As atypical antipsychotics include reducing serotonin as part of their action, the secondary impact is raising dopamine levels in certain brain areas. Specifically, "serotonin 2A (5-HT$_{2A}$) antagonism hypothetically stimulates downstream dopamine release in the striatum" (Stahl, 2013, p. 143). In other words, even with dopamine antagonism, the reduction of serotonin availability can increase dopamine levels, thereby mitigating the net reduction of dopamine availability. And dopamine and serotonin are not the only neurotransmitter systems at play in the use of antipsychotics.

Despite the uncertainty about how they "work," and very limited information about their impact on the developing central nervous systems of young people, the use of antipsychotic medications in this group has grown considerably over the years. This highlights the practice of "off-label" prescribing, as once the medication is approved by the Food and Drug Administration, prescribers can use them as treatments beyond their established indications. In the case of antipsychotics, there are limited approvals for pediatric populations, but they are commonly prescribed to young people for behavioral control, for which there may be no evidence.

It is also worth noting that the American Academy of Pediatrics has established key cautions against the use of antipsychotics beyond their FDA indications. As many young people have been exposed to trauma, these experiences often result in dysregulated and disruptive behaviors. Indeed, these symptoms can be difficult to manage and commonly confused with other diagnoses. But in 2020, the AAP cited the use of antipsychotics as "treatment pitfalls to avoid" across those situations in which dysregulated behaviors may be the targeted symptoms (Keeshin et al., 2020, p. 8) such as in PTSD, depression, anxiety, and ADHD.

Psychosis

To start, let us define psychosis or psychotic conditions. The most common psychotic diagnosis is schizophrenia, but there are other disorders that can include psychotic symptoms. A schizophrenia diagnosis is rare in pre-adolescents, as the typical age of onset is late adolescence into young adulthood. Schizophrenia requires symptoms such as hallucinations and/or delusional beliefs but also requires a significant impact on one's functioning across domains such as educational, occupational, interpersonal, and self-care. It's worth noting that our accuracy in diagnosing schizophrenia has diminished over time. In the DSM-III era, inter-rater reliability for schizophrenia was 0.81. With the DSM-IV, it dropped to 0.76. The DSM-5 made significant changes to the diagnostic category, eliminating subtypes such as paranoid or disorganized. Inter-rater reliability for this version of the DSM plummeted to 0.46, well below the expected standard of 0.60 for acceptability (Frances, 2012).

"Psychosis" is a term to capture when a person is struggling, or currently unable, to accurately perceive and respond to the events and interactions around them. Their experiences seem to "break" from reality, as they may be hearing voices that others do not hear; believe they have special powers that they do not possess; behave erratically; or express emotions in an odd manner. The severity of these conditions can vary in significant ways, but as a society, we have many assumptions about psychosis that affect our expectations of what "effective treatment" should look like.

In my work as an administrator in a residential treatment center, I had a particular interest in the youth struggling with psychotic symptoms. Starting early in my career, my curiosity of psychotic symptoms fueled a compassion for those struggling, as well as an astonishment of the resiliency and persistence of these individuals to wake up each day and put one foot in front of the other despite these frightening experiences. There was no clearer example than seeing a teenage boy struggling to walk from his cottage to the cafeteria each day.

Every day, this young man would walk with his peers to the cafeteria, but in just a few steps, they would pass him, making their way to the meal. He walked slowly, with intention. Rocking back and forth before raising his rear foot to plant his next step. Watching his effort day after day from my office, I approached him as he made his way to dinner one evening. He made pleasant conversation as he took each arduous step.

In speaking with his therapist, I learned that he "didn't want to talk much in therapy." But he kept his appointments. He was compliant with his medications (and he was on several and had been on many before being placed in residential care). He had some friends, but many of his peers thought he was "weird" and with his slow, methodical walking, he was regularly left behind or left out of activities.

As I slowly walked with him, I simply described how I observed him to be walking. "You rock back and forth before you take each step." *(This simple reflection is something I learned from psychologist Dr. Garry Prouty, who created an approach called Pre-Therapy)*. He glanced up from watching his feet and made eye contact with me. "They won't let me go," he responded. He cautiously explained that spirits were holding him by his ankles and his rocking motions were to break free from their grasp. In trying to gather more details and acknowledging that I knew he wasn't talking a lot in therapy, he stoically said, "They won't let me tell you; they will kill me if I tell anyone." Believe it or not, this was not the first time that someone had described voices that make such serious threats, but the intensity feels very real to those experiencing them. Knowing I was reaching the threshold of what this young man was comfortable sharing, I said, "Well, the next time you talk to them, ask them if they'll kill me instead, and then you can just talk about that stuff with your therapist." I then changed the topic and continued to accompany him to the cafeteria.

A couple of days later, I was walking across campus and saw him slowly walking back to his cottage from the school at the end of the day. He spotted me and waved, so I approached him. Still taking his very planted steps, he smiled as I got closer and proclaimed, "They said they'd do it!" Not quickly recalling the details of our previous discussion, he said, "I talked to them. They said they'd kill you instead of me!" While hiding my internal burst of anxiety about the prospects of what he said, I encouraged him to make the most out of their agreement and to start sharing his thoughts and feelings in therapy. He had a long road ahead but was able to be discharged several months later to his home.

The experience of psychosis is horrible. Thoughts become confusing. Trusted relationships may feel threatening. Voices may fill one's mind with commands, criticisms, mumbling, or odd sounds. Reality may become distorted—or in direct contrast to the way others see it. One may feel as if everyone can read their thoughts. They may feel like the radio or television is giving them personal messages. One of my mentors considered schizophrenia to be a "chronic terror condition" (Karon and VandenBos, 1981).

I spent many years, early in my career, developing skills in the psychotherapy of schizophrenia. With my hours upon hours of conversations with adults and adolescents with these conditions, I was confident that these symptoms were more than just misfiring of neurons. There was significance in their perceptions and beliefs, and I learned that there were clinicians in the field that believed these symptoms could be unraveled, deciphered, and better understood to improve the quality of life for people struggling to manage this terror. In addition to being mentored by some of the experts of the psychotherapy of schizophrenia, I also became involved in organizations that included therapists, educators, and psychiatrists that shared a like-minded approach to understanding and treating schizophrenia. While not the mainstream in the fields of psychiatry and psychology, there are clinicians who can offer these skills and support to the client, their families, and the systems of care trying to assist them.

For family members, psychosis can be equally frightening. Psychotic symptoms may not abruptly take over a person's beliefs, perceptions, and emotions, but they usually begin to show up slowly. They may also become more pronounced, only to recede and be less disruptive. For parents struggling to help their child, fears of "losing their child" can be overwhelming.

The stigma of a psychotic diagnosis is also damaging. People with the diagnosis are often inaccurately characterized as being frightening or violent (even though they are more likely to be victims of violence). And knowing that effective treatments are elusive, the entire family can become consumed with trying to manage these difficult, unpredictable experiences.

In my role as a professor of clinical psychology, it is rare to hear anyone question the use of antipsychotic medications in the treatment of psychosis. Largely assumed to be a genetically based, neurological condition, students presume that the most effective strategy is indeed medication. Moreover, entertaining the idea of a placebo being effective in relieving symptoms of schizophrenia is laughable.

Predictability Decreases Anxiety

For someone that is experiencing psychotic symptoms, managing the anxiety and fear associated with these symptoms is critical. In all my years of working in hospitals, residential treatment centers, and my private practice, I've had the opportunity to work with many people experiencing psychotic symptoms.

I quickly learned that being overt or obvious in my behavior helped alleviate anxiety. For example, if a person was sitting at a table eating their meal, and I had to walk around them to retrieve something from across the room, I would describe my actions. "Hey Billy, I just need to step behind you. I am going to get the paper I left across the room." Even without an acknowledgment from Billy, it makes my actions predictable. As a result, my activity is one less thing they need to be anxious about. And when they see me retrieve the paper and sit back down, it is an incremental step to make me reliable and trustworthy.

Decreasing anxiety is but one aspect of calming the terror of psychotic symptoms. When the world feels threatening and understanding the motivations of others is confusing, creating an environment where the person feels safe is essential. It can be difficult, particularly when those around the person are not struggling to make sense of the world. From their view, the room may appear safe, certain noises may be meaningless, but that may not be how the person experiencing psychosis may perceive things.

Recognize them as the expert of their experience. If someone is struggling with psychotic symptoms, it is unlikely that you will have your own experiences to compare to what they describe. Approach what they say with a genuine curiosity and with an appreciation that what they are saying is true to them. Simply trying to correct them, or refute beliefs that appear to be delusional, will only create interpersonal distance, and may make them perceive you as someone that cannot be trusted. Conversely, if you approach those discussions with a genuine intention to understand their experiences, you are creating a safe environment to share their thoughts and feelings. And, when that safe space is established, you may be able to share, "I think there could be other ways to explain what you're experiencing, but we can discover that together." A statement like that is not passing judgment but planting the seed for more flexible discussions about their beliefs and perceptions in the future. It also confirms that you are willing to explore those options, and you are not claiming ownership of what is "true" but that it will be discovered in partnership with them.

Our understanding of psychosis is woefully incomplete. I have worked with some individuals that have reported that their medications have given them a tremendous advantage, making the world safer, their relationships more predictable, and overall improving their quality of life. I have also worked with those that have felt medication interfered with their path toward health. Both positions, and those in between, are valid and need to be valued. The experiences of our clients must inform our approach to treatment.

The Cause of Psychotic Disorders

Despite over one hundred years of studying psychotic experiences and schizophrenia, we don't know what causes this spectrum of disorders. That's a frustrating reality. Millions of dollars, countless researchers, scientists, clinicians, theorists, and families have struggled to decipher the mysteries of schizophrenia yet identifying a "cause" of psychosis or schizophrenia remains unknown. All manners of exploration have been employed to find the cause; neuroimaging, neurochemistry, genetics, biochemical measures, psychological and neuropsychological tests, etc., yet there are no clear indications of what may cause these conditions. In fact, the most recent *Diagnostic and Statistical Manual* (DSM) published in 2022 summarizes the latest updates of this science:

> There is a strong contribution for genetic factors in determining risk for schizophrenia, although *most individuals who have been diagnosed with schizophrenia have no family history of psychosis.* Liability is conferred by a spectrum of risk alleles, common and rare, with each allele contributing only a small fraction to the total population variance. The risk alleles identified to date *are also associated with other mental disorders*, including bipolar disorder, depression, and autism spectrum disorder.
>
> Pregnancy and birth complications with hypoxia and greater paternal age are associated with a higher risk of schizophrenia for the developing fetus. In addition, other prenatal and perinatal adversities, including stress, infection, malnutrition, maternal diabetes, and other medical conditions, have been linked with schizophrenia. However, the vast majority of offspring with these risk factors do not develop schizophrenia.
>
> (p. 118, italics added)

Given this lack of understanding, the field's emphasis on medications as the primary intervention strategy exemplifies the role of these medications to contain symptoms rather than treat the condition. Specific neurological and neurochemical features have not been determined to be pathognomonic for schizophrenia. Even when anomalies are identified, they are never across the entire sample of those with the diagnosis, nor have any of those abnormalities been identified as the cause or result of psychotic experiences. In other words, we know that challenges in living can alter brain structure and function (neuroplasticity), and no doubt living with psychotic symptoms creates a range of difficulties in social contacts, educational and occupational opportunities, and engagement in the world around you, which can alter brain physiology. To this point, evidence suggests that exposure to trauma can cause neurobiological changes and create inflammation and dysregulation from oxidative stress (Inyang et al., 2022).

With the concept of neuroplasticity, even though our understanding of this dynamic process is in its infancy, it is difficult to discern what the product—or the cause—of the condition of schizophrenia is, even when examining the brain with our most advanced neuroimaging. For example, when a person participates in a neuroimaging study, they must meet the "inclusion criteria." Those criteria establish who are appropriate candidates to participate in the research. Often, researchers will select a group of those with the diagnosis (e.g., schizophrenia) and a control group; those without a psychiatric diagnosis. After conducting the experiment, researchers then compare the results between groups. If a difference is found in those with the diagnosis, it is attributed to the disorder. Keep in mind, even some of those with the diagnosis may *not* show the difference, but the study may still make an argument to support the correlation as an indicator of the disorder.

This methodology makes sense, but it largely neglects the developmental process of someone *before* they have the diagnosis. Think of all the factors that influence our brain development: early attachment, exposure to trauma, friendships, educational opportunities, healthy diet, substance use, being in nature, community engagement, hobbies, artwork, music, and so on. When people are in distress, many of these areas of their life are affected or compromised. This could occur years before a diagnosis is given. Our available science does not provide a roadmap to understand how deteriorating functioning across these domains is represented in neuroimaging. I am a fan of the amazing science of neuroimaging, but from my vantage point, we should be extremely cautious about assumptions and conclusions we may commit to.

Schizophrenia is considered heterogeneous in presentation and etiology. In other words, the presentation of symptoms may vary across individuals and there are also wide-ranging factors that may contribute to the condition's cause and progression. For some, there may be a genetic foundation for the condition while for others, early experiences of adversity may set the course toward psychosis, yet some others claim happy, uneventful childhoods. No one knows. There are factors that correlate with the condition, such as poverty, abuse, living in an urban environment, or season of birth, but none of these factors creates a direct line to causation.

With our limited understanding of what may cause schizophrenia, we must be mindful not to accept a one-size-fits-all approach to treatment. Moreover, our intervention strategies should be in close collaboration with the client and their family. Many clients are "non-compliant" with treatment. In most cases, it's not that they don't want help, but they want something different from what is being offered. Additionally, many therapists are not well trained in providing psychotherapy to individuals struggling with psychosis. These factors lead to a complicated process in understanding and addressing the needs of some of our most vulnerable clients.

The Role of Trauma

With the lack of conclusive evidence for neurological or genetic foundations for schizophrenia, there is growing recognition that traumatic experiences can dramatically influence the emergence, severity, and ongoing course of schizophrenia. Approaching schizophrenia as a chronic terror condition becomes even more poignant from this vantage point. It further strengthens the value of psychotherapy as a meaningful intervention strategy, which has diminished in recent decades.

As discussed in the chapter on trauma, the research on Adverse Childhood Experiences has provided keen insights into our understanding of trauma's impact on schizophrenia. "The severity of positive and negative symptoms appears to be correlated with the severity of Adverse Childhood Experiences, such as trauma and neglect" (APA, 2022, p. 118). Additional research has revealed that exposure to multiple Adverse Childhood Experiences linearly increases the severity of positive symptoms (Baldini et al., 2023). In other words, the more experiences of trauma one endures, the worse their symptoms become.

Recent research also reveals that Adverse Childhood Experiences are correlated with fewer negative symptoms, but greater suicidality and auditory hallucinations that are even less responsive to medication treatment (Prokopez et al., 2020). Indeed, significant correlations have been identified between hallucinations and childhood sexual abuse and childhood physical abuse (Grindey & Bradshaw, 2022). In these circumstances, while medication may suppress the intensity of the symptom, it may also diminish an emotional response to them. When these symptoms emerge from traumatic experiences, access to the emotional dimensions is critically important. In other words, powerful antipsychotics may reduce acute distress though they may still interfere with a psychotherapy process of healing.

The severity of symptoms is not limited to just ACEs. "There is evidence that social deprivation, social adversity, and socioeconomic factors may be associated with increased rates of this disorder" (APA, 2022, p. 118). Poverty, insufficient access to health care, a lack of educational resources, and unsafe communities can all contribute to the emergence and severity of psychotic symptoms.

Knowing the systemic impact of adversity and social challenges, clinicians should conceptualize interventions for schizophrenia through a trauma-informed lens. This perspective would also facilitate modifications to our diagnostic constructs in that a psychotic symptom could be a specifier in posttraumatic stress disorder, rather than attributed to schizophrenia spectrum disorders. The traumagenic neurodevelopmental model for schizophrenia has been proposed to further support a trauma-informed approach to treatment (Read, Fosse, Moskowitz, & Perry, 2014). With recognition of the impact of trauma, neuroplasticity, and neurological implications, the traumagenic neurodevelopmental model transcends the overly simplistic medical model that prevails today.

In the fascinating book *Mad in America*, Robert Whitaker (2019) provides a detailed account of this evolution in our beliefs and treatments for schizophrenia. Early attempts to explain psychotic symptoms would be seen as unsophisticated, misguided, or even abusive by today's standards. However, those models for understanding the psychotic experience were developed by leading thinkers of the time. That is an important perspective to maintain across our ideas of mental health, mental illness, and our best strategies to intervene. We definitely know more than we did a few hundred years ago, but we don't know as much as we will in another hundred years (or even ten).

How Antipsychotic Medications "Work"

Billions of dollars are spent on antipsychotics each year, so they must work, right? But defining how they "work" quickly becomes complicated. The mechanism of action varies across antipsychotic categories (e.g., first generation, etc.) and across specific medications within those classes. As part of this discussion, we'll first look at how medications attach to different neurotransmitter sites. This "receptor affinity" will help compare and contrast the ways these medications "work," at least as they interact with brain chemicals. Some popular antipsychotics are described in Table 6.2

To revisit the complexity of what these details mean, the "+" signs indicate the strength of the receptor affinity. Those with more "+" signs represent higher potency, in that a much smaller dose can achieve 50 percent occupancy of the specific receptor. For partial agonists, / is used instead of + to denote relative binding values.

Table 6.2 Antipsychotic Receptor Site Affinity

	Risperdal	Seroquel	Zyprexa	Geodon	Abilify	Haldol
D1	+++	++	+++	+++	?	+++
D2	++++	++	+++	++++	/////	+++++
D3	+++	++	+++	++++	++++	++++
D4	++++	-	+++	+++	+++	+++
5-HT$_{1A}$	++	//	+	///	////	+
5-HT$_{2A}$	+++++	+++	++++	++++	++++	+++
5-HT$_{2C}$	+++	+	++++	+++	+++	+
5-HT$_7$	++++	++	++	++++	++++	++
H$_1$	+++	+++	++++	+++	+++	+

Key: Ki (nM) > 10,000 = -; 1,000–10,000 = +; 100–1,000 = ++; 10–100 = +++; 1–10 = ++++; 0.1–1 = +++++. Table is adapted from: Elbe, D., Black, T., McGrane, I., and Choi, S. (Eds.). (2023). *Clinical Handbook of Psychotropic Drugs for Children and Adolescents*. Hogrefe Publishers.

Antipsychotics also influence histamine, alpha-adrenergic and muscarinic sites (APA, 2021). However, the purported therapeutic effect of atypical antipsychotics is often described as: "the drug's therapeutic activity in schizophrenia could be mediated though a combination of dopamine Type 2 (D$_2$) and serotonin Type 2 (5-HT$_2$) receptor antagonism" (Janssen, n.d.). While third-generation antipsychotic (Abilify) explains that "the efficacy of aripiprazole could be mediated through a combination of partial agonist activity at D$_2$ and 5-HT$_{1A}$ receptors and antagonist activity at 5-HT$_{2A}$ receptors" (Otsuka Pharmaceutical, n.d.).

One quickly realizes that some antipsychotic medications block dopaminergic and serotonergic activity while others increase the availability of these neurotransmitters. Beyond highlighting the contradictory approach to managing the neurochemistry of psychosis, it raises additional questions about treatment goals and behavioral outcomes. Of course, attributing the effects of antipsychotics solely to the reported receptor affinities is overly simplistic. There are many downstream effects, some known and many unknown. But before we review the evidence of effectiveness, it's worth noting that antipsychotics have problematic side effects across many physiological systems in the body.

When you consider the use of antipsychotics, they are usually to control disruptive, frightening, psychotic, and dysregulated symptoms. But they come at a cost. Side effects impact many systems in the body including the central nervous system (CNS), cardiovascular, endocrine, gastrointestinal, among others. As a child's full-time job is being a student, we should appreciate these side effects not only in their impact on the developing physiology but also on their day-to-day demands of being someone's child, someone's friend, a student, etcetera. With this, let's look at just some CNS side effects that would directly affect these domains:

- Behavioral activation
- Agitation, irritability
- Anxiety, nervousness
- Disturbed sleep, insomnia, nightmares
- Sedation and fatigue
- Poor concentration, confusion, and disorientation
- Extrapyramidal side effects, which can include dystonia, akathisia, pseudoparkinsonism, tardive dyskinesia, and other movement disorders
- Headaches
- Paresthesias (e.g., burning sensations)
- Seizures (Elbe et al., 2023).

Finally, in 2013 Dr. Henry Nasrallah published an article, "Haldol Clearly Is Neurotoxic: Should It Be Banned?" In this work, he details over two dozen studies documenting that Haldol damages brain physiology and function. While there are differences between Haldol and newer antipsychotics, there are also similarities. In fact, medications like Risperdal and Zyprexa have demonstrated similar neurotoxic effects in animal studies.

Measuring Antipsychotic Effectiveness

Research examining the effectiveness of antipsychotics regularly uses a symptom measurement tool called the Positive and Negative Symptom Scale (PANSS). The PANSS has been used for many years and has been established as a reliable and valid tool, measuring symptoms across thirty categories, scoring the severity of symptoms on a 7-point scale (7 being the most severe). The total range is 30 to 210. It also includes subscales of positive and negative symptoms (having 7 items in the positive, 7 in the negative, and 16 in the general psychopathology subscales). Generally, a positive treatment response is considered to be a 20 percent reduction in score from baseline. However, connecting clinical presentation to a PANSS score raises additional questions. Let's explore this in more detail.

Even with the established reliability and validity of the PANSS, using it to understand clinical implications had long been a challenge. But in 2005, in an analysis of PANSS scores and the Clinical Global Impressions (CGI) measure, authors established the following basic parameters for symptom severity (Luecht et al., 2005):

Severity Level Total PANSS Score
Mildly Ill ~55 to ~74
Moderately Ill ~75 to ~94
Markedly Ill ~95 to ~114
Severely Ill ~115 to ~144
Extremely Ill ~145+

Figure 6.1 from Leucht and colleagues (2005, p. 234) visualizes this range. Brackets were added to illuminate the approximated point range of moderately ill to markedly ill when correlating the CGI and PANSS scores.

The following discussion is not intended to be an exhaustive review of antipsychotic research. Rather, the goal is to provide a snapshot, using large review studies, or those that may directly relate to their use in adolescents. While I have tried to examine those with larger samples, the hope is that these

Figure 6.1 From: Leucht, S., Kane, J., Kissling, W., Hamann, J, Etschel, E. and Engel, R. (2005). What does the PANSS mean? *Schizophrenia Research*, 79(2–3), 231–238.

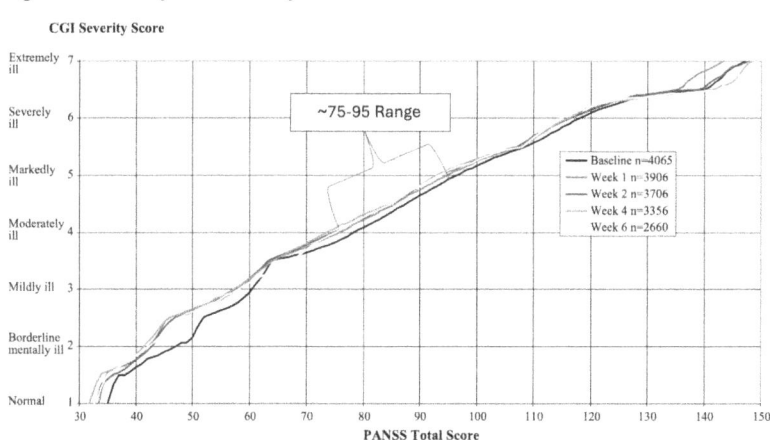

will provide a glimpse into their use and effectiveness as well as a foundation for critically thinking about how we're using them across the field.

As the field evolved from typical antipsychotics, researchers would often compare the newer drugs to the older ones. This research would hope to demonstrate that "newer is better" and lay a foundation for increased utilization of the newer medications. For example, an older comparative analysis between Risperdal and Haldol found Risperdal to be more effective. In this review of a dozen medication trials, Risperdal patients had an average baseline score of 94.7 and achieved a 20.9 (average) score reduction in the total PANSS score. In contrast, Haldol had an average baseline score of 92.2 and achieved a 14.3-point average reduction (Glick et al., 2001). Another way to summarize this information is that Risperdal achieved an average 22 percent reduction in PANSS total score (and averaged a 27 percent reduction in positive symptom score), while Haldol achieved an average 15.5 percent reduction in overall score (and averaged a 20 percent reduction in positive symptom score). With the assumption that a 20 percent reduction in PANSS score indicates effectiveness, both achieved that goal, with Risperdal outperforming Haldol.

However, even though this comparison argues for the increased effectiveness of Risperdal over Haldol, the clinical implications are less clear. In using the symptom severity parameters, positive responders essentially stayed within the range of "moderately ill," being at the upper end of that category at baseline, and at the lower threshold at endpoint. While there was clear improvement in numeric score, generating statistical significance, the clinical significance becomes another factor of analysis if the symptom severity is basically within the same category.

In 2008, a pooled analysis of adult studies of Abilify demonstrated similar efficacy. With an average total PANSS baseline of 93.8 (upper end of moderately ill), it achieved an average reduction of 14.4 points (15%) (still within the moderately ill range). But this analysis explored Abilify's performance against placebo, which generated some interesting details. Overall, authors concluded 37.4 percent of Abilify-treated patients achieved a response of greater than or equal to 30 percent improvement from baseline, while 21.4 percent of placebo-treated patients achieved that same level of response by week four of the study. No doubt, Abilify outperformed placebo, but one-fifth of patients on placebo achieved the threshold of response. Also of note, Abilify achieved a 1.0-point improvement on the scale for hallucinatory behavior, while placebo achieved a 0.7-point improvement (Kane et al., 2008).

Also in 2008, researchers completed a placebo-controlled study of Abilify in adolescents with schizophrenia. These authors concluded that two different doses (10 mg and 30 mg) of aripiprazole were superior to placebo (Findling et al., 2008). This study involved 302 patients (85% of them completed the six-week study). The average PANSS baseline across groups was 94.5 (recall that a PANSS score of 95 is the cutoff between moderately and markedly ill). A closer look at this study reveals that *all groups improved into the PANSS category of mildly ill*. Wait. Even the placebo group? Table 6.3 has a breakdown of the scores.

While all groups started at the PANSS threshold of being "markedly ill," all groups were in the category of "mildly ill" at study endpoint. Statistically significant differences were found numerically, but the clinically significant differences were less clear. Moreover, using the PANSS measure of thirty items, with 7-point scales, the differences between the placebo and 30 mg groups could simply represent just a one-point difference across seven of the thirty items. As authors note, "a statistically significant difference from placebo was observed in the 10-mg aripiprazole arm at study endpoint only. The 30-mg aripiprazole dose was superior to placebo at weeks 3 and 4 but not at endpoint (week 6 or last observation)" (Findling et al., 2008).

Geodon (ziprasidone) is an atypical antipsychotic medication. In 2013, researchers evaluated its efficacy in a placebo-controlled trial with 283 adolescents diagnosed with schizophrenia (193 received Geodon, 90 received placebo). This study included participants across different international regions (the United States, Europe, Asia, and Central/South America). In this six-week trial, Geodon *did not outperform placebo*. Participants in both groups achieved a PANSS total score improvement of just over 20 points (Findling et al., 2013).

One of the newest antipsychotic medications, Rexulti (brexpiprazole), published their outcome data for adults with schizophrenia online. Again, the medication demonstrated statistically significant differences over placebo. At two different doses, both 2 mg/day and 4 mg/day improved about 20 points on the PANSS. Placebo achieved an average of 13.3 points improvement. This online data also provided results from a long-term maintenance study. In this

Table 6.3 PANSS Scores at Baseline, Study Endpoint, and Average Improvement

	Placebo	Abilify 10mg	Abilify 30mg
PANSS Average Baseline	95	93.7	94.9
PANSS Average Endpoint	73.8	67	66.3
Average Point Improvement	-21.2	-26.7	-28.6

project, over two hundred participants had a baseline average PANSS score of approximately 82. After thirty-six weeks of medication, their average PANSS total score was approximately 57 (lower threshold of mildly ill). At this point, 105 patients were switched to placebo, while the others (97 patients) were maintained on Rexulti to be monitored for fifty-two weeks. While the Rexulti patients showed a slight, insignificant worsening of about 4 points, those patients who were switched to placebo only deteriorated approximately 10 points by the study endpoint. Importantly, the placebo patients remained in the "mildly ill" category throughout the remaining fifty-two weeks of the study (data available at https://rexultihcp.com/sz/efficacy).

The effect of placebos is fascinating, particularly in a condition like schizophrenia. While research regularly demonstrates statistically significant improvements in scores when comparing antipsychotic medications to placebo, careful examination of the severity rating should also inform our expectations in treatment response. As discussed, a 20 percent improvement in PANSS total score is considered to represent a positive response. Generally, this is a reduction of symptom severity from one category to the next. In no way does this represent an alleviation of the condition, but a reduction in severity. That, of course, is important, but may change one's thinking about the term "anti"-psychotic medication. Maybe "less-psychotic" would be more accurate.

In 2012, questions emerged about the effectiveness of placebos in clinical trials in schizophrenia. Authors observed that there were increasing trends of placebo effects in schizophrenia medication trials (Alphs et al., 2012). Remarkably, these authors detailed the progressive, increasing potency of placebos over time, noting that in 1993, a placebo may worsen total baseline PANSS score, but by 2007–2008, placebo was averaging a 16-point improvement. Meta-analytic review of the placebo response in schizophrenia has demonstrated 27 percent to 59 percent of patients diagnosed with schizophrenia achieved a 25 percent score reduction on the PANSS, also confirming that the placebo response has become more robust in recent decades (Hird et al., 2023). Incredible. A quarter to almost two-thirds of patients diagnosed with schizophrenia surpass the benchmark for a "positive response" when taking a placebo.

Methodologies in antipsychotic research are also worth considering. In many placebo-controlled trials, researchers use a "washout period" prior to randomly assigning participants to the medication or placebo groups. This is, basically, a process over several weeks in which people that were taking their medications have them abruptly discontinued. Rather than a gradual process, in just weeks participants are off their medications. Guess what happens. Rapidly discontinuing medications can lead to significant clinical deterioration. In some ways, this creates a potential for more severe symptom presentations, which raises additional questions about the relief observed by placebos.

The research on antipsychotic effectiveness needs to be integrated with a perspective offered by Drs. Harrow, Jobe, and Tong (2021). Looking at long-term outcomes in adults, they observe, "antipsychotic medications have proven relatively successful in randomized controlled trials up to a reach of 2 years in duration, but that success does not hold up beyond that time period as shown in a large series of prospective and retrospective naturalistic studies" (p. 1). These authors raise significant questions around the continuous use of antipsychotic medications, citing multiple studies demonstrating poorer outcomes for those maintained on medications. These findings directly conflict with standard practices. In fact, through all my years in the field, the goal of most psychological interventions for schizophrenia was to provide support and encourage compliance with their prescribed medication.

Antipsychotic Deactivation

Early in my career, I was exploring research related to the psychotherapy of schizophrenia. In all my clinical training opportunities in graduate school, I intentionally sought out opportunities to work with those diagnosed with schizophrenia and severe conditions. As a result, virtually all of those I worked with were medicated. This compelled me to understand the interaction of medications and the psychotherapy process, looking to determine the advantages and disadvantages with these combined interventions. Keep in mind, relatively few clinicians were trained in providing psychotherapy to clients struggling with psychotic conditions when I was in my graduate education, and even fewer have this training today.

In looking at the effects of antipsychotic medications, I found the concept of deactivation (Breggin, 2008). Deactivation is characterized as "a continuum of phenomena variously described as disinterest, indifference, diminished concern, blunting, lack of spontaneity, reduced emotional reactivity, reduced motivation or will, apathy, and, in the extreme, a rousable stupor" (p. 31). Breggin, a psychiatrist, provides extensive detail about the damaging neurological factors at the foundation of deactivation, and how it is created by antipsychotic medication. These are not therapeutic effects. Quite the opposite, as Breggin would consider them disabling.

The concept of deactivation should also be considered in the context of children and adolescents being exposed to these powerful medications. As noted above, there is little understanding of the long-term impact of antipsychotics on the developing nervous system of young people, although animal studies have demonstrated neurotoxic effects from medications like Haldol, Risperdal, Zyprexa, and others. Without a clear, demonstrable benefit for their use, mental health service providers, as well as policymakers, should closely monitor their utilization.

In conceptualizing psychosis as a "chronic terror condition," creating indifference and reduced emotional reactivity may have some advantages. Dulling the response to these symptoms may alleviate the intense distress they're feeling. However, if psychotherapy is going to be offered in their treatment, deactivation may be a challenging hurdle to overcome, thereby compromising the potential benefits of therapy.

The framework of deactivation informed my work when clients would want to come off their medications. Again, this work only happened with close collaboration from my clients' prescribers, but in my years of practice, I have been able to create a network of trusted clinicians in this challenging task. As this process began, effort was directed to educating the client and their family/support system about what to expect. As the medications have likely suppressed their emotional reactivity, behavioral spontaneity, etc., reducing medications may create resurgence of thoughts, feelings, and behaviors they may not have experienced for a long time. This discussion is explored in additional detail in Chapter 8 on deprescribing.

Antipsychotics in Other Conditions

As noted above, antipsychotic medications are used for many conditions. Aggression and irritability are common clinical targets. Indeed, "problems with aggressive behavior affect 10–25% of youth and constitute one of the most common causes for referral to a child and adolescent psychiatrist" (Gurnani et al., 2016, p. 65). Early reviews of antipsychotics for disruptive behavior disorders yielded weak evidence. In fact, a 1999 meta-analysis did not find evidence to support their use and later trials found that the drugs were not superior to placebo (Rajkumar, 2022). A Cochrane Database Review was completed in 2017. In reviewing ten studies, these authors found that risperidone (Risperdal) led to reduced aggression but cited low quality of evidence. They also noted this significant risk of serious side effects of this medication. Research to support the use of any other antipsychotics was lacking (Loy et al., 2017). Summarizing the available research, Rajkumar (2022) noted that off-label use of antipsychotics, besides Risperdal, is unsupported by the available evidence due to the lack of reliable safety and efficacy data. Rajkumar's comprehensive review concludes, "despite forty years of clinical trials in this area, there is, as of yet, no sufficient evidence to recommend the use of antipsychotics in DBDs (disruptive behavior disorders) in general" (p. 15).

There is a study that I regularly discuss with my students. It was published in the prestigious *Lancet* journal and compared Risperdal versus Haldol versus placebo in the management of aggressive behaviors in adults with intellectual disability (Tyrer et al., 2008). This is particularly interesting because, arguably, these clients may be less responsive to verbal de-escalation strategies and may be more susceptible to a placebo effect. The results are stunning. While a relatively small study, there were twenty-eight assigned to the Haldol group, twenty-nine to Risperdal, and twenty-nine to placebo. Researchers monitored aggressive behaviors but also considered factors like quality of life and impact on caregivers. Authors found, "although we noted a reduction in aggression with all treatments after four weeks, the greatest decrease was with placebo . . . no differences between groups in terms of aberrant behaviour, quality of life, general improvement, effect on carers, and adverse drug effects" (p. 61). They conclude, "antipsychotic drugs should no longer be regarded as an acceptable routine treatment for aggressive challenging behaviour in people with intellectual disability" (p. 57).

The Treatment of Early Age Mania (TEAM) Study

Pediatric bipolar disorder saw skyrocketing prevalence in the late 1990s– early 2000s. Angry, impulsive, moody youth were commonly diagnosed with bipolar disorder. During this time, a large study was conducted to compare lithium, Risperdal, and divalproex sodium (Depakote) to manage the symptoms of mania in 279 6- to 15-year-olds (Geller et al., 2012). This randomized trial lasted eight weeks and data were collected at multiple sites. At study endpoint, Risperdal was more effective than lithium and Depakote. A subsequent analysis of TEAM study outcomes raised questions about the reliability of the original findings.

Vitiello et al. (2012) noted that in this diagnostic group, roughly half of youth receiving antipsychotics have a clinically significant improvement, mood stabilizers (anticonvulsants) even less. These researchers found the response to Risperdal effectiveness was influenced by the site of the research and whether the patient had co-occurring ADHD. At certain sites, Risperdal was observed to have a larger effect size, making the response ratio much larger at some sites compared to others. The authors concluded that "these data suggest that factors other than specific treatment have a powerful influence on outcome" (Vitiello et al., 2012, p. 877).

It's worth remembering that disruptive mood dysregulation disorder is the condition that emerged out of the failure of pediatric bipolar disorder. Now, young people with DMDD are commonly prescribed antipsychotic medications to control disruptive, problematic behaviors characteristic of the disorder. But alternative strategies have been demonstrated.

As a clinician and administrator in residential treatment centers, I have found that if a youth ever had an incident of aggression, one of the first questions responding staff would ask is, "Did they take their medications this morning?" Of course, this question presumes that if someone is compliant with their medications, it will control aggression, maybe even anger. With respect, despite very sedating doses of medications, many youth feel passionate enough to make their way through the day able to express themselves. Again, if you critically examine "outcomes" for antipsychotic medications, "anti-anger" is not one of them. But for the painful lives lived by those placed in residential treatment, assuming that being compliant with medication can totally suppress those feelings is foolish.

Bellonci and colleagues (2013) conducted a study to reassess the psychotropic medication use in 531 youth, placed in residential treatment centers at two different locations. Of the participants, over half of them (292) had their medications decreased or discontinued. Youth in residential care are those with complicated and challenging symptom presentations, often have multiple psychiatric diagnoses, a history of failed treatments, and poor response to previous interventions. Decreasing or discontinuing medications would presumably risk considerable deterioration. But this isn't what researchers found. Instead, "youth in the medication reduction group experienced a significant 79% reduction in physical restraints and a corresponding 78% reduction in assaults" (Bellonci et al., 2013, p. 1777). While the classes of psychotropics were not reported, the use of antipsychotics is common in residential treatment settings.

In research I conducted about the Adolescent Subjective Experience of Treatment in residential care (the ASET study), eighty-four youth across seven different treatment centers were interviewed. Of them, 70 percent were on an antipsychotic, many on more than one. Some of the antipsychotic medications in my sample included Geodon, Abilify, Risperdal, and Zyprexa, as well as older typical antipsychotics such as Haldol, Trilafon, and Thorazine. Over 40 percent of youth in this study were on three or more psychotropic medications, a practice for which there is virtually no evidence for improvement.

We Need to Know More

Throughout this discussion, examples of large studies have been examined, many included funding from the pharmaceutical industry. But we're left with more questions than answers. Thinking about "effective treatment" with antipsychotics is altered when we realize that success is measured by an incremental decrease in symptom severity, nothing near a cure. But there is much more to understanding the spectrum of symptom presentations that represent schizophrenia.

- Why do some people benefit from antipsychotic medications? While some do not?
- Why do some people with a diagnosis of schizophrenia recover just using psychotherapy? Why do some not?
- How could dietary changes create relief or even remission in schizophrenia, while for others it's meaningless? (Sethi et al., 2024; Palmer, 2022).
- Why do some people with a diagnosis of schizophrenia have odd neurological findings, when most do not?
- Why does Avatar Therapy provide significant relief from auditory hallucinations? (Garety et al., 2024).
- What is the role of inflammation in psychosis?

I have worked with many clients, across the lifespan, diagnosed with schizophrenia or a psychotic disorder. Assuming that a one-size-fits-all approach will work fails to understand the vast spectrum of people struggling with these challenges. In my decades of experience in the field, I've realized we know so very little about schizophrenia. This is in no way to dismiss the decades of research, tireless hours, intense commitment and compassion, and dedication of those in the field that have researched and provided care to people with schizophrenia. But we are a long way from the outcomes we desire, or that these people deserve.

- I worked with an adolescent boy, diagnosed with schizoaffective disorder from a prestigious medical center in Chicago, prescribed Clozaril, Risperdal, and Clonidine. After many months of difficult, collaborative work, he was able to be taken off his medication. He had a sharp sense of humor and was a bit awkward interpersonally but continued to do well.
- I worked with a woman who was diagnosed with schizophrenia, unable to work, living at home with her husband. After months of

psychotherapy, she came into a session saying she was feeling so much better, she took a part-time job. She continued to make gains and was ultimately able to discontinue her medication.

- I worked with a young man, diagnosed with schizophrenia. Intelligent, personable, great sense of humor, and close connections to his family. He experienced hallucinations so intense they would wake him up at night. He found tremendous value in psychotherapy and while he continued to experience significant symptoms (while on medications), he was able to reduce his medication and later able to maintain employment, continue his studies to complete his undergraduate degree, and engage in an enjoyable relationship.

- I worked with a teenage boy, who upon discharge from a hospital, cautiously walked around me, looking to see if I had gills. He told me he couldn't trust anyone with gills. He was prescribed the highest possible dose of Seroquel but was still actively psychotic.

- An elderly woman, having been diagnosed with schizophrenia for decades, went to her room one night in a psychiatric hospital. She suffered from tardive dyskinesia, from long-term exposure to antipsychotics. As I was doing checks to make sure everyone was doing well, I found her sitting on the edge of her bed. Her sad expression captured my attention. Asking how she was, she said, "I'm just tired. I have been in the hospital so many times. I don't think any treatments will help me. I'm so tired."

- I worked with a young man diagnosed with schizophrenia. Most times, he was doing exceptionally well. Successful in his work, enjoying a relationship, and very active in the community. At times, he would hear voices that would drive him to disorganized behavior, believing that he had to be in the basement of a building because the voices couldn't reach him there. His psychiatrist would prescribe Remeron (an antidepressant) for several weeks, alleviate the hallucinations, and he would return to long periods of optimal functioning.

- I worked with a man who had been diagnosed with schizophrenia for many years before he started individual psychotherapy with me. He was educated, personable, and able to use psychotherapy very productively. While he believed that going off his medications completely was not an option, he was able to maintain a very small dose of Navane (a low-potency typical antipsychotic) and returned to full-time work.

- In my clinical training, there was a woman diagnosed with catatonic schizophrenia who was continuously hospitalized for seven years. Every morning, she would emerge from her room, only to shuffle over to "her" chair in the dayroom of the unit, where she would sit staring at the floor. After just a few months of consultation from an expert in the psychotherapy of schizophrenia, she was discharged from the hospital to a community-based living center. Her psychiatrist proclaimed, "the medications finally kicked in!"

- I worked with an adolescent boy who was diagnosed with schizoaffective disorder in a group home who refused his medication but was doing quite well. He was personable, had an enjoyable sense of humor, and was very supportive with his peers. Unmedicated, he came to me, requesting a therapy session one day. He sat on the couch, but then curled up into the fetal position, facing the back of the couch. He unleashed a torrent of accusations, shouting and swearing, but then went quiet. I could see him taking deep breaths, and then sitting upright facing me, he simply said, "I bet you didn't expect to hear that today."

- I worked with a veteran who was diagnosed with schizoaffective disorder and had alienated most of the caregivers in a case management program. He was invited to a community-based drop-in center but would be disruptive and belligerent when he attended. I invited him to participate in individual psychotherapy sessions. At first, he was accusatory and oppositional, yet he continued to drive over an hour (one way) twice a week for sessions. Once we positioned our chairs to be side by side, facing out a window, our sessions became positive and productive.

The list goes on. I am describing these situations because they highlight the vastly different circumstances that clients may present with. All different, all deserving to achieve their own success, all in different ways. In these situations I was able to work with them while reducing medications, the work was carefully coordinated with psychiatrists whom I trusted and could easily be reached to manage the collaborative work. The courageous people that I have had the opportunity to work with inspire me and continuously remind me that our science is insufficient. We need to continue devoting our efforts to better understanding strategies to optimize the outcomes of our clients and be extremely cautious of the assumptions we make about our available treatments.

Walk Away Message

Clinical Challenges: The use of antipsychotic medications has become common in the United States. Billions of dollars are spent annually on them, and they are used for many conditions beyond diagnoses of schizophrenia or psychosis. This off-label use undermines the connection of their mechanisms of action to any known neurochemical abnormalities in schizophrenia, which remain unknown. That is, if they are believed to be beneficial in many conditions, it would be foolish to believe all these conditions share a similar neurochemical foundation being ameliorated by antipsychotics. Rather, it could be argued that the suppressive, or deactivating, functions of antipsychotic medications are creating the response. In the treatment of schizophrenia, studies with adolescents have shown mixed results, and while medications (usually) outperform placebos in statistically significant outcomes, the clinical significance requires further study. As placebos have become more effective in recent decades, research often demonstrates placebos achieving noteworthy symptom improvements. This leads to more uncertainty in their use, as the wide-ranging side effects of antipsychotic medications are well-established. Finally, as detailed above, a "response" to antipsychotics within drug research may not be commensurate with the expectations in a naturalistic setting. Improving by one category of severity on the PANSS is important, but improving from "severely ill" to "markedly ill" means the patient is still experiencing serious, impairing symptoms, despite being a responder and compliant with treatment. This research highlights the need to challenge our assumptions about treatments and presumed outcomes.

Implications for Psychotherapists: If you are a therapist providing services to someone taking antipsychotic medications, my goal in providing this information is in hopes that it will expand your view of what *should* work versus what *could* work. We don't know enough to reliably predict outcomes, so careful evaluation, ongoing assessment, and client-centered strategies should guide your work. Listen to their voice. Listen to their experiences of success and failure and help those guide your interventions. As we are not prescribers, it is essential that you establish collaborative relationships with those prescribing medications to your clients. Ongoing and transparent communication between treatment providers, your client, and their system of support will provide the essential building blocks to make clear and positive steps toward their success. Be persistent. Our system of care makes it difficult to coordinate meetings and phone calls, as everyone is busy, but open, ongoing collaboration will help achieve the goals your clients deserve.

References

Alphs, L., Benedetti, F., Fleischhacker, W., & Kane, J. (2012). Placebo-related effects in clinical trials in schizophrenia: What is driving this phenomenon and what can be done to minimize it? *International Journal of Neuropsychopharmacology, 15*: 1003–1014.

American Psychiatric Association. (2021). *The American Psychiatric Association practice guideline for the treatment of patients with schizophrenia* (3rd ed.).

American Psychiatric Association. (2022). *Diagnostic and statistical manual of mental disorders* (5th ed., text rev.).

Baldini, V., Di Stefano, R., Rindi, L., Ahmed, A., Koola, M., Solmi, M., . . . Ostuizzi, G. (2023). Association between adverse childhood experiences and suicidal behavior in schizophrenia spectrum disorders: A systematic review and meta-analysis. *Psychiatry Research, 329*.

Bellonci, C., Huefner, J., Griffith, A., Vogel-Rosen, G., Smith, G., & Preston, S. (2013). Concurrent reductions in psychotropic medication, assault, and physical restraint in two residential treatment programs for youth. *Children and Youth Services Review, 35*: 1773–1779.

Breggin, P. (2008). *Brain-disabling treatments in psychiatry: Drugs, electroshock, and the psychopharmaceutical complex* (2nd ed.). Springer Publishing.

Elbe, D., Black, T., McGrane, I., & Choi, S. (Eds.). (2023). *Clinical handbook of psychotropic drugs for children and adolescents*. Hogrefe Publishers.

Findling, R., Cavus, I., Pappadopulos, E., Vanderburg, D., Schwartz, J., Gundapaneni, B., & DelBello, M. (2013). Ziprasidone in adolescents with schizophrenia: Results from a placebo-controlled efficacy and long-term open-extension study. *Journal of Child and Adolescent Psychopharmacology, 23*(8): 531–544.

Findling, R., Robb, A., Nyilas, M., Forbes, R., Jin, N., Ivanova, S., . . . Carson, W. (2008). A multiple-center, randomized, double-blind, placebo-controlled study of oral aripiprazole for treatment of adolescents with schizophrenia. *American Journal of Psychiatry, 165*: 1432–1441.

Frances, A. (2012, May 8). Newsflash from APA meeting: DSM-5 has flunked its reliability tests. *HuffPost*. https://www.huffpost.com/entry/dsm-5-reliability-tests_b_1490857

Garety, P. A., Edwards, C. J., Jafari, H., et al. (2024). Digital AVATAR therapy for distressing voices in psychosis: The phase 2/3 AVATAR2 trial. *Nat. Med., 30*: 3658–3668. https://doi.org/10.1038/s41591-024-03252-8

Geller, B., Luby, J., Joshi, P., et al. (2012). A randomized controlled trial of risperidone, lithium, or divalproex sodium for initial treatment of bipolar I disorder, manic or mixed phase, in children and adolescents. *Archives of General Psychiatry, 69*(5): 515–528.

Glick, I., Lemmens, P., & Vester-Blokland, E. (2001). Treatment of the symptoms of schizophrenia: A combined analysis of double-blind studies comparing risperidone with haloperidol and other antipsychotic agents. *International Clinical Psychopharmacology, 16*(5): 265–274.

Grindey, A., & Bradshaw, T. (2022). Do different adverse childhood experiences lead to specific symptoms of psychosis in adulthood? A systematic review of the current literature. *International Journal of Mental Health Nursing.* https://doi.org/10.1111/inm.12992

Gurnani, T., Ivanov, I., & Newcorn, J. (2016). Pharmacotherapy of aggression in child and adolescent psychiatric disorders. *Journal of Child and Adolescent Psychopharmacology, 26*(1): 65–73.

Harrow, M., Jobe, T. H., & Tong, L. (2021). Twenty-year effects of antipsychotics in schizophrenia and affective psychotic disorders. *Psychological Medicine, 52*(13): 1–11. https://doi.org/10.1017/S0033291720004778

Hird, E., Diederen, K., Leucht, S., Jensen, K., & McGuire, P. (2023). The placebo effect in psychosis: Why it matters and how to measure it. *Biological Psychiatry: Global Open Science,* October (*3*): 605–13. https://doi.org/10.1016/j.bpsgos.2023.02.008

Inyang, B., Gondal, F., Abah, G., Dhandapani, M., Manne, M., Khanna, M., . . . Mohammed, L. (2022). The role of childhood trauma in psychosis and schizophrenia: A systematic review. *Cureus, 14*(1). https://doi.org/10.7759/cureus.21466

Janssen Pharmaceuticals. (n.d.). Risperdal prescribing information. https://www.janssenlabels.com/package-insert/product-monograph/prescribinginformation/RISPERDAL-pi.pdf

Kane, J., Assuncao-Talbot, S., Eudicone, J., Pikalov, A., Whitehead, R., & Crandall, D. (2008). The efficacy of aripiprazole in the treatment of multiple symptom domains in patients with acute schizophrenia: A pooled analysis of data from the pivotal trials. *Schizophrenia Research, 105*(1–3): 208–215.

Karon, B., & VandenBos, G. (1981). *Psychotherapy of schizophrenia: The treatment of choice.* Jason Aronson, Inc.

Keeshin, B., Forkey, H., & Fouras, G. (2020). Children exposed to maltreatment: Assessment and the role of psychotropic medication. *Pediatrics, 14*(2): E20193751

Leucht, S., Kane, J., Kissling, W., Hamann, J, Etschel, E., & Engel, R. (2005). What does the PANSS mean? *Schizophrenia Research, 79*(2–3): 231–238.

Loy, J., Merry, S., Hetrick, S., & Stasiak, K. (2017). Atypical antipsychotics for disruptive behaviour disorders in children and youths. *Cochrane Database of Systematic Reviews,* Issue 8. https://doi.org/10.1002/14651858.

Otsuka Pharmaceutical Company. (n.d.). Abilify prescribing information. https://www.accessdata.fda.gov/drugsatfda_docs/label/2016/021436s041%2C021713s032%2C021729s024%2C021866s026lbl.pdf

Nasrallah, H. A. (2013). Haloperidol clearly is neurotoxic. Should it be banned? *Current Psychiatry, 12:* 7.

Palmer, C. (2022). *Brain energy: A revolutionary breakthrough in understanding mental health—and improving treatment for anxiety, depression, OCD, PTSD, and more.* BenBella Books.

Prokopez, C., Vallejos, M., Fuentes, P., Caporusso, G., Alberio, G., Cozzarin, L., . . . Daray, F. (2020). The role of adverse childhood experiences in the development of a more severe type of schizophrenia. *Schizophrenia Bulletin, 46*(Suppl 1): S302. https://doi.org/10.1093/schbul/sbaa029.744.

Rajkumar, R. (2022). Antipsychotics in the management of disruptive behavior disorders in children and adolescents: An update and critical review. *Biomedicines, 10*: 2818. https://doi.org/10.3390/biomedicines10112818

Read, J., Fosse, B. D., Moskowitz, A., & Perry, J. (2014). The traumagenic neurodevelopmental model of psychosis revisited. *Neoropsychiatry, 4*(1): 65–79. https://doi.org/10.2217/npy.13.89

Sethi, S., Wakeham, D., Ketter, T., Hooshmand, F., Bjornstad, J., Richards, B., . . . Saslow, L. (2024). Ketogenic diet intervention on metabolic and psychiatric health in bipolar and schizophrenia: A pilot trial. *Psychiatric Research, 335*.

Stahl, S. (2013). *Stahl's essential psychopharmacology: Neuroscientific basis and practical applications*. Cambridge University Press.

Substance Abuse and Mental Health Services Administration (SAMHSA). (2019). *Guidance on strategies to promote best practice in antipsychotic prescribing for children and adolescents*. HHS Publication No. PEP19-Antipsychotic-BP. Rockville, MD: Office of Chief Medical Officer, SAMHSA.

Tyrer, P., Oliver-Africano, P., Ahmed, Z., Bouras, N., Cooray, S., Deb, S., . . . Crawford, M. (2008). Risperidone, haloperidol, and placebo in the treatment of aggressive challenging behaviour in patients with intellectual disability: A randomized controlled trial. *Lancet, 371*. 57–63.

Valenstein, E. (1998). *Blaming the brain: The truth about drugs and mental health*. The Free Press.

Vitiello, B., Riddle, M., Yenokyan, G., Axelson, D., Wagner, K., Joshi, P., . . . Tillman, R. (2012). Treatment moderators and predictors of outcome in the treatment of early age mania (TEAM) study. *Journal of the American Academy of Child & Adolescent Psychiatry, 51*(9): 867–878.

Whitaker, R. (2019). *Mad in America: Bad science, bad medicine, and the enduring mistreatment of the mentally ill*. Basic Books.

Zaim, N., Findling, R. L., & Sun, A. (2020). Antipsychotics for treatment of adolescent onset schizophrenia: A review. *Curr Treat Options Psych., 7*: 23–38. https://doi.org/10.1007/s40501-020-00198-9

7
Child Welfare and Intensive Services

Child welfare systems across the country work to meet the needs of some of our country's most vulnerable and troubled youth and families. The system is stretched thin, under-resourced, and continually faces complicated challenges, distressing headlines, and frustrating outcomes. There are no simple remedies to fix our nation's child welfare system, as some states manage this work well while others do not. All dimensions of the child welfare system cannot be addressed here but to start this discussion, let's look at some established facts.

- There are approximately 400,000 children and adolescents placed in foster care within the United States. This number fluctuates each year but has remained fairly consistent in this range for years. In 2018, there were 437,010 youth in care and in 2022 there were 368,530. In these five years, it has trended down (U.S. Department of Health and Human Services, 2023).
- "Nearly all children in foster care have experienced maltreatment or neglect and trauma from being separated from their families of origin, all of which can be developmentally disruptive" (Radel et al., 2023, p. 1107). Children are typically removed from their home because of safety concerns.
- The Family First Prevention Services Act (FFPSA) was initiated recently to keep children in their homes, avoiding removal to foster care. The FFPSA is designed to use evidence-based, trauma-informed interventions to support youth and families to keep families intact. These services are not yet in place in every state.
- Young people in the child welfare system are much more likely to receive psychiatric medications. In fact, they are also more likely to be receiving multiple psychiatric medications (polypharmacy). From a

recent analysis, adolescents (12–17-year-olds) in the child welfare system were more often medicated compared to other Medicaid-enrolled youths (34.3% versus 12.8%, respectively). Further, 19.1 percent of child welfare adolescents received polypharmacy versus 5 percent of other Medicaid-enrolled in this age group (Radel et al., 2023).

- The best available data indicate that the use of psychiatric hospitalization for children and adolescents has increased significantly from 2009 to 2019. A review of this service revealed an increase of over 40,000 hospitalizations annually (from 160,499 in 2009 to 201,932 in 2019) totaling $1.37 billion in 2019 (averaging approximately $6,800 per hospitalization). Hospitalized youth have also become more commonly diagnosed with multiple conditions (Arakelyan et al., 2023). It should be noted that this 2023 data does not include hospitals exclusively designed for psychiatric purposes, so these numbers are undoubtedly underestimated. For example, a specific nationwide psychiatric provider highlighted data from over 112,000 adolescent inpatient admissions in 2021 (Universal Health Services, 2021). This adds 50 percent to the above nationwide review when considering just one large psychiatric provider.

The prescription practices within this system of care have blown past established Practice Guidelines. Indeed, experts have voiced concerns over the high rates of antipsychotic use in pediatric populations as well as noting that "most pediatric psychotropic medication use (67%) is not approved by the US Food and Drug Administration and is therefore prescribed off-label" (Pennap et al., 2018, p. E2). This deviation from Practice Guidelines is concerning and warrants increased scrutiny. Many believe that too many medications are being used within the child welfare system, particularly with severely troubled young people.

The Challenges of Youth in Care
The Diagnostic Dilemmas

There is little debate that children and teens within the child welfare system can present with distress, emotional extremes, and many difficult-to-manage behaviors. Of course, we should approach these challenges with a trauma-focused approach. Through this lens, our priorities should be providing safe, stable, nurturing relationships. This must be the foundation of our intervention strategies.

In addition to trauma, or because of it, children within the child welfare system often have multiple diagnoses—that is, comorbid disorders. Each disorder has prominent symptoms that raise concerns for others—behaviors or emotions that are uncomfortable to manage. Even though a youth may have two, three, or four diagnoses, a prescriber may choose medications that target prominent symptoms within each separate diagnosis. There is an additional consideration here: psychiatrists in residential treatment have told me that for Medicaid-funded youth, they require a diagnosis to obtain reimbursement for a medication that the psychiatrist believes would help. This, of course, artificially complicates the diagnostic picture. Moreover, the diagnoses that a child receives could stay with them for a long time.

A common feature of youth in care is called "comorbidity." That is, they present with such complicated symptoms that they are often given multiple diagnoses. They have comorbid conditions. This raises the challenge of prioritizing interventions in order to achieve the most significant outcomes that can lessen the severity across their presentation. For example, if someone is diagnosed with a substance abuse condition, major depression, and trauma exposure, a treatment plan may prioritize any one of these "disorders" as a primary target with the hope that, by improving one, you may benefit the others. One's substance use may be exacerbating their depressive symptoms, so by prioritizing your intervention on the substance abuse, the depressive symptoms may also improve. Or not. Because of the complicated, comorbid presentations in youth, the formulation of the treatment plan must explore these various options and conceptualize what interventions may initially reap the greatest benefit. However, as this is often speculative, close monitoring of their response is essential so the team of providers can quickly pivot to "plan B" if the outcomes are not being achieved.

Unfortunately, much of the research available to guide intervention strategies is not developed for the challenging youth within the child welfare system, or those with comorbid conditions. Most interventions are studied to observe their effects on a specific diagnostic presentation. But the stakes are high. These young people need help and support, in many forms, requiring providers to communicate, collaborate, and closely monitor outcomes.

Consider a teen that is depressed. They have expressed suicidal ideation and feel like they can't trust adults. A prescriber may offer an antidepressant like Prozac. But this teen also has shown aggression. A prescriber may add an atypical antipsychotic, such as Risperdal, to control aggressive outbursts. With these challenges, the teen may admit to their struggles in school, unable to focus or complete homework. You guessed it: a prescriber may offer Concerta to address the difficulties related to a proposed ADHD diagnosis.

In isolation, the medication prescribed for each one of these behavioral presentations aligns with expected prescribing strategies. However, in combination, the medications described in the above scenario, albeit common, create a situation where each medication works against the others. That is, when you understand the mechanism of action of each of these medications, you realize they are each competing. Take a look:

- Prozac increases the availability of serotonin, as the package insert describes, "Although the exact mechanism of action of Prozac is unknown, it is presumed to be linked to its inhibition of CNS neuronal uptake of serotonin." See the chapter on antidepressants for more detail.
- Risperdal reduces the availability of both serotonin and dopamine. From the package insert, "The drug's therapeutic activity in schizophrenia could be mediated through a combination of dopamine Type 2 (D_2) and serotonin Type 2 ($5\text{-}HT_2$) receptor antagonism."
- Concerta (methylphenidate) increases the availability of dopamine and norepinephrine. From the package insert, "Methylphenidate is thought to block the reuptake of norepinephrine and dopamine into the presynaptic neuron and increase the release of these monoamines into the extraneuronal space." The chapter on stimulants explores this mechanism in additional detail.

This typical combination increases the availability of dopamine (stimulant), increases the availability of serotonin (antidepressant), and blocks the availability of dopamine and serotonin (antipsychotic).

In research that I coordinated several years ago, exploring the subjective experience of adolescents in residential treatment, this combination of these three medication classes occurred in 12 percent of the group studied. Also concerning, the combination of a stimulant and antipsychotic medication (having competing mechanisms of action) occurred in 28 percent of the sample.

In this common clinical situation, how would one reliably expect a positive outcome of this medication combination? Would each medication be expected to achieve its desired outcome despite other medications competing with its mechanism of action? It may be the case that symptom relief could occur in this example of polypharmacy, but an explanation of how extends beyond what seems to be understood about how these medications may interact. Even though all these presenting problems could be the result of traumatic experiences, a strategy to suppress them with medications will likely result in less-than-optimal outcomes, without devoting sufficient focus on addressing the trauma.

Health Is Not the Absence of Symptoms

Most of our models of intervention are developed with the goal of reducing the severity or impairment from symptoms. This is obviously important but insufficient to create positive, durable outcomes. The absence of depression is not happiness. The absence of anxiety is not calm and confident. The absence of aggression is not close, caring relationships. *Those* outcomes are our true targets. Those outcomes take time, they require different interventions toward skill development, and they can only be achieved in safe, positive, supportive environments.

On this point, *No Method to the Madness* tries to tackle the questions around our use of psychotropic medications in youth. Throughout, we have explored medications' ability to control symptoms of various disorders, often with dubious long-term advantages. However, as we explore how to cultivate strength-based outcomes, it's worth noting that despite the claims of sophisticated understanding of depression, psychosis, ADHD, etc., no one purports to have a medication remedy, or neurochemical understanding, of courage, honesty, commitment, enthusiasm, intimacy, etcetera. You get the point. Those assets come from relationships.

Data-Driven Decisions

Given the complexities of integrating systems of care, the clinical issues, and family dynamics, case managers that endeavor to organize and guide services face incredible challenges in gathering, analyzing, and using the information to make decisions to improve outcomes for youth and families. It is not difficult to find regular headlines about case managers being stretched thin, often under-resourced, trying to help some of our most vulnerable families.

States are incentivized to become compliant with the Comprehensive Child Welfare Information System, or CCWIS final rule. The Administration for Children and Families (ACF) created the standards for data collection, use, and framework for the CCWIS initiative. If states choose to modernize their data systems in compliance with CCWIS standards, costs of the project can be supplemented by the federal government. So far, states are moving in the direction of modernizing, but very few have completed the process. As a result, it remains unclear whether these efforts will help create positive, durable outcomes, but the modernization of data collection and analysis is a big step in the right direction.

As noted, few states have completed the CCWIS modernization. Because it emphasizes technology development and implementation, large companies, filled with skilled programmers and developers have stepped up to tackle the problem. However, simply complying with the standards within the final rule may not fully embrace the challenges of child welfare workers in the front lines. Some have integrated algorithms into the decision-making process, only to find that even these algorithms can be biased, generate the wrong decisions, or further complicate a process.

We need to enhance our ideas of outcomes. As a prevailing goal, our treatments look to reduce symptoms with the assumption that health is some default outcome that is buried beneath all the clinical diagnoses. But *health is not the absence of symptoms*. It must be pursued. In this way, simple symptom control, while necessary, is insufficient. And if we aggressively embraced a health-based framework, we would commit our energies to relational success, creating skills in both youth and their parents, create financial stability in these families, and establish a trajectory of success. Meeting needs is different from responding to problems.

A Strength-Based Model

"Have you had more opportunities to succeed, or to fail?"

Throughout *No Method to the Madness*, I've referred to the Circle of Courage. I believe this model could be applied across our systems of care, throughout the child welfare system and intensive services in the continuum of care. As discussed, I had the privilege of being mentored by the creators of this model early in my career. With their expertise as psychologists, educators, and researchers, they have continued to promote and train a values-based model that stands up against rigorous research. In fact, looking at models of psychological development over time, the Circle of Courage synthesizes the key ingredients and creates a methodology to implement and measure effectiveness and success.

Having had the privilege of working with the creators of the Circle of Courage for many years, I've seen its effectiveness in a variety of settings. In my first exposure, working as an administrator in a residential treatment center, the organization sought out consultation with experts in a strength-based approach to create a therapeutic environment, one that would meet the fundamental needs of youth to cultivate resiliency, promote positive relationships, and create a trajectory of success. It was the Circle of Courage. Simple but not simplistic. The task is to create an environment that responds to the universal needs of belonging, mastery, independence, and generosity so that people will thrive.

The Circle of Courage is a model, a paradigm, and a philosophy that identifies the essential values that cultivate strength, resiliency, and resourcefulness. The values and needs identified within the Circle of Courage have been synthesized into this model through "Indigenous wisdom, perspectives of youth work pioneers, and leading-edge research on resilience, neuroscience, and positive youth development" (Brendtro, Brokenleg, & VanBockern, 2019, p. 1). In contrast to so many popular treatments, it was not developed as an innovation from an established model of psychotherapy. Rather, it was distilled from generations of indigenous wisdom focused on understanding and responding to universal human needs, critical for healthy development of youth, or to support their recovery after adversity.

Getting to know the creators of the Circle of Courage, I quickly appreciated their decades of commitment to supporting at-risk youth. By training, they were psychologists and educators. But the ability to recognize the unique strengths in youth is not in the standard training of mental health professionals. The prevailing deficit-based model focuses on identifying diagnoses, disorders, and dysfunction. Looking past these problems to embrace the strengths of troubled young people and cultivate these assets amid challenges requires genuine optimism in the potential of our young people. In this model, it's not about suppressing symptoms but cultivating strengths and resiliency to create a successful path forward.

Imagine a model in which we focus on meeting the universal needs of youth—needs of Belonging, Mastery, Independence, and Generosity to reduce the impact of trauma and modify maladaptive behaviors. This approach also appreciates the reality that symptoms have meaning. Problematic behaviors, confusing emotions, and disturbed thoughts emerge from troubling experiences and unmet needs. When our method is to address these needs, healing can occur. This is real treatment versus simply containing problematic behaviors through medication.

Belonging—This universal value is rooted in creating safe, cooperative, and fulfilling connections with others. Caregivers, peers, the community, and beyond, feeling safe and connected to the world around you allows you to meet a universal need for interpersonal closeness, trust, and belonging. When this need is unmet, relationships can become conflictual and untrustworthy. Youth feel rejected. This unmet need over time can create a wary approach toward others, seeming to be an unwillingness to connect, but may be rooted in a feeling of being unsafe.

Mastery—Meeting the universal need for Mastery means developing the skills of our youth and cultivating their unique talents and interests. When this need is unmet, youth experience challenges in school, in social situations, and in completing tasks that may otherwise seem expected. A key to both Belonging and Mastery is to embrace and appreciate the individual child, with all their unique differences, talents, challenges, and aspirations. All youth need opportunities to succeed.

Independence—This universal need focuses on self-control, self-confidence, autonomy, and assertiveness. This unmet need emerges as impulsivity, insecurity and a lack of confidence, challenges in decision-making or feeling powerless, and problematic relationships. Being responsible doesn't emerge without being given responsibilities.

Generosity—In this need, caring, respect, and collaborative support are at the forefront. When a child has their needs met for Generosity, they share, respect others, and offer their help in the support of others' needs. As they mature, youth can begin to offer their unique interests and abilities in the support and promotion of others. It may be small activities or more sophisticated endeavors to support the success of others (Brendtro, Brokenleg, & VanBockern, 2019).

Another rich exploration to support the Circle of Courage is the private logic of the youth. Their internal thoughts, aspirations, fears, ambivalence, desires, etcetera, fuel their behaviors and inform how they engage with the world around them. Clinician and expert trainer, Mark Freado, has created an insightful methodology to understand the internal world of youth, called *The Art of Kid Whispering*. Written with colleague J. C. Chambers, this process creates a process to explore the internal world of youth and integrate it into the approach of meeting their universal needs (Chambers & Freado, 2015).

Like a canvas for a painting, the treatment environment (or milieu) is essential for the effectiveness of any intervention offered. But today, the treatment environment is an afterthought. A secondary factor to the offering of "evidence-based treatments." Nothing therapeutic occurs if people do not feel safe. This oversight may indeed be one of the key weaknesses in our current models of care. We seek to create a solution to a complicated problem with one tool, rather than a focused effort to change the ecology around the child and family.

Consider trauma. Our research models look to use one psychotherapy intervention or one medication to reduce a score on a trauma scale to measure success. The methodology of a randomly controlled trial is laudable but fails to appreciate the power of the environment in which the intervention is delivered. Inpatient and residential treatment settings that do not provide a clear sense of safety will be far less effective, even when utilizing a trauma-informed, evidence-based intervention. It could be argued that any intervention would be markedly more effective in an environment in which the child felt safe, compared to one in which there were unsafe conditions. It seems obvious but is largely ignored in professional discussions.

The complexity of the milieu is multifaceted. From the administration to direct care workers, they must have a shared vision, devote resources, and operate in a concerted way to fulfill that shared vision. When an organization's administrative level is driven by profits, it is rarely a shared vision of the direct care staff.

Profiteers in the System

If you have been involved in working with youth with severe emotional and behavioral challenges, you've likely heard the term, "troubled teen industry." This phrase represents providers of inpatient and residential services ostensibly driven by profits rather than outcomes. I've had conversations with them. In fact, an administrator in one of these organizations said it that clearly: "We don't get paid for outcomes; we get paid for bed occupancy." I was stunned but not surprised.

To further emphasize the financial exploitation in the system, the U.S. Senate Committee on Finance initiated an investigation into four of the largest providers of behavioral health care services in the United States. Investigators reviewed over twenty-five thousand documents, interviews, and audit data. Upon concluding the investigation, this Senate Committee released their report, and it revealed wide-ranging incidents of abuse, inadequate care, poor training, insufficient staffing, and business models set up to exploit placement and payment strategies to maximize profits (U.S. Senate Committee on Finance, 2024).

Another problem in this segment of the industry is that they are often accredited. Organizations such as CARF or The Joint Commission offer reputable standards designed to increase the quality of care. However, as demonstrated in these organizations, accreditation can be achieved while still providing substandard or abusive practices. The Senate Committee investigation found that while violations were identified in an accreditation review, these providers would create a remediation plan yet never fulfill it. These plans are difficult to enforce from an accreditation standpoint, so it requires that the provider organization carry the onus in modifying their practice. A responsibility found to be frequently ignored in these organizations.

A system exploiting profits from our most vulnerable youth and families is reprehensible. People should be paid for their services. If you provide better services, it should leverage better revenue. But substandard, inadequate, and abusive services should never be rewarded. I am sure, at many levels within these complex, nationwide organizations, moments of therapeutic interaction occur. I am sure that many staff in these organizations want better outcomes for these young people. I've spoken with them. Specifically, another administrator of one of these identified organizations expressed high aspirations for what they can accomplish. Yet here we are.

A system of care that is *not* focused on meeting the needs of these youth and families has failed. If the approach of responding to crises or clinical challenges is to suppress problematic behaviors, rather than responding to needs, the approach may achieve short-term success but will fail in the long-term.

Data to Drive Placements

Multiple hospitalizations, polypharmacy, and repeated failed placements do not reflect "best practices." Multiple, ineffective hospitalizations occur because most large health care providers are not paid for their outcomes, they are paid for bed occupancy. In other words, repeated hospitalizations are good for business. When a young person is hospitalized, the priority is to ensure safety and suppress any "out of control" behaviors that are difficult to manage, typically with medications. With limited lengths of stay (averaging 4.7 days in 2019; Arakelyan et al., 2023) little psychotherapy occurs, meaning that youth don't gain insight into their problems and don't develop new skills to manage their feelings. As a result, hospitals have become a form of crisis management—to contain a problem rather than create a lasting solution. It's not uncommon that a youth may be re-hospitalized weeks or months after a hospitalization. It's worth asking: is it that hospitalizations don't provide sufficient outcomes? Or do some youth simply require repeated hospitalizations? When a child is repeatedly hospitalized, they are often described as "treatment resistant." They may be, or they might be a perfect fit in an industry often driven by profits.

Data should be collected throughout a youth's involvement in care, from the first contact until the need for care disappears. While a hospitalization is routinely justified to address suicidal, dangerous, or grossly disorganized behaviors, the crisis must be managed. But if the improvement only lasts a week or two after discharge, shouldn't we demand more of this level of care? Short-term successes and long-term failures are data points.

Consider this simplistic overview of crisis behaviors (Figure 7.1). Assuming a score of 1 represents calm, while an 8 is a crisis (such as aggression). So, over a month in this example, this youth has periods of crisis with multiple days in between of calm behavior.

Figure 7.1 An Example of Episodes of Crisis Behavior (provided by the author)

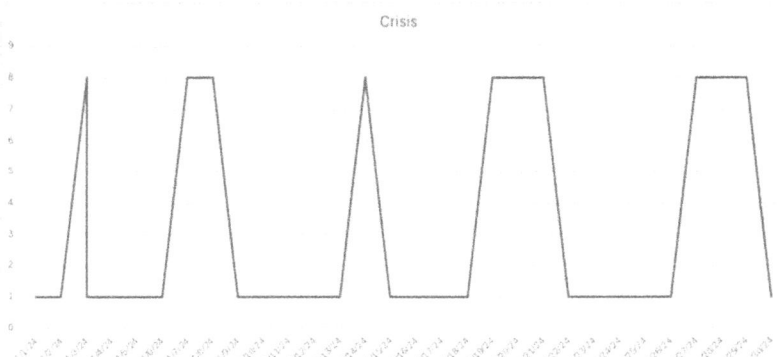

Our typical model of intervention is to apply treatments at the point of a crisis. Let's assume that at the first point of crisis, this youth was prescribed Abilify to control the behavior. As he returned to baseline, we often attribute that improvement to the use of medication. As a result, with the repeated incidents of crisis over time, a common response would be to increase the dose or add medications. Little attention is paid to the periods of calm, such as what is creating and maintaining them. It's as if "no news is good news."

When data can be collected, analyzed, and provided in a way to drive decision-making, our ability to shape outcomes will improve. Imagine if the following domains of information were regularly collected and available for real-time analysis and reporting. Imagine being able to quickly decipher the factors that immediately precipitated a behavioral crisis in a young person or family. Imagine then, over time, being able to recognize individualized patterns that would support more durable, long-lasting success, rather than feeling as if we're "reinventing the wheel" with each new treatment encounter.

Trauma Exposure—As discussed throughout *No Method to the Madness*, we must focus on a youth's exposure to trauma. The type of trauma, the developmental timing, and duration of those experiences all provide key information to better understanding how to effectively intervene and support them. Assessment of trauma exposure in the caregivers is also important to recognize if they may have unmet needs to address.

Clinical Symptoms—challenging behaviors, beliefs, and emotions are all important to monitor. A diagnosis is more unreliable in this regard. Temporal instability of diagnoses clouds the accuracy of our perspective. Tracking symptoms, however, provides a more accurate representation of the youth's functioning.

Ability to Manage These Symptoms—Even though symptoms may present, a person's ability to manage them should also be closely monitored. I worked with a young man who was experiencing persistent auditory hallucinations. On a symptom scale, he would have scored high, as the symptom was not controlled with medications, and it was persistent. However, this bright, ambitious young man was able to take college courses, hold down two part-time jobs, and enjoy a dating relationship. As symptoms should be tracked, so should the individual's ability to manage them.

Medications—The introduction, dose changes, and discontinuation of all medications should be closely monitored. It is well established that slight changes in dose can have a downstream effect on other behaviors. As medications are thought to offer benefits, they come with many side effects.

Psychological Services—All psychotherapy services (individual, family, group) and psychological evaluations should be incorporated into the overall approach formulation in creating a treatment plan. In my experience, many of my clients have had previous therapy experiences. What worked, and what didn't, from the client's perspective is valuable information. It's important to recognize that if therapy wasn't successful before, it does not mean that it may not be helpful now. Many factors influence the effectiveness of psychotherapy. Psychological evaluation data offers key data points that not only establish a baseline in functions (e.g., cognitive functions, emotional factors) but can also assist in integrating multidimensional aspects.

Family Resources—Financial stability, housing, access to food, transportation, emotional resources, communication, etc., are key factors that influence a youth's ability to effectively engage in services, respond to interventions, and create a successful path forward. Not knowing about these issues could lead to faulty assumptions about a child and their "symptoms." For example, a hungry child, or a child that has not slept well, will likely show problematic behaviors. Moreover, setting up appointments for services without access to reliable transportation may be assumed to be "non-compliance" with recommendations when they don't show up.

Community Resources—Access to services varies across communities. Providers should be well-versed in those resources. Urban areas may have a much more robust range of services than rural areas, and this should influence the formulations for intervention, and expected outcomes. Being familiar with food and clothing resources, housing, and transportation can provide vital components that enhance a child and family's sense of safety and control in their lives.

Interpersonal Relationships—The quality of one's relationships is an important measure of their well-being. They can be a source of influential feelings such as joy, support, frustration, or danger. Assuming that once a crisis is averted, or symptoms have been reduced, that other dimensions of a youth's life are fulfilling ignores the function of symptoms; that they reflect one's internal stress, fears, and so on.

Sense of Purpose—Having goals, aspirations, and a feeling of purpose in one's day-to-day life is essential. This dimension may not be considered by service providers, but is a factor in "grit," resiliency, a sense of mastery, and connection to the world around you.

Community Engagement—Finding ways to engage in your community, whether through volunteering, employment, or recreational activities can serve as an important source of distraction, a sense of generosity, connection with others, or fulfilling activities.

Happiness/Enthusiasm—Being happy and feeling joy is not a default mode. For example, if someone is struggling with depression, part of the challenge is to alleviate that distress, but another part of that challenge is to cultivate experiences that generate happiness, joy, and a sense of enjoyment.

Hobbies—Activities that can build skills, enhance enjoyment, and provide connections with others are important. Giving the youth something to look forward to, activities to fill free time, skills to continue to develop, and opportunities to cultivate unique, individual talents may all emerge from engaging in hobbies.

Resiliency—Coping with, and adapting to stress, is essential. Evaluating a youth's ability to manage stress provides another important dimension in creating a trajectory for success. Moreover, rather than symptom suppression, this is an outcome that needs to be developed, enhanced, and monitored.

Self-Reflection/Self-Care—Connected with resiliency, a person's ability for self-reflection supports an awareness to alert them as to when they need help. With this, many people can use self-care strategies when they feel stressed, but we all have a threshold where we need to seek the assistance of others. Having this dimension as a factor for monitoring also provides caregivers with insights toward further supporting the youth in care.

Modern technologies exist to collect, analyze, and report this data to drive decision-making. While states embark on their modernization processes for CCWIS, many have not incorporated sufficient data collection and analytics. While their systems of care will benefit from the increased efficiencies, key data points are critical to improve outcomes. The above list is only a partial list but speaks to how our intervention models should evolve to embrace strengths and address the clinical challenges. These positive, prosocial aspects of a child's functioning should be targeted outcomes, emphasized even more than the reduction of symptoms. Indeed, durable, positive, happy futures require it.

Phased Implementation with Improved Data

Residential Treatment

When done right, residential treatment offers an exceptional opportunity to create lasting change. Having spent over fifteen years of my career within residential treatment settings, I've seen the value of this level of care. I've also seen its failures. Some of the best clinicians I've known in my career have been within the residential treatment environment. Forced to think beyond evidence-based strategies, the creative, dedicated, resilient, and resourceful staff at all levels in these settings can deliver great value. But residential treatment has also been a target of criticism.

The clinical challenges found in residential centers are some of the most complicated. When I started working in these settings, children and teens could spend years in placement. Times have changed dramatically, as the recommended lengths of stay are now much more compressed, often with a goal of six to nine months. Creating arbitrary time constraints for residential placement may be misguided. No doubt, spending years in residential treatment is not necessary for most youth placed in care. It should be a rare exception. But part of this dilemma is driven by the "failing upward" mentality of this most intensive level of care.

In most cases, youth that end up in residential treatment have endured multiple failures in previous placements, plagued by failed foster homes, repeated psychiatric hospitalizations, an inability to establish reliable caregiving relationships, trauma exposures, multiple medications, and poor outcomes. Only after months or years of these failures and frustrations, is a youth considered for residential placement. As research demonstrates that children have better outcomes when they remain in their homes, reluctance to placement is understandable, and it can be expensive as well (although a day in care is not as expensive as a day of hospitalization). Indeed, residential treatment is often considered an intervention of last resort.

Under the right conditions, residential treatment is also an opportunity for a fresh start. This process requires recognizing that previous efforts have not been successful. It requires understanding that the clinical issues that the child first faced are likely quite different now. Time has passed, circumstances have changed, and relationships have evolved. The placement process should begin with an evaluation period, but rather than diagnostic interviews over the first days of placement, the multidimensional evaluation should take weeks.

And while current practices include the "shotgun approach" of throwing all interventions at the youth upon placement, this may not be the most effective utilization of resources.

When done right, the residential milieu can be a potent tool. As discussed above, if the milieu has a reliable and well-implemented strength-based, trauma-informed framework, such as the Circle of Courage, a sense of community will be established. Safety will be integrated throughout program areas. Staff communicate and reinforce these ideas with youth and each other, and administrative processes fully support the milieu as a vital component of treatment. Training and fidelity to the model are essential.

Upon admission, the focus should be on integrating the youth into the residential community and establishing a sense of safety for them. Interpersonal dynamics need to be closely monitored, as these will always fluctuate with admissions and discharges. With emphasis on the youth's acclimation to the treatment community, this becomes their primary focus and the emphasis of safety, prosocial values, and the cultivation of strengths and resiliency is at the forefront.

Emphasis on the milieu as the first phase of intervention also provides an opportunity to pull back and reevaluate other interventions. For example, while it's rare to deprescribe medications, a phased approach could create this opportunity (see chapter 8 on deprescribing for additional details). The youth's experience of a safe, controlled, predictable environment can offer a profound benefit on feelings of anxiety, feeling unsafe, and uncertainty. Reducing or alleviating these distressing symptoms, simply through an effective, therapeutic milieu, changes what interventions may be needed in the next phase. No doubt, establishing trust and connection with youth who have "failed upward" in the system is a delicate process. It requires Attention, Intention, and Repetition (AIR).

While this first phase may require weeks, it could significantly alter the youth's remaining time in residential treatment. While the first phase of acclimating the youth into the safe, strength-based environment continues, so does the evaluation process. There is careful examination of their interpersonal skills, coping and resiliency, evolving symptom presentation, family resources, educational aptitude, and management of their stress and symptoms.

Imagine if these data points were available to the clinicians to determine their next intervention steps. A youth who feels that their environment is controlled, predictable, and safe may not engage in aggressive behaviors. A youth in an environment that looks to highlight their unique strengths and interests may start to feel proud of themselves, elevating their self-esteem, and possibly reducing feelings of inadequacy and rejection. Clinicians may now determine that psychotherapy is the next, least intrusive intervention. Recognizing that the youth's traumatic history continues to impact them, psychotherapy is the preferred intervention.

Now acclimated to the safe, effective milieu, the youth receives psychotherapy and the evaluation continues. Looking to continue cultivating strengths, the treatment team continues to formulate how to support the youth's recovery. Symptoms may still be present, but the severity, function, and impact may be mitigated by other factors in this phased approach. Data would inform the process: Does the youth struggle to manage depressive feelings? Do they lack substantive friendships to rely on to talk about problems? Do they have an unstable sleep schedule that is affecting them? Are they engaging in self-harm behaviors?

With modernized strategies, data could be available in real-time versus waiting for a staff meeting every few months. Technology could alert treatment team members to any observed changes as direct care staff, clinicians, educators, or caregivers can enter data into the system. With designated indicators, any concerns could be immediately communicated to stakeholders. This technology exists.

A phased approach may seem unrealistic. Youth that are challenging enough to warrant residential treatment are believed to only benefit from all treatments, all at once. That has been the method for decades. Phased implementation may extend the length of stay in residential care, but it could result in more long-lasting benefits. Moreover, more reliable, valid data, throughout a youth's involvement in the systems of care, would also be able to discern more accurately who needs residential care, rather than spending months or years "failing upward."

The discussion throughout *No Method to the Madness* has focused on the evidence (or lack of) to support our treatment decisions. It's important to note that the interpersonally dynamic milieu of a residential treatment center has not been well-researched. Nor are there "best practice" standards that can be universally deployed across different agencies. The relationships among staff, among youth, and between youth and staff make this a particularly complex environment. We are at a point, however, when technology can begin to answer these questions. With that comes the chance to fully understand how to leverage relationships and the myriad factors to optimize outcomes, even in our most complicated and vulnerable youth.

I have maintained my belief in the power of the milieu after my many years working in residential treatment and subsequent years of consulting with agencies. Throughout these years, what has been clear is that certain staff, those who have genuine connections with you, can have powerful influences on youth. Aggression, depressive feelings, feelings of rejection, happiness, connection, and even symptoms of psychosis—I've seen these improve as youth engage with different staff within the milieu.

Beyond the scope of discussion here, my observations are not unique but confirmed by my earlier studies in interventions for psychosis. Programs like Soteria, Gifric, the Windhorse Program, and Geel, Belgium have all demonstrated effective therapeutic interventions in the treatment of psychosis, with little emphasis on the use of medications. There is a long history demonstrating the power of the environment to mitigate the impact of the most severe psychological conditions. Further, Bellonci and colleagues (2013) were able to decrease medication use with severely troubled youth in a residential setting with significant benefits. That study will be discussed in more detail in Chapter 8 on deprescribing. To this point, authors conclude, "Residential treatment can provide a treatment milieu that allows for thoughtful reassessment of the clinical basis for behavioral disorders in children that can achieve the dual goals of medication reduction and behavioral stabilization" (Bellonci et al., 2013, p. 1778). Now with the technology platforms available for sophisticated data collection and analysis, it's time that we use these advancements to truly maximize the power of this foundational service in congregate care settings.

References

Arakelyan, M., Freyleue, S., Avula, D., McLaren, J., O'Malley, A. J., & Leyenaar, J. (2023). Pediatric mental health hospitalizations at acute care hospitals in the U.S., 2009–2019. *Journal of the American Medical Association*, *329*(12): 1000–1011.

Bellonci, C., Huefner, J., Griffith, A., Vogel-Rosen, G., Smith, G., & Preston, S. (2013). Concurrent reductions in psychotropic medication, assault, and physical restraint in two residential treatment programs for youth. *Children and Youth Services Review*, *35*: 1773–1779.

Brendtro, L., Brokenleg, M., & VanBockern, S. (2019). *Reclaiming youth at risk: Futures of promise* (3rd ed.). Solution Tree Press.

Chambers, J. C., & Freado, M. (2015). *The art of kid whispering: Reaching the inside kid*. CreateSpace Independent Publishing Platform.

Pennap, D., Zito, J. M., Santosh, P. J., Tom, S. E., Onukwugha, E., & Magder, L. S. (2018). Patterns of early mental health diagnosis and medication treatment in a Medicaid-insured birth cohort. *JAMA Pediatrics*, *172*(6): 576. https://doi.org/10.1001/jamapediatrics.2018.0240

Radel, L. F., Ali, M. M., West, K., & Lieff, S. A. (2023). Psychotropic medication and psychotropic polypharmacy among children and adolescents in the US child welfare system. *JAMA Pediatr.*, *177*(10): 1107–1110. https://doi.org/10.1001/jamapediatrics.2023.3068

Universal Health Services, Inc. (2021). Our impact in 2021 by the numbers. https://uhs.com/wp-content/uploads/2022/03/UHS_2021-By-the-Numbers.pdf

U.S. Department of Health and Human Services. (2023). AFCARS report #30. https://acf.gov/sites/default/files/documents/cb/afcars-report-30.pdf

U.S. Senate Committee on Finance. (2024). Warehouses of neglect: How taxpayers are funding the systemic abuse in youth residential treatment facilities. https://www.finance.senate.gov/imo/media/doc/rtf_report_warehouses_of_neglect.pdf

8
Deprescribing: Is It an Option?

As a psychologist, I cannot prescribe medication. Any medication changes need to be done under the supervision of a licensed prescriber. What will be explored here are observations and suggestions made by psychiatrists and other professionals. They should not be considered as specific instructions or to replace guidance from your prescribers. I will be exploring this topic from my role as a psychologist, working with many clients who have been medicated. I've had many opportunities to collaborate with prescribers in the process of deprescribing. I will emphasize my experience working with prescribers in this discussion. It's not common, though, that psychologists or therapists are trained for collaboration in this process.

In *No Method to the Madness*, my goal has been to challenge the assumptions about the safety and effectiveness of our overuse of psychotropic medications in youth. Through an analysis of research, the intention is to raise awareness, question what we consider established science, and pose questions about our common practices. Looking at specific classes of medications has raised serious concerns. But using multiple medications at the same time (polypharmacy) raises even more questions. Indeed, "much polypharmacy seen in practice is untested or not supported by clinical trials" (Bellonci & Huefner, 2020, p. 3). But now concerned about our overreliance on medications, you may be asking, "OK, great. What are we supposed to do?"

If you are a psychologist or therapist (e.g., a non-prescriber), and you are working with clients who are exploring the idea of not being on medications in their treatment, it is essential that you have an established network of psychiatrists that you can lean on for collaboration in this process. It will require phone calls, meetings, and active discussion about strategies to consider supporting your client's goals, minimizing any negative outcomes, and creating a framework of success for them. Moreover, with what we have seen in *No Method to the Madness*, we need to modify our expectations of medication effectiveness. While benefits may be seen in the short-term, clinicians should be prepared for diminished long-term gains. Further, it is also clear that non-prescribers working with medicated clients must have knowledge about the benefits and drawbacks of medication use, particularly during the process of discontinuing medication, as increased symptoms may simply be reflective of medication discontinuation rather than a re-emergence of an impairing disorder.

What We Know

The overuse of psychotropic medications in children and adolescents has raised alarm. As the practice of aggressive prescribing, polypharmacy, and off-label use has increased, growing concern has been expressed from prescribers, therapists, parents, and youth. Using adult research has proven inadequate to guide the prescribing practices for youth and robust evidence for long-term, durable benefits from psychotropic use in youth has been lacking. While the ideal recommendations would be discontinuing medication when the child has developed sufficient control of the problematic symptoms through skill development (Bellonci & Heufner, 2020), this is not often seen in day-to-day practice.

While deprescribing is an inherent part of a psychiatrist's function, there is limited data or guidance when it comes to children and adolescents (Stimpfl et al., 2025). From my vantage point, very few treatment strategies look toward a non-medication outcome. That is, thinking about successful treatment ending with the discontinuation of medication is uncommon. Our medical model seeks to (a) make a diagnosis based on symptoms and (b) provide a treatment. If symptoms are reduced after treatment starts, it's attributed to the treatment. As a result, removing the treatment would be assumed to result in the return or increase of symptoms. In this framework, we've painted psychiatrists (and prescribers) into a corner. Their journey through medical school is fueled by a passion for helping people, alleviating distress, and enhancing well-being. No doubt, a noble and respected pursuit. Our society, though, assumes that the practice of medicine is firmly established in reliable, replicated science and that the methodology of scientific research minimizes risk and maximizes benefits. This is even more emphatically expected when there is a crisis. If someone presents at an emergency department with aggressive, psychotic behaviors, the expectation is that there is a medicine to contain them. But "crisis" becomes relative. No one wants to feel distress, but we all do. We want to alleviate it as quickly as possible. So, the phrase "a pill for every ill" becomes the expected product of psychiatry. And as Whitaker and Cosgrove have established, it's good for business (Whitaker & Cosgrove, 2015).

Decades ago, psychiatrists were trained in psychotherapy; many trained in psychodynamic or psychoanalytic approaches, when seeking to understand unconscious processes was seen as valuable. The expectation was that, as medical professionals, they were the most highly trained to understand the trauma, chaos, and malaise of the human condition. Their training has evolved. Now it is rare that psychiatrists receive substantial training in psychotherapy strategies, save for knowing the popular therapy approaches such as CBT. But understanding the human condition, such as from existential or phenomenological perspectives, has virtually disappeared in today's practice.

Throughout the mental health field, we're vulnerable to the bewilderment from sophisticated concepts like neuroscience. As discussed elsewhere in our discussion, the brain is inextricably involved in everything we do. So is air. But we devote billions of dollars, countless hours, and untold numbers of careers to understanding the brain. We know a lot about the brain, but relatively little about what can drive actionable treatment strategies in psychiatry or psychology. Yet the public puts trust in experts and when we use terms like limbic system, amygdala, prefrontal cortex, hippocampus, or hypothalamic pituitary adrenal axis, it sounds impressive. To this end, I devote considerable energy to educating my clients about what we know, what we don't know, and where science seems to be trending (a.k.a., good guesses).

The use of medications is here to stay. But when other options become necessary, practitioners may begin to ask, "how do we get back to baseline?" That is, we've tried all these medication strategies, but we want to reevaluate things and determine if the challenges of years ago are still priorities today. This person, diagnosed with anxiety at 8 years old is now 14. Have their needs changed in this developmental process? How can we figure this out? How do we begin?

Whenever a medication is initiated, there should be a clear understanding of the specific target of that treatment. For example, saying that "it's to treat the ADHD" or "to help their depression" is insufficient. The prescriber should have a goal(s). Simply addressing a diagnosis is vague, as the constellation of symptoms that make up any of these disorders is complicated and no medication effectively manages all the symptoms. In depression, is it the anhedonia? The hopelessness? Thoughts of death? Low self-esteem? If those are the articulated targets, does the chosen medication have evidence of affecting that symptom? For ADHD, is the child often interrupting? Is the concern impulsivity? Is it incomplete homework? You get the point. This type of planning also establishes outcome measures. That is, knowing if medications are achieving their goal. The same is true for psychotherapy or other interventions.

Our diagnostic formulations are also important here. Conceptualizing the varying treatment needs within a diagnostic framework are not well understood. For example, "there are no data in youth regarding differing treatment duration for those experiencing single versus recurrent mood episodes, severe symptoms, or prolonged duration of symptoms" (Stimpfl et al., 2025, p. 6).

Once a treatment is applied, sufficient time should be provided to see the results. But during this time, it is imperative to monitor other dimensions of the young person's life. For example, have they started in a new classroom? Did summer break just start? Did one of their parents just lose their job? Did one just start their dream job? Did their best friend just move away? Knowing how the young person's life is progressing also helps further our understanding of their goals, aspirations, frustrations, and so on. Tracking these events, their reactions, and their ability to cope with change is very valuable. But in time, those involved in the youth's care may realize that the medication that was started doesn't seem to be helping. Or, more commonly, the gains that were seen in the first few months have seemed to diminish. We're not sure it's helping anymore. Too often, at this point, therapists and parents alike may assume, "Well, it was helping a few months ago. Maybe we should increase the dose or add something else." In my years of experience, rarely does the treatment team conclude, "I guess the medication stopped working. Time to discontinue it."

Unfortunately, deprescribing psychotropic medications is uncommon in the treatment of severely troubled youth. There seems to be a belief that the more troubled a child or adolescent is, the more they need medication (and more types of medication). This polypharmacy practice is not supported in evidence-based practices but is common across the field. However, Bellonci and colleagues (2013) have demonstrated that even in residential treatment settings, reducing or eliminating medications can actually result in a reduction of aggressive behaviors and an increase in diagnostic clarity. That's right. Despite popular (mis)perception, reducing medications does *not* necessarily result in more problematic behaviors and can help clarify clinical priorities. In a project conducted across two residential centers, medication reductions were conducted for almost 300 youth (of a sample of 531). Dramatic reductions were seen in assaultive incidents and the use of physical restraints.

Moreover, a valuable analysis and recommendations from Bellonci and Huefner (2020) add strategies that need to be considered in our delivery of services to troubled youth. When medications fail, the common response is to increase the dose, change the medication, or add additional medications. But Bellonci, a psychiatrist, and Huefner, researcher of at-risk youth and their treatment, both nationally respected, have established guidelines to assist practitioners in the process of deprescribing. Not only can this help inform and optimize outcomes, but it also creates an opportunity to avoid long-term exposure to medications with known (and unknown) impact on the developing central nervous systems of our young people.

Following the prescribing framework from the American Academy of Child and Adolescent Psychiatry (AACAP), the deprescribing framework remains consistent with that standard of care. Bellonci and Huefner summarize these parameters, including:

- Comprehensive assessment.
- Biopsychosocial formulation. This is essential in understanding if the current medication regimen may be contributing to side effects, clouding the clinical picture.
- Ongoing reassessment.
- Knowledge of the disorder's course and application of this information to guide deprescribing. This would include review of the best available evidence and practice guidelines.
- Developmentally appropriate decision-making with the youth and caregiver.
- Assent from the youth and caregiver, keeping them fully informed of the process.

When considering situations of polypharmacy, Bellonci and Huefner specify:

- Start tapering medication that has the least evidence of efficacy and/or greatest evidence of side effects or risk of side effects (e.g., SGAs);
- Start tapering medication that is prescribed at a supra-therapeutic dose without obvious justification;
- Start tapering medication that is prescribed at doses that are sub-therapeutic or has limited or no evidence of effectiveness for the condition for which it is prescribed (e.g., SGAs for sleep).
- When deprescribing medications, the half-life of the medication can affect the speed at which it can safely be deprescribed.

- When anticonvulsants (including Benzodiazepines) are used for psychiatric reasons, it is important to remember that rapid tapering can precipitate seizures even if patients have not previously had seizures. (p. 352).

Before Bellonci and Huefner's work, Drs. Breggin and Cohen (1999) provided guidance when considering discontinuing psychotropic medications. While a controversial figure, Breggin is a renowned expert in psychopharmacology, having decades of experience as a clinician, author, and expert witness.

Gradual withdrawal: Highlighting the inherent compensatory neurological activity that occurs when psychotropic drugs enter the central nervous system, Breggin and Cohen note that this activity does not cease immediately upon discontinuing a medication. These activities persist for some time, potentially causing withdrawal symptoms. The brain attempts to compensate physically for the disabling effects of biopsychiatric interventions, frequently causing additional adverse reactions and withdrawal problems. The brain does not welcome psychiatric medications as nutrients. Instead, the brain reacts against them as toxic agents and attempts to overcome their disruptive impact (Breggin, 2008, p. 9). To minimize this risk, they recommend "a slow, gradual withdrawal . . . the longer the withdrawal period, the more chances you have to minimize the intensity of the expected withdrawal reaction" (p. 134).

One drug at a time: First, these authors note that discontinuing multiple medications simultaneously should be reserved for acute, serious toxicity. Otherwise, the prescriber should carefully consider how the combined medications may interact, mechanisms of action, pharmacodynamics, etc. Their training in pharmacology is particularly important here to minimize negative outcomes.

Careful selection of the sequence of drug discontinuation: Similar to the above point, at times, certain medications may be used to lessen negative effects of another medication, such as a side effect, or work to overlap/ enhance receptor occupancy, etcetera. There may be many reasons that medications were first prescribed but discontinuing them will raise new questions about the appropriate sequence. A prescriber's training here is of critical importance. Beyond the expertise of non-prescribers, understanding the neurophysiological impact of these medications will help drive the decision-making process.

The 10 percent method: While not an absolute rule, Breggin and Cohen refer to pharmacology textbooks recommending decreasing the dose of a medication in 10 percent increments, when possible, and taking one to several weeks for each step in this process. The authors note that the longer one has been on medications, the longer this discontinuation process may need to be done without significant deterioration.

Prescribers are encouraged to fully review these sources for additional guidance. Further, as a therapist, if you can collaborate in this process, it is reasonable to expect behavioral or emotional deterioration. In my own experience, I would increase the frequency of my contact with the youth and caregivers. Not only would this provide a more focused, intensive opportunity to support the client through the process, but it would also increase the frequency of supervision of their status. If they were struggling or in distress, ongoing communication with the prescriber may allow a slower taper, additional support, etcetera.

Most recently, there have been contributions to the process of deprescribing. Theall, Ninan, and Currie (2024), while incorporating the Bellonci and Huefner (2020) recommendations above, add to the discussion of deprescribing. In conducting a focus group with experts in child and adolescent psychiatry, the following themes emerged. Authors observe that there has been an overreliance on psychotropic medications in youth, with particular concerns about polypharmacy in those at-risk youth in the child welfare system. Of concern, authors note "existing resources for deprescribing with child/youth patients are largely theoretical and untested, especially for polypharmacy" (Theall, Ninan, and Currie, 2024, p. 3).

The Medication

Noted above, conducting a thorough evaluation of current clinical priorities, a comprehensive review of previous medications, as well as successes and failures, creates a foundation of understanding. Reviewing the medication should also leverage the expertise of prescribers, their training, and experiences of observing withdrawal effects, challenges, and so on. This also allows prescribers to critically evaluate the original intention of the medication, FDA indications, off-label patterns, and the relevance of practice parameters. Indeed, some practice guidelines have not been updated in years and will require a thoughtful review of the available, most current literature (Theall, Ninan, and Currie, 2024).

The Setting

In the focus group, psychiatrists within inpatient settings felt more confident about abrupt discontinuation of medications, as they believe there is enhanced monitoring of the youth. This is true, in that there are more staff observing the hospitalized children and teens. However, in my own experience, medication changes that occur within psychiatric inpatient settings are very concerning. Nurses are excellent caregivers and have a well-rounded knowledge of medications but from my vantage point, they are susceptible to the popular beliefs of medication use. Moreover, the other direct care staff (e.g., psychiatric technicians) likely have very little education on the adverse effects of psychotropics, and even less about the potential complications of medication withdrawal.

I would argue that the confidence of psychiatrists in the focus group may be exaggerated. In fact, in my role as professor of graduate clinical psychology students, I have the opportunity to supervise their work in advanced clinical training. Many of these students are placed in psychiatric hospitals to conduct psychological assessments or therapy. I have repeatedly been presented with cases of young people being admitted to an inpatient setting, only to have multiple medications discontinued—with new medications started within a week. This practice is quite clearly against all the abovementioned recommendations. Presumably, this is based on the assumption that because the youth is hospitalized in a crisis, the medications they were previously prescribed were "ineffective." Rather than devoting the time to the comprehensive evaluations discussed above, it would appear that very little retrospective analysis is completed. In my opinion, this process is replete with failures to provide outcomes-driven care. In fact, for those youth receiving psychological evaluation, they are typically discharged before the results are reported to the treatment team. My graduate students also report high rates of recidivism.

Outpatient settings create different challenges. In contrast to the high level of monitoring available in inpatient settings, outpatient settings create less focused observation. This can lead to potential failures in identifying side effects or complications from medication withdrawal. In my own clinical work, I would often schedule more frequent sessions with clients who were in this process of discontinuation. Not only would this allow for more observation and collaboration with their parents/caregivers but allow for more focused skill development in the process.

The Timing

The feedback offered in Theall, Ninan, and Currie (2024) recognized the importance of trauma anniversaries, developmental considerations, family events, and the duration of the deprescribing process. These thoughtful dimensions of the youth's life represent not only how life events will influence the response to any treatment (e.g., medications or psychotherapy), but also knowing that a change in circumstances could also enhance or facilitate the ability to discontinue medications.

Changes to treatment strategies should consider timing. Is the young person going through any transitions that may negatively influence the process? For example, is it the beginning of a new school semester or beginning of summer break? Are there events occurring at home that may affect the youth's response to intervention? Thinking systemically will further inform the various influences that may enhance or reduce a youth's response.

Stepwise Approach

Theall, Ninan, and Currie (2024) provided important components of taking incremental, thoughtful steps in the deprescribing process. Part of this includes creating a baseline of the targeted behaviors. For example, if a medication was chosen to discontinue, originally prescribed for sadness related to depression, creating a baseline measure of that symptom is important to monitor the process, determine a threshold of tolerance, and have ways to document progress. In this stepwise process, targeting one medication at a time was also noted to be important, acknowledging that antidepressants and antipsychotics may require more time to discontinue. With insight, the authors highlight having a crisis plan in place. This crisis plan should also embrace the potential of deterioration but may not necessitate the re-implementation of medication. With sufficient support in place, the crisis could be managed and deprescribing can continue. I have seen this in my own clinical experiences. Preparing parents is particularly important as increased symptom acuity can be unsettling, but having a crisis plan in place can alleviate this anxiety.

 Walk Away Message

As emphasized above, discontinuation of any medication should be under the close supervision of the prescriber. If you are a therapist, be an advocate for your client but listen closely to their experience. Over the years, I have had many clients who felt as though their medications provided vital relief. But in my work, I always prepared for when the medication stopped providing this relief. I also spent time developing a network of psychiatrists that I could refer to, and rely on, knowing they would be conservative in their prescribing strategies and also be responsive to me in the event they chose to begin a deprescribing process. It takes time, effort, and focus. Knowing your community resources is also important as clients and families will want to access additional resources to support their process, develop compensatory strategies, and optimize their outcomes.

References

Bellonci, C., & Huefner, J. (2020). Best practices for prescribing and deprescribing psychotropic medications for children and youth. In *Handbook of research on emotional and behavioral disorders: Interdisciplinary developmental perspectives on children and youth*. Routledge, 341–358.

Bellonci, C., Huefner, J., Griffith, A., Vogel-Rosen, G., Smith, G., & Preston, S. (2013). Concurrent reductions in psychotropic medication, assault, and physical restraint in two residential treatment programs for youth. *Children and Youth Services Review, 35*: 1773–1779.

Breggin, P. (2008). *Brain-disabling treatments in psychiatry: Drugs, electroshock, and the psychopharmaceutical complex* (2nd ed.). Springer Publishing.

Breggin, P., & Cohen, D. (1999). *Your drug may be your problem: How and why to stop taking psychiatric medications*. Perseus Books.

Stimpfl, J., Walkup, J., Robb, A., Alford, A., Stahl, S., McCracken, J., . . . Strawn, J. (2025). Deprescribing antidepressants in children and adolescents: A systematic review of discontinuation approaches, cross-titration, and withdrawal symptoms. *Journal of Child and Adolescent Psychopharmacology, 35*(1). https://doi.org/10.1089/cap.2024.0099

Theall, L., Ninan, A., & Currie, M. (2024). Findings from an expert focus group on psychotropic medication deprescribing practices for children and youth with complex needs. *Frontiers in Child and Adolescent Psychiatry, 3*:1481446. https://doi.org/10.339/frcha.2024.1481446

Whitaker, R., & Cosgrove, L. (2015). *Psychiatry under the influence: Institutional corruption, social injury, and prescriptions for reform*. Palgrave Macmillan.

Index

10 percent method 174–5

AACAP (American Academy of Child and Adolescent Psychiatry) 4, 40–1, 44–5, 90, 92–3, 173
AAEs (adverse adolescent experiences) 45
ABC diagnoses 24–5
Abilify 104–5, 123, 133, 136–7, 142, 161
abuse *see* child abuse sexual abuse
academic achievement 72, 75–6
accuracy of diagnosing 21–2
ACEs (Adverse Childhood Experiences) 42–4, 131–2
ADD *see* attention deficit disorder
Adderall 53–4, 69
Adderall XR 53–4, 62
adenosine 65
ADHD *see* attention-deficit hyperactivity disorder
Administration for Children and Families (ACF) 155
adolescence 26–7, 31
    AACAP 4, 40–1, 44–5, 90, 92–3, 173
    ACEs 43–4
    ADHD and academic achievement 75–6
    practice parameters 44–5
    "rule out trauma, then diagnose" methodology 41
    treating depression 83–120
    see also hyperkinetic reaction of childhood
Adolescent Subjective Experience of Treatment in residential care (ASET study) 142
adverse adolescent experiences (AAEs) 45
Adverse Childhood Experiences (ACEs) 42–4, 131–2
African drapetomania 24
Ahmad, F. 88–9
AIR (Attention, Intention, and Repetition) 165
algorithms 155–6
allostasis, allostatic load 44

Almeida-Montes, L. 93, 94
Alza Corporation 67
American Academy of Child and Adolescent Psychiatry (AACAP) 4, 40–1, 44–5, 90, 92–3, 173
American Academy of Pediatrics 45, 49, 51, 63, 64, 66, 86, 124–5
American Board of Psychiatry and Neurology 97
American Psychological Association, Working Group on Psychoactive Medications for Children and Adolescents 75–6
American Psychological Association (APA)
    antipsychotics 131–2, 133
    "best guess" diagnoses 15
    diagnosis leading to treatment 19
    diagnostic ambiguity 16
    DMDD 103–4
    ethics 4
    evolution of diagnosing 23
    foundations of critically examining the science 6–7
    function of a diagnosis 17–18
    genetics, ADHD 60
    guidelines for adolescent depression 91
    major depressive disorder 87
    neurological basis for ADHD 58–60
    persistent depressive disorder 100–1
    stimulant use disorder 76–7
    Working Group on Psychoactive Medications for Children and Adolescents 75–6
    see also Diagnostic and Statistical Manual of Mental Disorders
Amill-Rosario, A. 85
amphetamine 69–70
Anatomy of an Epidemic (Whitaker) 30
Anda, R. 35
anhedonia 38, 171–2
antagonism, agonists 65, 122, 124, 132–3, 154
anticonvulsants 141–2, 174

Index

antidepressants 83–120
  and function 106–11
  see also selective serotonin reuptake inhibitors
antipsychotics 103–4, 121–49
  causes of psychotic disorders 129–31
  deactivation 139–40
  deprescribing 174–5
  effectiveness 134–9
  and function 132–4
  other conditions 140–1
  predictability and anxiety 127–8
  psychosis 125–7
  role of trauma 131–2
antisocial personality disorder 22
anxiety disorders 27, 29, 127–8
  of childhood or adolescence 28
  see also trauma
APA *see* American Psychological Association
Aptensio 66–7
Aptensio XR 62
Arakelyan, M. 152, 160
aripiprazole 123, 133, 136–7
arriving at a diagnosis
  accuracy of diagnosing 21–2
  diagnosis leading to treatment 19–21
  diagnostic ambiguity 16–17
  diagnostic/statistical manuals of mental disorders 25–33
  evolution of diagnosing 23–5
  function of a diagnosis 17–18
  leading to treatment 19–21
  "rule out trauma, then diagnose" methodology 18–19
The Art of Kid Whispering (Freado & Chambers) 158
ASET (Adolescent Subjective Experience of Treatment in residential care) 142
asylums 23
Atkinson, S. 95, 96
attention deficit disorder (ADD) 28, 55, 66
Attention, Intention, and Repetition (AIR) 165
attention-deficit and disruptive behavior disorders 30–1
attention-deficit hyperactivity disorder (ADHD) 49–81, 171–2
  antipsychotics 141–2
  causes 58–61
  "common-ness" 50–1
  diagnoses 54–8
  diagnosis leading to treatment 20

DSM-5 31
DSM-5-TR 33
DSM-III-R 29
DSM-IV 30–1
Inter-Rater Reliability Scores 22
marketing 52–4
medications/treatments 49, 61–4
  academic achievement 75–6
  effectiveness 61–4
  stimulants 70–8
MTA study 70–5, 78
"often" definitions 57–8
"rule out trauma, then diagnose" methodology 41
stimulants 64–70
trauma and 51–2
universal and exclusivity concepts 8–9
youth in care 153, 155
see also Multimodal Treatment Study of Children with ADHD
atypical antipsychotics 123, 133, 137, 142
  see also individual second generation antipsychotics...
auditory "pseudo-hallucinations" 39–40
autism spectrum disorder 7, 22, 28–9, 30–1, 104–5, 121–2, 129
Avatar Therapy 143

Baldini, V. 131
Behavior Disorders of Childhood and Adolescence 26–7
behavioral despair 107
behavioral treatment 71, 72–3
Bellonci, C. 142, 167, 169–75
Belonging (Circle of Courage) 45–6, 116, 157
"best guess" diagnoses 15, 171
bipolar disorder 22, 29–30, 42, 105–6, 121–2, 142
Black, T. 109, 133
The Boy Who Was Raised as a Dog 86
Bradshaw, T. 131
Brainard, J. 9
Breggin, P. 123, 139, 174–5
Brendtro, L. 45–6, 157, 158
Brokenleg, M. 45–6, 157, 158
Bruno, A. 103, 104–5
bupropion (Wellbutrin) 111, 113
"business" of academia 9–10
  see also marketing

caffeine 64–6
Camerer, C. 8

Index

caregivers *see* family/caregivers
CARF 159
Cartwright, S. 24
cause(s)
   ADHD 58–61
   function of a diagnosis 17–18
   of psychotic disorders 129–31
CBT (cognitive behavioral therapy) 45, 90–3, 97–9, 171
CCWIS (Comprehensive Child Welfare Information System) 155–6, 163
CDRS-R (Children's Depression Rating Scare-Revised) 93–4, 97–8
Celexa 91, 108, 109
Centers for Disease Control and Prevention (CDC) 88–9
central nervous system (CNS) 64–70, 109, 154
   antipsychotics 133–4
   see also stimulants
CGI (Clinical Global Impressions) 135
Chambers, J. C. 158
chemical imbalance 3–4, 23, 85, 111–16
child abuse 32, 39–40, 131
   see also trauma
child welfare and intensive services 46–7, 151–68
   challenges of youth in care 152–63
      data-driven decisions 155–6
      data-driven placement 160–3
      diagnostic dilemmas 152–4
      health and absence of symptoms 155
      strength-based models 156–9
      troubled child industry 159–60
   phased implementation 164–7
Children's Depression Rating Scare-Revised (CDRS-R) 93–4, 97–8
Choi, S. 109, 133
chronic terror conditions 126–7, 131, 140
Cicchetti, D. 37
Cipriani, A. 96–7
Circle of Courage 45–6, 116, 156–9, 165
citalopram (Celexa) 91, 108, 109
clinical challenges, antipsychotics 146
Clinical Global Impressions (CGI) 135
clinicians, depression in adolescents 115–16
clinicians and ethics 5
Clonidine 143
Clozaril 143
cocaine 64, 68–9
Cochrane Collaboration 96–7
Cochrane Database 140

cognitive behavioral therapy (CBT) 45, 90–3, 97–9, 171
Cohen, D. 174–5
collaboration 4–6, 40–1, 177–8
combined treatment 71, 72–3
community care and engagement 71, 162, 163
comorbid disorders 17, 32, 88, 94, 103–4, 153
Complex PTSD (C-PTSD) 39–40
Comprehensive Child Welfare Information System (CCWIS) 155–6, 163
concentration 39
   OCD 9, 108
   see also attention-deficit hyperactivity disorder
Concerta 62, 66–7, 154
   see also methylphenidate
conduct disorder 22, 28
   see also oppositional defiant disorder
confirmation bias 24–5
   see also predictability
containment vs. treatment 121–49
Corkum, P. 75–6
Corrigan, M. 59
Cortese, S. 74–5
Cosgrove, L. 170–1
COVID pandemic 85
C-PTSD (Complex PTSD) 39–40
crisis behaviors 160–2
Currie, M. 175–7
Curtin, S. 88–9
cutting 38
Cymbalta 95–6, 111

Dabney, J. 54
Danese, A. 44
data-driven decisions 155–6
   see also evidence-based treatments
data-driven placement 160–3
Davies, J. 83–4
Daytrana 66–7
DBDs (disruptive behavior disorders) 29, 140–1
DEA (Drug Enforcement Agency) 69
deactivation 139–40
The Death of Expertise (Nichols) 10
decision-making 85, 86–7, 173–4
   data-driven 155–6, 161, 163
   DMDD 105
   evolution of diagnosing 23–4
   genetics, ADHD 61
   persistent depressive disorder 100–1

popular beliefs in academia 12
"rule out trauma, then diagnose" methodology 19
strength-based models 158
defectives 24
dementia 59
Depakote 141–2
depersonalization/derealization 40
depletion studies 112
deprescribing medication(s) 169–78
depression 26
   in adolescents 83–120
      diagnostic framework 84–7
      DMDD 101–6
      fluoxetine (Prozac) 91–7
      function of antidepressants 106–11
      impact of depression 88–90
      major depressive disorder 87–8
      persistent depressive disorder 100–1
      TADS 97–9
      treatment guidelines 90–9
   major depressive disorder 26, 87–8
   universal and exclusivity concepts 9
desvenlafaxine (Pristiq) 96–7, 111
Dexedrine 69
diagnoses
   ADHD 54–8
   "best guess" diagnoses 15, 171
   "rule out trauma, then diagnose" methodology 18–19, 41–2, 115
   see also arriving at a diagnosis
Diagnosis by Response 33
diagnostic ambiguity 16–17
diagnostic dilemmas
   ADHD 77
   depression in adolescents 115
   youth in care 152–4
diagnostic frameworks, depression in adolescents 84–7
diagnostic interviews 20
diagnostic manuals of mental disorders 25–33
Diagnostic and Statistical Manual of Mental Disorders (DSM) 6, 15–16, 18, 23, 25, 26
Diagnostic and Statistical Manual of Mental Disorders, 2nd Edition (DSM-II) 26–7, 54–5
Diagnostic and Statistical Manual of Mental Disorders, 3rd Edition (DSM-III) 22, 27–8, 50, 54–5, 125
Diagnostic and Statistical Manual of Mental Disorders, 3rd Edition, Revised (DSM-III-R) 15, 28–9, 55

Diagnostic and Statistical Manual of Mental Disorders, 4th Edition (DSM-IV) 22, 29–31, 49, 55–6, 77, 84–5, 125
Diagnostic and Statistical Manual of Mental Disorders, 4th Edition, Text Revision (DSM-IV-TR) 31, 85
Diagnostic and Statistical Manual of Mental Disorders, 5th Edition (DSM-5) 15–16, 22, 31–2, 49, 87, 101–2
Diagnostic and Statistical Manual of Mental Disorders, 5th Edition, Text Revision (DSM-5-TR) 26, 32–3
   cause(s) of psychotic disorders 129
   depression in adolescents 84–5, 86
   diagnosing ADHD 56–7
   diagnosis leading to treatment 20
   diagnostic ambiguity 16
   DMDD 101–2, 105
   function of a diagnosis 17
   genetics and ADHD 60–1
   neurological basis for ADHD 59
   responding to trauma 37–8
   serotonin 114–15
   stimulant use disorder 76
disorders usually first evident in infancy, childhood, or adolescence 31, 49
disruptive behavior disorders (DBDs) 29, 140–1
disruptive mood dysregulation disorder (DMDD) 22, 25, 84, 101–6
   antipsychotics 121–2, 142
   DSM-5 31–2
   DSM-5-TR 32–3
   "rule out trauma, then diagnose" methodology 42
distress
   and diagnosis 20–1
   see also trauma
divalproex sodium (Depakote) 141–2
DMDD *see* disruptive mood dysregulation disorder
dopamine 64–9, 76–7, 109, 111, 113, 122–4, 133, 154
dosReis, S. 85
drapetomania 24
drug abuse 53, 68, 69, 76–7, 153
Drug Enforcement Agency (DEA) 69
DSM *see Diagnostic and Statistical Manual of Mental Disorders*
duloxetine (Cymbalta) 95–6, 111
Dyanavel XR 69
dysphoria 38, 101–2
dysregulation 129–30

TDD 32, 101–2
  see also disruptive mood dysregulation disorder
dysthymia 100–1

"effective treatment" 61–4, 134–9, 143
Effexor 111
Elbe, D. 67–8, 109, 133, 134
emotion, regulation 38, 40, 163
  see also depression
Emslie, G. 93–6
Engel, R. 135
escitalopram (Lexapro) 91, 100, 108, 109
ethics 4–6
etiology see cause(s)
Etschel, E. 135
Evekeo 62, 69
evidence-based treatments 89–90, 155–6, 160–3, 173
evolution of diagnosing 23–5
exorcisms 23
external validity 7

"failure to replicate" dilemmas 8
"Fake Scientific Papers are Alarmingly Common" (Brainard) 9
Family First Prevention Services Act (FFPSA) 151
family/caregivers 41
  abuse 32, 39–40, 131
  depression in adolescents 116
  youth in care 162
Faust, D. 18
FDA see Food and Drug Administration
Fifth International Conference on Bipolar Disorder 105–6
Findling, R. 93, 94, 103, 105, 136–7
Finlay, S. 44
first generation antipsychotics see typical antipsychotics
fluoxetine (Prozac) 91–9, 108–9, 111–12, 113, 154
fluvoxamine (Luvox) 108
fMRI (functional magnetic resonance imaging) 8
Focalin 66–7
Focalin XR 62
focus see concentration
Food and Drug Administration (FDA) 85
  ADHD treatments 61, 64
  antipsychotics 124–5
  child welfare 152
  deprescribing medication(s) 175
  escitalopram (Lexapro) 100

fluoxetine (Prozac) 95
impact of depression 89
NDRIs 111
SSRIs 107–10
forced swim test 106–7
Forns, J. 113
Fosse, B. D. 132
Freado, M. 158
Freedman, R. 103
Friederichsen, A. 94
function of a diagnosis 17–18
functional magnetic resonance imaging (fMRI) 8

Garner, A. 45
Garnett, M. 88–9
Geel, Belgium 167
Geller, B. 141
generalized anxiety disorder 22
  see also anxiety disorders
Generosity (Circle of Courage) 45–6, 116, 157, 158
genetics 60–1
  see also nature versus nurture
Geodon 123, 133, 137, 142
Gifric program 167
Giordano, J. 26–9
Glick, I. 136
"gold standards" for medication trials 63
Grindey, A. 131
group delinquent reaction of childhood 27
Gurnani, T. 140

Hadland, S. 54
Haldol 123, 133, 134, 136, 139–42
"Haldol Clearly Is Neurotoxic: Should It Be Banned?" (Nasrallah) 134
Hales, D. 97
hallucinations 39–40
Hamann, J. 135
happiness/emthusiasm 163
  see also emotion, regulation
Harrow, M. 139
Hays-Grudo, J. 46
health and absence of symptoms 155
Herman, J. 37
Heron, M. 88
heterogeneity of psychiatric disorders 16
  see also diagnostic ambiguity
Higgins, E. 68
hobbies 163
homeostasis 44, 110
homogeneity of psychiatric disorders 15–16
Hoy, J. 49

Index

Huefner, J. 167, 169–75
humors 23
hyperkinetic reaction of childhood 26, 50, 54–5
   see also attention-deficit hyperactivity disorder
hypervigilance 38, 40, 52

iatrogenic 122–3
"impairment" 55
inattentive and hyperactive types 56–7
inclusion criteria 130
Independence (Circle of Courage) 45–6, 116, 157, 158
inflammatory response 44, 77, 129–30, 143
insanity 23
Insel, T. 89
insight-oriented psychotherapy 11
intellectual disabilities 18, 141
   see also IQ scores
internal validity 6–7
internalization 72–3, 158, 162–3
International Classification of Diseases (ICD) 20, 22, 55–6
interpersonal relationships 25, 37, 40–2, 162–3
   Belonging (Circle of Courage) 45–6, 116, 157
   residential treatment 165–6
   trauma and ADHD 51–2
   see also family/caregivers
interpersonal therapy (IP) 20, 90–1
Inter-Rater Reliability Scores (DSM-5) 22
intranasal methylphenidate abuse 68
IQ scores 59

Janssen Pharmaceuticals 133
Jensen, P. 73
Jewish Problem 24
Jobe, T. H. 139
Joint Commission 159
Jornay 66–7
journals 9, 50, 59, 141
jumpiness 39

Kane, J. 135
kappa scores 29, 87–8, 103
Karon, B. 126–7
Karr-Morse, R. 43
Kawa, S. 26–9
Keeshin, B. 124–5
Kirchner, J. 85
Kirsch, I. 113–14

Kissling, W. 135
Kluger, J. 12
Kupchan, J. 26

Lancet journal 59, 141
Langley, C. 86
learned helplessness 107
Lee, H. 85
Leucht, S. 135
Levine, P. 37
Lewis, S. 44
Lexapro 91, 100, 108, 109
Lilly, E. 93, 94
lithium 141–2
lobotomies 23, 122
"location" of depression 106–11
Long, M. 113
Loy, J. 140

McGonnell, M. 75–6
McGrane, I. 109, 133
Mad in America (Whitaker) 132
MADRS (Montgomery and Asberg Depression Rating Scale) 99
major depressive disorder 26, 87–8
major neurodegenerative disorder 22
Mallet, C. 49
marketing 9–10, 159–60
Mason, N. 112
Mastery (Circle of Courage) 45–6, 116, 157–8
medications 3–4
   ADHD 49, 61–4, 70–7
   chemical imbalance 3–4, 23, 85, 111–16
   deprescribing 169–78
   "gold standards" for medication trials 63
   MTA study 71–2
   neurotoxicity 77, 134, 139–40
   placebos 7, 61, 63, 89–100, 116
      antidepressant function 106–7
      antipsychotics in other medications 141
      critique by Davies 83–4
      DMDD 104–5
      measuring antipsychotic effectiveness 136–7, 138
      placebo effect 99, 114, 116, 138, 141
      power of placebos 113–14
      Prozac studies 92–7
   SNRIs 111
   TADS study 97–9

polypharmacy 104, 151–2, 154, 160, 169–70, 173–4, 175
youth in care 162
see also antidepressants; antipsychotics; *individual drugs...*
memory disorders 39
dementia 59
mental health institutions 23
meta-analyses 92–7
methylphenidate 53, 66–8, 71, 154
see also Ritalin
Meyer, J. 108
minimal brain dysfunction 54–5
see also hyperkinetic reaction of childhood
mirtazapine 113
Mojtabai, R. 101
Molina, B. 74
Moncrieff, J. 114–15
Montgomery and Asberg Depression Rating Scale (MADRS) 99
Mood Disorder 26
Moral Therapy 23
Moreno, C. 29
Morris, A. S. 46
Morrison, A. P. 39–40
Morton, W. 66, 68
Moskowitz, A. 132
Multimodal Treatment Study of Children with ADHD (MTA) 70–5, 78
at eight years 74
at three years 73
young adult outcomes 74–5
Mydayis 69

Nasrallah, H. 134
Natarajan, A. 49
National Committe for Mental Hygiene 23
National Institute of Mental Health (NIMH) 77, 89, 100
nature versus nurture 1–2
NDRIs (Norepinephrine-Dopamine Reuptake Inhibitors) 111, 113
negative moods 38
see also anhedonia; dysphoria
Negro-White Intermixture 24
neurodevelopmental disorders 31, 49
neuroinflammation 77
see also inflammatory response
neurological basis for ADHD 58–60
neurons/neurotransmitters 67–9, 107–8, 111, 133

see also dopamine; norepinephrine; serotonin
neuroplasticity 122–3, 129–30, 132
Neurosequential Model of Therapeutics (NMT) 37
neurotoxicity 77, 134, 139–40
see also substance abuse
New York Times 122
Nichols, T. 10
NIMH (National Institute of Mental Health) 77, 89, 100
Ninan, A. 175–7
NMT *see* Neurosequential Model of Therapeutics
norepinephrine 64, 67, 68, 69, 108, 109
NDRIs 111, 113
SNRIs 111
youth in care 154
norepinephrine-dopamine reuptake inhibitors (NDRIs) 111, 113

obsessive compulsive disorder (OCD) 9, 108
Odeh, S. 51
off-label prescribing 124
Olfson, M. 101
one-size-fits-all approaches 130–1, 143
oppositional defiant disorder (ODD) 17, 22, 27–31, 41, 72–3, 103
other disorders of infancy, childhood, or adolescence 28
other reaction of childhood 27
Other Specified ADHD 20
overanxious reaction of childhood 27
over-reactiveness 39
Owen, R. 104–5
oxidative stress 129–30

PACEs (protective and compensatory experiences) 46–7
PANSS (Positive and Negative Symptom Scale) 134–5, 136, 138, 146
paper mills 9
paranoid thoughts 2, 40, 69, 125
see also schizophrenia
Parent Training in Behavior Management (PTBM) 64
parent-child relations 72
see also family/caregivers
paroxetine (Paxil) 91, 108
Pelham, W. 76
Pennap, D. 152
Perry, B. 37
Perry, J. 132

persistent depressive disorder 100–1
pervasive developmental disorders 28
   DSM-III-R 28–9
   DSM-IV 30
Pfizer 85
pharmaceutical industry 52–4, 69, 75, 85, 106–7, 133
   see also individual drugs...; marketing; medications; treatments
The Pharmaceutical Journal 50
physical and/or verbal aggression 38
pill versus liquid 67
placebos 7, 61, 63, 89–100
   antidepressant function 106–7
   antipsychotics in other medications 141
   critique by Davies 83–4
   DMDD 104–5
   measuring antipsychotic effectiveness 136–7, 138
   placebo effect 99, 114, 116, 138, 141
   power of placebos 113–14
   Prozac studies 92–7
   SNRIs 111
   TADS study 97–9
pleasure chemical *see* dopamine
Polak, M. A. 39
polypharmacy 104, 151–2, 154, 160, 169–70, 173–4, 175
popular beliefs in academia 10–12
Positive and Negative Symptom Scale (PANSS) 134–5, 136, 138, 146
posttraumatic stress disorder (PTSD) 18, 22, 35–7, 39–41
   C-PTSD 39–40
   practice parameters 44–5
   "rule out trauma, then diagnose" methodology 41
practice parameters 44–5
predictability 24–5, 127–8
prescribers 40–1, 140, 175
   deprescribing medication(s) 169–78
   off-label prescribing 124
pre-synaptic neurons 67, 68–9, 107–8
Pristiq 96–7, 111
profiteers *see* marketing
Prokopez, C. 131
protective and compensatory experiences (PACEs) 46–7
providers 37
   ethics 5–6
"Provisional" diagnoses 21
Prozac 91–9, 108–9, 113, 154

psychologists and ethics 4–6
psychosis 69, 122, 125–7, 133, 140, 167
   see also schizophrenia
psychotherapists, and antipsychotics 146
psychotropic medications *see* antipsychotics
PsyD 1
PTBM (Parent Training in Behavior Management) 64
PTSD *see* posttraumatic stress disorder
"publish or perish" culture 9

quickness of temper 38
Quillivant 66–7
Quillivant XR 62

Radel, L. F. 151–2
Rajkumar, R. 140–1
Rapaport, M. 97
Read, J. 39–40, 132
receptor affinity 132–3
reckless or self-destructive behavior 38
relationships *see* interpersonal relationships
Remeron 113
residential treatment 164–7
reuptake process 107–11
   see also antagonism, agonists
Rexulti (brexpiprazole) 123, 137–8
Reynolds Adolescent Depression Scale 98
Risperdal 7, 104–5, 123, 133, 136, 139–42, 143, 154
Ritalin 53, 66–8
Ritalin LA 62
Ross, C. A. 39–40
Ruhé, H. 112
"rule out trauma, then diagnose" methodology 18–19, 41–2, 115
runaway reaction of childhood 27

Safe, Stable, Nurturing Relationships (SSNRs) 45, 86
   see also family/caregivers
SAMHSA (Substance Abuse and Mental Health Services Administration) 123
Santarsieri, D. 109–10
Schachar, R. 75–6
Schene, A. 112
schizophrenia 10–12, 69
   Inter-Rater Reliability Scores 22
   see also antipsychotics
Schwartz, T. 109–10
Science journal 9

scientific research papers 9–10, 23–4, 133, 135
  see also journals
second generation antipsychotics *see* atypical antipsychotics
selective serotonin reuptake inhibitors (SSRIs) 40–1, 44–5, 85, 90–1, 97, 107–10, 111–12
  serotonin depletion studies 112
  see also individual SSRIs...
self-control, confidence 27, 56, 158
self-destructive behavior 38
self-reflection/self-care 37, 163
  see also interpersonal relationships
Senate Committee on Finance 159
sense of purpose 163
sensitivity 38
Sequenced Treatment Alternatives to Relieve Depression (STAR*D) 100
Seroquel 123, 133, 144
serotonin 68, 107–16, 124, 133, 154
  depletion studies 112
  see also selective serotonin reuptake inhibitors
Serotonin Norepinephrine Reuptake Inhibitors (SNRIs) 111
sertraline (Zoloft) 85, 108, 109
sexual abuse 42, 131
Shea, S. 104–5
Shire Pharmaceuticals 53–4, 69
short- or long-acting 67
SKAMP (Swanson, Kotkin, Agler, M-Flynn, and Pelham) Scale 61–3
sleep disturbances 39
Smith Kline & French Laboratories 122
social skills 72
Son, S. 85
Soteria program 167
SSNRs *see* Safe, Stable, Nurturing Relationships
stability in relationships *see* interpersonal relationships
Stahl, S. 121, 124
STAR*D (Sequenced Treatment Alternatives to Relieve Depression) 100
Statistical Manual for Institutions for the Insane (1918) 23
statistical manuals of mental disorders 25–33
stepwise approaches 177
Stimpfl, J. 170, 172
stimulants 54, 64–70, 103–4

stimulant use disorder 76–7
  as treatment for ADHD 70–7
Stockton, G. 66, 68
strength-based models 156–9
  see also Circle of Courage
students and clinicians, ethics 5
substance abuse 42, 53, 68, 69, 76–7, 123, 153
Substance Abuse and Mental Health Services Administration (SAMHSA) 123
suicidal ideation 89
Swanson, J. 74
systematic umbrella reviews 114–15
systems of care 37

TADS (Treatment for Adolescents with Depression Study) 97–9, 101
TEAM study 141
temper dysregulation disorder (TDD) 32, 101–2
  see also disruptive mood dysregulation disorder
TF-CBT (Trauma-Focused Cognitive Behavioral Therapy) 45
Theall, L. 175–7
therapeutic dose 67
third generation antipsychotics 123
  see also individual third generation antipsychotics...
Thorazine 122–3, 142
threats/hypervigilance 38, 40, 52
Tong, L. 139
trauma
  and ADHD 51–2
  Circle of Courage 45–6, 116, 156–9, 165
  depression in adolescents 86
  role of 35–48
    ACEs study 42–4
    and antipsychotics 129–32
    Circle of Courage 45–6
    PACEs 46–7
    practice parameters 44–5
    responding to trauma 35–41
    "rule out trauma, then diagnose" methodology 41–2
  youth in care 161
Trauma-Focused Cognitive Behavioral Therapy (TF-CBT) 45
trauma-informed 37
Treatment for Adolescents with Depression Study (TADS) 97–9, 101
treatment dilemmas

Index

ADHD 78
  depression in adolescents 115–16
  treatments 19–21
    ADHD 49, 61–4
      stimulants 71–7
    decision-making 85, 86–7, 173–4
      data-driven 155–6, 161, 163
    DMDD 105
    evolution of diagnosing 23–4
    genetics, ADHD 61
    persistent depressive disorder 100–1
    popular beliefs in academia 12
    "rule out trauma, then diagnose" methodology 19
    strength-based models 158
  depression in adolescents 83–120
    guidelines 90–9
  evidence-based treatments 89–90, 155–6, 160–3
  evolution of diagnosing 23
  residential treatment 164–7
  see also medications
Trilafon 142
troubled child industry 159–60
typical antipsychotics 123
  see also individual first generation antipsychotics...
Tyrer, P. 141

United Nations (UN) 53
universal and exclusivity concepts 8–9
unsocialized aggressive reaction of childhood 27

Valenstein, E. 122–3
van der Kolk, B. 37
van der Zwaard, R. 39
van Os, J. 39–40
VanBockern, S. 45–6, 157, 158

VandenBos, G. 126–7
Vazquez, J. 65–6
venlafaxine 111
verbal aggression 38
Versiani, M. 113
vilazodone (Viibryd) 91
Vitiello, B. 141–2
Vogin, G. 105–6
Vyvanse 53–4, 62, 69

Walter, H. 88, 90, 91
Weihs, K. 95, 96
Wellbutrin 111, 113
What Happened to You? 86
Whitaker, R. 23–4, 59, 67, 122, 132, 170–1
  Anatomy of an Epidemic 30
  Mad in America 132
Wiley, M. 43
Windhorse Program 167
witchcraft 23
withdrawing reaction of childhood 27
Wolraich, M. L. 49, 63
World Health Organization (WHO) 20, 39–40

Xu, L. 113

young adults
  MTA study 74–5
  see also adolescence
youth in care *see* child welfare and intensive services

Zhang, C. 85
Zhang, L. 113
Zhou, X. 92–5
ziprasidone (Geodon) 123, 133, 137, 142
Zoloft (sertraline) 85, 108, 109
Zyprexa 123, 133, 134, 139–40, 142